ANALECTA BIBLICA

INVESTIGATIONES SCIENTIFICAE IN RES BIBLICAS

—————————— 142 ——————————

ROBERT NORTH, S.J.

MEDICINE IN THE
BIBLICAL BACKGROUND

and Other Essays on the Origins of Hebrew

EDITRICE PONTIFICIO ISTITUTO BIBLICO - ROMA 2000

IMPRIMI POTEST

Romae, die 2 iulii 1999

R.P. ROBERT F. O'TOOLE, S.J.

Rector Pontificii Instituti Biblici

Periodical names in this volume
(except where there was a special reason for giving them in full)
are usually abbreviated as in S. SCHWERTNER,
Internationales Abkürzungsverzeichnis (IATG² 1992, = TRE)

ISBN 88-7653-142-4

© E.P.I.B. – Roma – 2000

EDITRICE PONTIFICIO ISTITUTO BIBLICO

Piazza della Pilotta, 35 - 00187 Roma, Italia

Medicine in the Biblical Background

and Other Essays on the Origins of Hebrew

Medicine and Healing in the Old Testament Background
Revised and updated conference
Medicina y terapias en el Antiguo Testamento
from the Madrid Alcalá University
Almería Summer Course, July 20, 1992

CONTENTS

1

Medicine and Healing in the Old Testament Background

"Physician, heal thyself" (Lk 4,23), already proverbial as used by Jesus in the synagogue of Galilee, has become a byword everywhere for ineffectualness bordering on quackery (Nolland 1979). Actually not the worst thing that could be said about doctors is that some of them are so dedicated to healing others' ills that they neglect their own health. More devastating is the reference of Mk 6,26 to the poor woman who for years had spent all she had on physicians and got worse instead of better.

Even if disparaging, both these references serve as a valuable indication that there did exist a flourishing medical practice in the Judaic-biblical background. And yet surprisingly amid the almost-endless procession of people seeking from Jesus a miraculous cure, there is hardly ever a reference to any normal human means of remedying such ills. In comparison to this, the Old Testament references, though themselves also sparse and fragmentary, are imbedded in neighboring cultures and thus contribute more usably to our picture.

I. Some recent sources

In turning to these Old Testament mentions, we are fortunate in having at our disposition some very recent and thorough studies. The excellent scholarly dictionary called *ThWAT*. recently completed, has a key-word on *rapa'*, "heal" (Brown 1990); and the English translation now in course has reached *hālâ*, "sick" (Seybold 1976). The great *TRE* enterprise in an inevitably slow course of publication, has now reached the article on *Krankheit*, "sickness" (Scharbert 1990). These articles give a succinct summary of the data and a very recent rich bibliography. Similar earlier articles retain a certain usefulness (Harrison 1962, Hübner 1989, Leibowitz 1976, Stoebe 1992, Oepke 1966, Stählin 1964).

Also valuable for us are the published Acta of several recent meetings devoted to biblical medicine (Kottek 1985, Castrén 1989, Baader 1990, Guillermand 1987, Hankinson 1988, Hart 1983, Horstmanshoff 1992). A similar composite volume begins with OT medicine (Wiseman in Palmer 1986). And of course there is *IDB* and the impressive new *AnchorBD*. One might well think that with researches like these available, there is nothing further to be done.

But the clock has not stood still, even in the few months since these works were published. Notably in the field of archeological excavation, there is some relevant find or explanation in almost every volume (North 1994). Though the medical tool-kits found in shipwrecks or other unlikely situations are often far removed from the actual Palestine of the time of King David or Ezra, still they form important links in the chain of our reconstruction. Even ancient coins are being used to suggest the diagnosis of a disease.

We may note in advance how varying is the approach of the apparently similar studies mentioned above. What do they consider it important to take up first ? Obviously when we are sick, after home-remedies fail, the first thing we think of is to see the doctor. Anyway persons are more interesting than things. Specifically, sympathetic and helpful doctors make easier reading than unpleasant sicknesses, or medicines, or scalpels. Hence it is natural that some researches in making an outline of their material put first the physician and his preparation, his social class, his tools and assistants.

But upon reflection, we might find it more logical to put first the sick person or rather his various sicknesses. It is those which really make the doctor relevant (Ramsey 1970). In strict logic we might say that even prior to the sickness come its causes, thus eventually the normal physiology and anatomy of which the sickness represents a distortion.

In fact all of us like to accentuate the positive, to talk about living rather than dying (though "the art of dying" has also its place in medical research: Kruse 1989; Westermann 1974). It would seem more up-to-date to discuss first of all what the Bible has to say about *health* and the means of preserving it, "preventive medicine" (Jackson 1988, 32; Ebstein 1901/3), or "public health" (Kottek 1986/94; Cilliers 1993).

And indeed since it is the Bible we are talking about, obviously the primary source of health as well as of healing is "God the physician" (Ex 15, 26), variously presented on p. 32 below (Lohfink 1981; Niehr 1991).

Recognizing the value of all these divergent approaches, we may perhaps conclude that in a study of "medicine and healing", the first thing to analyze is the available data about the *sicknesses* and their origins, then for each the *remedies* which are found to be used, and last but far from least, the *person* of the physician and what meaning it has to speak of God as our physician.

II. The biblical experience of pain and malfunctioning

The Hebrew word meaning "to be sick" is *hālâh*. Before turning to the etymology and synonyms of this root, we wish to emphasize that our concern is primarily with "the sick person" (*hōleh*; "sickness" is *holî*). In this connection we may note in advance with Seybold (1978, p.9) that the sick person's condition is not solitary, but constitutes a triangle: to himself it is *aegritudo*, discomfort and need of help; to the doctor it is *páthos, nósos*, a clinical datum; but also to society it is *infirmitas*, a burden and a challenge: "as I am today, so you may be tomorrow" (Rothschuh 1975, 414).

Seybold adds that modern medicine has done wonders of differentiating sicknesses ever more precisely; but it has lagged behind in distinguishing what all sicknesses have *in common*; indeed, some doubt that any one definition of "sickness" can be given (Rothschuh p.420). Also, curiously, "sicknesses themselves are born and die"; some like AIDS (SIDA) are new to our own time; others like plagues have become almost unknown. As for leprosy, defective translations of the biblical terms have themselves *caused* untold suffering throughout the ages: a good stimulus for us here to take seriously the job of clarifying what was really meant by sickness(es) in the Bible.

The "triangle" mentioned above relates the sick person to the doctor and to society (Gourévitch 1984). This is an echo of Hippocrates, the most famous name in the whole history of medicine's origins. We must therefore note briefly in advance by what right we bring into a discussion of *biblical* medicine data from an outside environment. The worldwide medicine of Rome came from Greece, originally Cnidus in Ionia (Grmek 1988; Phillips 1987; Schumacher 1963; see below IV,4, p. 40). But the Greek specialists had quickly settled in Alexandria, where they inherited the insights of the previous medical center, Egypt (Saunders 1963).

In Alexandria Hippocrates (with Galen) is really the name of a school rather than just a person (c. 400 B.C.; see p. 41 below), from after the time of Ezra but early enough to have influenced Sirach and Maccabees. Egypt was Palestine's nearest and most powerful neighbor, and has left on papyrus a vast arsenal of medical experience (Grapow 1954 & 1958; Ghalioungui 1983; Edel 1976). All the excellent studies of Old Testament medicine to which we have alluded draw heavily on the history of medicine in pharaonic Egypt.

Mesopotamian data are also taken into consideration, though much more limited to the demonic or otherwise religious factors prominent also in the Bible (Biggs 1990; Oppenheim 1962; Herbero 1984; Sendrail 1953). Unexpectedly one research is devoted entirely to Babylonian medicine and its direct influence upon the Greek, with Egypt mentioned only casually for some comparative conclusions

(Goltz 1974). But upon second thought this will hardly surprise us, since many researches had already been devoted exclusively to Egyptian medicine or to its influence on Greek.

———

The biblical Hebrew word for "sick", *hōleh,* is from a root surprisingly unattested in the cognate Semitic languages, though rapprochements with Arabic *ḥelwa*, "sweet" have been attempted (Seybold 1976, 400); and in fact the Hebrew Piel with *pānîm* means "soothe". In a research on pain in the Old Testament *hôleh* is only one of fifteen Hebrew terms studied, and one of seven to which is given a meaning "sick(ness)"; but the book treats chiefly sorrow, grief, bereavement; also loss, punishment (Scharbert 1955).

The common Semitic root *dawah* occurs in the Bible mostly for a woman's malaise (Lev 15,33; 20,18); more generalized, sometimes with *lēb* (Lam 1,13; 5,17; Isa 30,22; Ps 41,4H). Absence from Hebrew of the quite common Semitic term for "sick", *marsu* in Akkadian (Arabic *marîd*) is sometimes attributed to its demonic implications. Common enough in the Bible is the word for "(feel) pain", *kā'ēb*; and also "being felled", *maggēpâh*, by sickness as "a blow struck", *nāgap.*

The Hebrew *hōleh* is perhaps more general than our word "sick". It is rather "not feeling so good", "weary and wan"; more like the Greek *asthenēs,* though in the Septuagint this represents rather Hebrew *qāšal. Hōleh* designates the opposite of *šālôm* -- one of the few Hebrew words which most people think they know, but which really means not so much "peace" but rather "well-being", overall state of completeness or "being as things ought to be". This very general sense of *hōleh* accounts in part for the difficulty which experts find in recognizing specific known diseases in the biblical symptoms. "It is seldom possible to make a simple equation between the ancient disease and a modern one" (Jackson 1988, p.184; though he often tries to, says Pilch 1990).

The most obvious reference to sickness which we would expect to find in the Bible or anywhere else would be headache or stomach-ache, especially but not only where children are involved. I have not found in any of the experts a confirmation for my suspicion that headache and stomach-ache as such simply do not exist in the Bible; in part doubtless because even in touching on vast realms of human experience it simply had no occasion to deal with them; more likely because the term *hōleh* of itself implies those vague symptoms of headache and stomach-ache which are to some extent characteristic of most sicknesses (Marconi 1990; von Soden 1989).

Another very good reason for the experts' non-mention of these discomforts is the sound norm of modern exegesis: we ought to deal with the biblical materials in *their own* categories and with *their own* emphasis, not insist on seeking in the Bible answers to questions which are not there asked. Nevertheless the exegete must also use a little ingenuity in envisioning *why* the Bible is silent on a subject which would seem so obviously relevant. In this spirit we will take up first the distresses relating to the head.

1. The head and its appurtenances

The Bible itself and the Ancient Near East in general usually enumerate the parts or ills of the body from the head down to the feet (Wiseman 1986,19). The famous Isaiah 1,6, "unsound from the sole of the foot to the head" is rather a metaphor for general (moral) corruption.

The most astounding thing about the ills of the head is that there is in biblical Hebrew absolutely no word for "brain" (North 1993). And yet in the fearful rending and outpouring of the innards which are often noted for the wounds of war and other violence, the biblical people must have often detected the gruesome spattered portions of the brain. The Mishnaic and Arabic term *moah* occurs only in Job 21,24 for the marrow within the bones as a metaphor for prosperity. In Talmudic Aramaic it is used six times meaning skull, twice meaning brain (Sokoloff 294).

The word *lēb, lēbāb*, usually or always translated "heart", is rather the organ of thought or will (along with emotion), and in not a single one of its 850 occurrences can be proved to refer specifically to what we call "heart" (Gil Modrego). Only relatively recently has this organ been known to be for pumping the blood. Since in the Bible its functions are rather of cognition and regulation of body-reaction, we have maintained that its operations should be equated with those of the brain (North 1995). Admittedly it was not localized within the head or skull, but it is not formally excluded among the "innards" which were "vital" in causing death but also in regulating conscious life. These may be regarded as including the bone-marrow which has some resemblance to the interior of the brain. The *lēb(āb)* was doubtless known in itself as one of those several "vital organs", chiefly in the stomach-area, as will be noticed below; and may thus continue to be translated "heart", though not exactly because it "beats" (Gen 45,26; de Sousa 1990, 74: or stops beating; *yāpāg < pûg* = ? "benumb").

An entirely different approach to the problem of the brain is afforded not by the Bible itself but by evidences of "trepaning" excavated in Lachish, Jericho, Arad, and Egypt (Jack 1937; Zias 1982; P. Smith 1990; Pahl; Wolska). It seems likely that these perforations of the skull were made to relieve pathological pressure on the brain. This explanation has been queried by some, but others maintain it can be traced even into the Stone Age (Seybold 1978, 17).

There also seems to be no Hebrew word for "nerve" or awareness of its importance. It is more natural that in battle-wounds no "nerve" as such would have been noticed; it is not a black line, as the frequent representations of the whole nervous system might lead us to assume, but a grayish string. Modern Hebrew dictionaries attempt a variety of terms for nerve, mostly in its derivative sense of "boldness", but also *'ēseb* (biblical II. "shape", "vessel"? or I. "pain").

Jacob's blow on the thigh in Gen 32,32H, which caused him to "limp" afterwards, is generally explained as having affected the sciatic nerve better known today. This Talmudic insight may be due to the Septuagint use of *neûron*, meaning "tendon" (Vulgate *nervus*) for Gen 32,32; but the final verse 33 in the Hebrew Bible uses the word *gîd*, "sinew, tendon", attested in Job 10,11; Ezek 37,6.8 and three other times in the Bible (Wharton).

There is no article on any of these terms, not even "Heart" nor on "Physiology" or "Anatomy" in the 1992 *Anchor Bible Dictionary* (but see Sussman). A recent doctorate on the biblical "mind", though claiming that Barr's research on "thought patterns" has discredited some anthropologists' views, is really about divine guidance in thought (Carasik 1997). For lack of better biblical information about the brain and nervous system, we will not attempt here to reduce to modern terms the various prominent cases of paralysis, stroke, epilepsy (Pinkus 1992; Sussman 6,11).

Nor do we have enough data to discuss mental disorder (*pace* A. Young 1989), often perhaps loosely designated in the Old and New Testaments as demonic possession or divine punishment (Pangas 1989; Simundson 1989). It is suggested that demon-possession may have been a real disorder due to *belief* in demons coupled with the frustration of subjection to foreign political authority (Theissen 1974, 253; Humbert 1964,111). There have of course been other studies of insanity in NT times (Pigeaud 1987; Hersant 1989).

Eyes. One of the ailments best attested in the Bible is to be blind, *'iwwer* (Münchow 1983), though it is often used metaphorically, as with us: "there's none so blind as those who *will* not see". One serious older research concludes that blindness is one of the few sicknesses (apart from injuries, of course) for which the Bible assigns a purely natural cause: Lods 1925,183: Gen 27,1; 48,17; 1 Sam 3,2; 1 Kgs 14,4), but even so it notices that most biblical etiologies and remedies were "magical" (further Horsfall 1995; Marganne 1994; Zaghloul on amblyopia 1992).

Anyway the cited examples are all due to old age; little or nothing is said about the pathetic children, until recently sometimes seen in Bible lands, with visible eye-disease to which they are so accustomed that they do not even reach up to brush away the flies. Blindness from weeping is perhaps metaphorical in Ps 88,9 or Job 17.7; and the "groping" of the blind evokes charity in Deut 27,18; Isa 59,10. Other "sociological implications" of eye afflictions in the Old Testament have been studied (Papagiannopoulos 1989).

Rubbing the eye-lens could have remedied cataract but with initial enlargement of things seen, "men like trees walking" Mk 8,24 (Fraser 1973; *AnchorBD* 6,14; but see p. 33 below). Ophthalmic spatulas made of bone are said to have been found at Jemme south of Gaza (Van Beek).

What the biblical writers call blindness was either the disease of ophthalmia (conjunctivitis or trachoma) or senile degeneration. For remedies the Babylonians used kohl and sophisticated bronze lancets (Stol 1989); the Egyptians used also malachite and stibium, and the Ebers Papyrus (1550 B.C.; Ebbell 1937) commends forceps for ingrown eyelashes (Harrison *IDB* 1,148; Helbing 1980); it seems implied that some of these cures may have influenced biblical Palestine. Though Pentateuchal hygienic enactments do not include ocular care (Gordon 1933), Lev 19,14 and Deut 27,18 deal with blindness as a social problem, and in Lev 21,20 impaired vision excludes priesthood.

A modern case of scorpion-ash as remedy is recorded (Amitai 1995). The most conspicuous biblical-era case of remedy for blindness is undoubtedly the (miraculously attained) fish-gall curing Tobit's "albugo" (*IDB* 1,849) from bird-dung (2,10; 6,4.7; 11,12). It must be remembered that we possess this (deuterocanonical) book only in Greek, reflecting a more advanced stage of cultural and medicinal influence on Israel, some of which may perhaps be hinted in the details of a story otherwise highly far-fetched.

Ears. Regarding the deaf, though there is a biblical word for it, *hereš*, attested roughly twice as many times as "blind", their pathology is barely mentioned, largely ritual as Lev 21,18; or metaphorical as Isa 6,10; 29,18 eschatological. The *IDB* renvoi under Deafness turns out to be a scant six lines (1,849) without verse-reference or factual data.

Nose. A "runny nose", and the "cold-in-the-head" to which it is due, are both virtually ignored in the Bible; as indeed also among us today they are so universally common, especially but not only in children, that they are hardly considered a disease at all, just one of the ups-and-downs of existence. We today are aware of the usual connection of colds with the lungs; "lung" again has no biblical Hebrew word at all, despite modern *rē'ah*. Colds have also a frequent connection with stomach-virus (Perizonius/Goudemit 1989), and especially fever.

Fever is in Hebrew *qaddahat* (Deut 28,22; Lev 26,16) or *hirhur* (Deut 28,22, in a list adjacent to *daleqet*, "inflammation"; modern distinctions in Harrison IDB 2,266, including *šahepet* despite lexica "consumption": Skoda 1994). Amid abridging twenty works of Galen, Maimonides dealt with fever (Langermann 1993).

Fever may often be due rather to the infection of a wound, as noted below. But a different kind of fever due to infection is that of contagious diseases like malaria (Borza 1987; Hellweg 1985). Such infection can reach the epidemic stage, as at Ebla (Pomponio 1989; Pettinato 1986,308). This kind is known from biblical examples, some narrated with clinical precision, others attributed to the angel of the divine vengeance (2 Kgs 19,35). We are here within the realm of dreaded "plagues", like the now-agreed bubonic plague of the Philistines in 1 Sam 5,9. Verse 8 there refers to the Ten "Plagues of Egypt" [Ex 7-11], which are variously claimed to reflect local pests or sandstorms (Hoffmeier 1992; Lemmelijn 1996; Schmidt 1990; but see p. 33 below).

Throat. The throat is not usually noted among disease centers, though it is subject to goiter and cancer. Its channels for air and food are certainly among the most important organs. The ills of the tongue in Scripture are usually limited to speech, and not to its physical aspects like stuttering, but to the content as display or often betrayal of the character (Brueggemann, *IDB* 4,670). The vocal chords are also of constant use, but rarely in need of medical care, except when they become deficient. But in one of the articles below (p. 73) we have tried to show that the voice itself, its loudness, is not just to be taken for granted but has its part in the formation of personality.

Teeth. The *šēn* (root "sharpen") / *odoús* are used often in quite varied senses, some of which have become famous: "skin of my teeth" (Job 19,20), "tooth for a tooth" (with eye in Ex 21,24), "sour grapes setting (others') teeth on edge" (Jer 31,29 = Ezek 18,2), "gnashing of teeth" (Mt 13,42 and often). Records of teeth (in Aristotle: Cootjans 1991) are intertwined with those of nutrition (Brothwell 1959). But none of these seem to imply the need of a dentist, whose functions in our day have been almost completely separated from those of the physician. In nearby Egypt, however, is noted the lofty station of "le grand des dentistes" as of "le grand des médecins du Palais" (Bardinet 1990, 230; Harris).

2. The innards ("heart") or stomach-area organs

The biblical people must have known the specific heart among the inner organs, and probably also its "beating", whether or not that is the meaning of

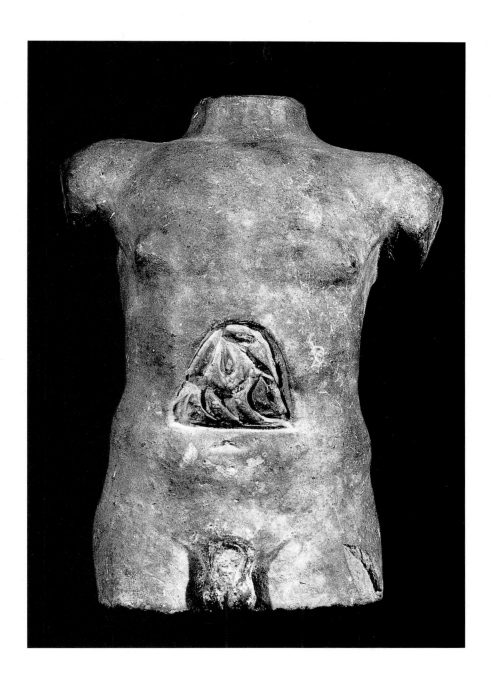

Fig. 1 – Madrid Etruscan torso

Fig. 2 – Organs of Decouflé statuette

Gen 45,26. So we are better-advised to continue translating *lēb* as "heart", one of the (most) vital organs in the stomach-area (for which we should really say "belly", but in recent English it has become mildly vulgar as used for humans). But the "heart" was not the organ of "romantic love", except insofar as emotion is a normal component of thought and will, of which the *lēb*, "innards" were organ(s) (Schipperges 1989); so also the Babylonian *libbu* (Labat 1951, p.xxx). These inner organs were only confusedly known, largely because operations involving blood-shedding or post-mortem were disapproved (Hempel 1958, 244).

Nor was the heart known as organ of what is currently understood as the circulation of the blood, and its connection with infections: all of which came to be known only much later. Blood, of course, is very familiar in the Hebrew Bible; indeed, "life itself is in the blood" (Deut 12,23; Gen 9,4). The word *dam* occurs 368 times, often as among us also today in the sense of "bloodshed, violence"; medically chiefly in relation to the wounds of war or other misfortunes, which we will notice under "bones". Blood in animal sacrifices is prominent in Lev 17 (though not in Num 6; Chiesa 1981). The favorite medieval practice of "bloodletting", well known already from Galen (P.Brain 1986), would not have been tolerated by the biblical people -- although they were aware of the "leech" (Prov 30,15). But it is unlikely that they knew of "hormones" produced for the blood-stream (Kellermann 1990).

For the Egyptians (whose medical progress was admirable but after all not perfect) the heart was a center for breathing and pulse; and even for the *Ka*, "soul, reality"; the animal-heart was valued for sacrifices (Fabry 416; Brunner). Something of the generalization of the functioning of "heart (or) inner organs" is found also in Greek (Richardson) and Hittite (Chen Xu 1995). Not only *kēr*, *kradíē* (S.Sullivan 1995), but also *thymós* (Caswell 1991) and other terms properly designating concrete inner organs had come to be used for "human vitality itself" or for "the personality; what it is that essentially makes the person in his or her distinctiveness" by the time Egyptian and Greek medical influences had encompassed Rome.

The Etruscans northward from Rome have left numerous statuettes, probably *ex-votos* for healing, some of which show the skin of the stomach partly removed and the interior organs neatly visible, as in a window or primitive X-ray (Baggieri 1996). The most notable of these (**Fig. 1**) dated 150 B.C., is in the Madrid National Museum, often reproduced (North 1994,372; 1995,33; Krug [2]1993,35; ital. [1]1990, also p.35). It shows rather what is beneath the heart and lungs, and experts have recognized various organs and given them their modern names. Though the statuette remains a product of imagination rather than dissection or X-ray, it is precious as giving us a fair idea of what the late-biblical people must have regarded as the (lower) inner organs or *lēb*.

More satisfying though unfortunately of no authenticated provenance is the statuette of a youth, clothed, with his arm beneath his chlamys, but with an oval of skin folded back between the breastbone and navel, revealing his internal organs **(Fig. 2)**. The photo (Decouflé 1964, fig.19; names indicated in fig. 21 and in North 1994, fig. 19,3) is accompanied by a clear drawing with the organs numbered (from the top) 1 to 26, and nearby these numbers are accompanied by the suitable modern terms. The real heart is called instead "No. 6, oreillettes; No. 7, ventricules". The lungs are numbered 3 only on our right (his left) but shown on both sides, long but rather thin to make place for nearby organs; the lung to our left shows the "the incisions" numbered 4 and 5 (also 27 right edge). The largest organ, in the center, is numbered 16, "Liver, [to us the] left lobe"; near its top is No. 11, right lobe. The kidney called 18 is expressly labeled [his] right (*and* "surrénal"; no other kidney is shown). A large circular low-center No. 21 is called "gall-bladder (*vésicule*) or rectum". This fascinating photo is one in a series of described terra-cotta statuettes similar to the one from Madrid.

There are also many other researches on Etruscan anatomical ex-votos from near Rome (S. Richardson 1993; Fenelli 1975AB; Gatti Lo Guzzo 1978; de Laet 1969; Tabanelli 1962). Though in date and place they are rather far on the fringe of the biblical center, they are precious as affording us a concrete view of what the *lēb* is likely to have meant there. It remains true that as organ of intellect and will, the biblical "heart" corresponds to what we call the brain; but these operations rightly are increasingly linked with the *emotions* and thus not only with the increased heartbeat but also with other sensations within the torso rather than the skull.

Liver. *Kābēd*, "the heavy thing" was notably differentiated from the other internal organs, doubtless because of the threat of its importance in the animal-divination procedures of Babylonian "hepatoscopy" (Ezek 21,21). In Lam 2,11 (where Revised Standard still has "heart" with LXX), the liver is singled out as seat of the emotions; and it is suggested that this vowel-pointing (as "soul, spirit") should be used instead of *kābôd*, "glory" in Gen 49,6; Ps 16,9; 57,8.

The frequent ills of the liver (hepatitis) are either not recognized or not mentioned in the Bible or even in Egyptian sources. *Yēreqôn*, "greenish-yellowishness" (of face, Jer 30,6) may be due to jaundice (or to anemia, Rosner 1972). Diabetes rather than gout may have been the illness of King Asa (1 Kgs 15,23; AnchorDB 6,14 prefers DeVries to Preuss-Rosner). Nothing in our sources seems identifiable as the dreaded cancer (of any bodily part).

Kidneys. Beside Decouflé above, on Egyptian sources see Park 1994. Also from Egypt. there are claimed to be "radiating" symptoms of gallstones (Miller & Ritner 1994).

Colon. What about constipation or diarrhoea ? From 2 Chr 21,19 we learn that King Joram had in his "intestines" (*me'eh*) an incurable disease, and they "came out" and he died. The symptoms seem to indicate amoebic dysentery. Symptoms of Antiochus IV in 2 Mcb 9,5.9 may have been similar, or perhaps rather cancer. It has been claimed that the "fiery serpents" of Num 21.6 were the guinea-worm (Lee 1973).

We are better informed about hemorrhoids, at least from Egyptian sources (Jonckheere 1947,41). The imagination-defying "golden emerods" of our earlier translations of 1 Sam 6,5 are now generally taken as "tumors". But as carriers of the Philistines' bubonic plague the term has been rendered rather "rodents" (Muntner in Rosner 1977,6).

3. Skin and bones

Leprosy. Perhaps the disease which would occur to us as most common in the Old and especially New Testament is the skin-rash or infection called "leprosy": *sara'at* 35 times, plus verbal usages; *lépra* only Mk 8,3 ‖ and *leprós* 9 times. Before investigating what this biblical word really means, we may note two more general allusions to skin-disease. Some Qumran Cave 4 fragments not in the known Geniza text of the Damascus Zadokite document seem to indicate that hair-sprouts on the skin are due to the entry of an evil "spirit", possibly physiological rather than demonic (Baumgartner 1990). And the Hippocratics are claimed to have wrongly and dangerously ascribed skin-disease to internal fluids; two marble plates in Epidaurus Asclepius temple describe 48 cures, most in a dream, only two involving the treatment by ointment which is usual today (Mustakallio in Castrén).

In dealing with biblical "leprosy", our hopes are aroused by the fact that the celebrated case of Naaman in 2 Kgs 5 was made the subject of a special research by one of the most esteemed scholars of recent times, Gerhard von Rad. But there we will be disappointed; he sees fit to deal chiefly with the social background of guru-style healers like Elisha, and with Naaman's own high status and the gifts he brings; not a word is said about what his "leprosy" really was, nor about its healing. But precisely this problem is treated by many (Mull 1992; Hulse 1975; Seidl *ThWAT*; Stol 1987).

We may take as our starting-point the trivial but significant fact that Leviticus speaks of the *sara'at* or "leprosy" of a garment (13,47-59) or of the mud-wall of a house (14,34-48).   Obviously there is question here of some discoloration due either to stain or to corruption of the material, and in this sense identical with a skin-rash such as Hippocrates and Polybius describe, which is a human disease, but more likely psoriasis or erysipelas.   The Babylonians describe similar conditions, e.g. "If the skin of a man exhibits white *pusu*-areas and is dotted with *nuqdu*-spots, such a man has been rejected by his god and should be rejected by mankind" (text copied, transliterated, and translated by Kinnier Wilson in Ishida 1982).

In Palmer's compilation the chapter by Browne on leprosy alone is almost as long as Wiseman's treating leprosy along with all other biblical diseases.   In view of the "leprosy" of garments or walls, Browne considers that *sara'at* refers to several *different* disorders, which cannot be reduced to any one definition or class.   He rightly notes also that it often means either "scab" or "eruption", both of which are clinically quite different from a mere rash or discoloration.   He appropriately emphasizes that although Naaman was publicly well known to have leprosy, this did not disqualify him from holding a high office involving frequent contact with important people, not only in Syria where the ritual regulations might have been quite different from those in Leviticus, but also in Israel where he came without concealment for healing.

Though the LXX *lepra* applied to various diseases (including possibly even our modern leprosy, or the similar elephantiasis *IDB* 3,112), there is *almost* a consensus that in *no* case do the biblical descriptions correspond to what is today known as leprosy.   Moreover in the whole background of the Middle East not a single sure case of (our) leprosy has ever been attested: even in Egypt, so sensitive and advanced in medical matters (Bucaille 1990).   Hundreds of well-embalmed skeletons have afforded modern physicians ample evidence for declaring they show no trace of what we call "leprosy" before some Coptic examples around 500 A.D. (Grmek 1983,154; Zias 1985).

A rendition like "dreaded skin disease" (Verbov 1976) for *sara'at* is preferred in modern translations of 2 Kgs 7,3; 15,5 and such.   This well indicates that we have to do here with a real sickness, probably contagious (in a way that real modern leprosy is not), and sometimes developing horribly, even if not to the gruesome extent favored by medieval and modern art.   In short, the term covered a variety of symptoms which caused *dread*, even in slight or initial stages.

Thus in Leviticus it is above all a *ritual* matter, something for the *priests* to decide (as Deut 24,8; Mk 1,43).   This need not necessarily imply the survival of some superstition akin to that which the Babylonians called "the disfavor of one's god" (even in the "curse" of 2 Sam 3,28).   It may merely imply that just as in the Middle Ages apart from population-centers only the priestly class had sufficient education to apply the necessary criteria.

Although in general the Bible, though perhaps no more than most people everywhere and always, tended to regard sickness as a divine punishment for sins, yet this was not specially the case with *sara'at,* as if it were a venereal disease. Hence it is surprising to see a serious archeological journal "correlating" leprosy and lust (Zias 1989; milder Baruch 1964).

Bones interest us chiefly because of the wounds of war and more casual everyday fractures (Geroulanos 1994; Salazar 1991; Majno 1975; Živanović 1982). These form the chief part of the Smith Medical Papyrus splendidly edited by Breasted, which gives us an idea of the best the biblical sufferer could hope for. The word *'ēsem* is normal Hebrew for bone, though it occurs only a dozen times to designate a specific or injured bone in the body; and "(his) bones" as with us is used some six times to designate the dead. But *'ēsem* is frequently used for the whole body or the substance, or also for "oneself". Thus a modern Hebrew speaker will say without any sense of oddness "I wash my bone" but may laugh to hear an Arab say "I wash my soul" (*nafs,* Hebrew *nepeš*).

The Arabic word for bonesetting has intriguingly come into our language(s) as algebra. Trajan's column in Rome, amid several touching scenes of soldiers helping their wounded fellows with almost tender brotherliness, shows a *capsarius* bandaging the thigh of a wounded comrade (Penso 1984, p.149, fig.73; Davies 1989). Penso's brilliant illustrations show also (p. 186-190) several paintings like X-rays, mostly of bones and skeletons, thus differing in style from the terracottas discussed above. The famous "Anatomy Lesson" fresco from Room 1 of Rome's Via Latina catacomb shows fourteen students, one bare-chested, paying close attention to the master with pointer, touching a nude body on the floor (Penso p. 242, pl. 18).

Bones and entire skeletons are constantly encountered by excavators but without much elation, since their study is specialized and expensive, and rarely yields the kind of information archeologists look for (Arensburg 1985AB; Rak 1976; Haas 1969). The Egyptians and the Babylonians seem to have known only 200 bones, whereas the medieval Jewish lore, benefiting by the Arabic as well as the Egyptian-Greek medical experience, counted 240 (Oholot 1,8; Preuss-Rosner 1973). The exact number is somewhere in between, but seems to be reluctantly specified by modern encyclopedias or doctors, in order to allow for some variation.

Such variation is mild and unnoticed except for the cases of having an extra finger or toe, an anomaly frequent enough to have been often represented in art, surely not in all cases by a simple mistake (Barnett 1986). Goliath had six fingers and six toes on each side, according to 2 Sam 21,20. The article on "Finger" in *EDB* (Hartman 1963) is surprisingly more informative than *IDB* 2,268. Of undoubted interest is the chapter "Medicine and the Birth of Defective Children; Approaches of the Ancient World" (Amundsen 1996, 50-69).

Cripples were strangely classed with athletes (Aigner 1988). Akin to such abnormalities are the hunchback and various forms of dwarfism (paralleled in Lev 21,20; Fohrer; Heymer 1993; Dasen). Dwarfs exerted a special fascination on the Egyptians (Seyfried 1986), and several are known to have reached prominence and power in the government (Rupp 1965). Herkhuf's report on a dwarf being brought by him to the boy pharaoh Pepi II (LexÄg 2,1129), or rather Pepi's bossy reply, was immortalized in stone near Aswan.

Interest in anatomy as such seems to have left no echo in the Bible (Barcía Goyanes 1987-9; religiously Finkel 1995), despite some in Mesopotamia (Scharf 1988; Ebeling 1932). There is a biblical word for skull, *gulgolet*, which became consecrated in its Aramaic form Golgotha, the skull-shaped hill of Calvary. But there is no word for skeleton; modern Hebrew uses *šeled*, not biblical (or *gerem*, really a biblical synonym for *'esem*). It has been sagely observed that we would never even know we have an anatomy or a physiology except for the experience we have of them in sickness. For this reason a physician wrote that we should value sickness as an irreplaceable form of education in the structures and skills of the human body (Barras 1992).

Weakness, misery. "Lord, heal me, my bones ache" in Psalm 6,2 is the prayer of one who is "languishing" in a way for which it is frequently impossible to find a specific disease or remedy. This is in general the case of the quite recognizable genre called "the Complaint Psalms". It is true that in many cases there is immediately question of "my enemies", as here in verse 7; but expressions like "my bones ache" are hardly the way one would refer to one or several actual bones broken or injured by an enemy. In Psalm 22,17, "I can count all my bones" is not a realistic way of referring to physical injuries, even if LXX "they have pierced my hands and feet" be admitted for the preceding verse; in any case there is in this Psalm magnificent eloquence in portraying not only the speaker's misery and rejection, but far more his own and others' confidently-awaited outcome.

"I lie awake [and] all the day my enemies taunt me" of Ps 102,7 seems to have unsympathetic cronies in mind rather than battle-enemies. "Men trample upon me .. my enemies trample upon me all the day long ... they seek to injure my cause ... they lurk, they watch my steps" might well refer to a business deal being blocked while he lies "tossing" in bed (Ps 56,1.2.6.8), though some see here mental-disease or persecution-complex (Kinnier-Wilson p.359). But it is possible that while the sufferer lies on his sickbed he is tortured by the thought that some enemy far away is using magic practices to cause his sickness (Mowinckel 1962 vol 2, p.2-5).

In Psalm 28,2.5 the "festering wounds" are ascribed to "the Lord's arrows", a metaphor which has been rightly said to resemble "the arrows of Apollo god of the plague" (Fohrer 1981; p.175 on Ps 91,5). In Psalm 32,4 the illness is quite plainly accepted as a punishment for the sufferer's own sins; so also in Ps 39,2.10; and even 61,8, where there is question of broken bones. In any case it is recognized that these symptoms are all vague and hard to reduce to specific diseases (Hempel 1958, 260). Ultimately the Psalmist is moaning about being just *hōleh*, "out of sorts", from headache or stomach-ache, or simply from the ever-present misery of being "human, therefore *subject* to diseases".

4. Genitality and childbirth

Expert studies of medicine in itself and in the Bible commonly devote notable space to reproduction, which is a common healthy human experience and not in itself pathological at all. "The Hebrew women are more vigorous in giving birth than the Egyptians", says Exodus 1,19. Vigor of the twins being born is noted in Genesis 25,26; nothing is said there (though perhaps hinted in the later struggles of Jacob and Esau) about twins being ill-omened in the anthropological findings of the Near East and elsewhere. Curiously in IDB twins get an article only in relation to Castor and Pollux (and Acts 28,11: 4,719).

There was of course always some possibility of danger in childbirth: miscarriage (1 Sam 4,19) or death (Gen 35,18), even double. High infant mortality is plausibly presumed rather than actually discovered in biblical narratives like 1 Kgs 14,17; 2 Kgs 4,22. In any case the strong and insistent desire of women to have many children is often expressed throughout the Bible, especially in the stories of Rachel and Anna (Gen 30,1; 1 Sam 1.6). Aphrodisiacs were known and used (Gen 30,14), though birth-control plants are claimed to have been in use ever since Eve (Riddle 1994). Qohelet 11,5 shows admiring awareness of the growth of the bones of the fetus within the womb.

"Bible-gynecology confrontation" (Adinolfi 1989) is an interesting title which perhaps promises more than it delivers; there are similar treatments for late antiquity (Nathan 1993) and the Middle Ages (Barkai 1991). Also to be noted are the Greek treatises of Soranus (Burguière 1988) and others (De Lacy 1992; Byl, Dean-Jones, Arthur-Katz: all 1989). The modern-sounding "evil of being a woman" (Gourévitch 1984) gains from a word-play in French, *mal* being both "evil" and "sickness". Griffiths treating "Love as a disease" cites Ct 2,5; 5,8, but adds that Greek parallels are more abundant "without great anatomical precision", he pregnantly concludes.

The overall biblical link between sickness and sin (downplayed by Jesus in Jn 9,3) was not as closely focused on sex-sins as our medieval-modern mentality would expect. Reference may perhaps be found to syphilis (Num 25,8; J.Flavius Ant 4,155; 3,264) and gonorrhea (Kottek 1994, 39; 43 & 76). Though virginality before marriage was stressed (Tigay 1993) especially in rabbinic practice, still the relative silence of the Bible on pre-marital intercourse and masturbation might lend some support to a current medical and social view that they are an inevitable even if undesirable part of normal growing-up.

Prostitution's evils and dangers, and inevitability, are prominent especially in relation to the "foreign woman" of Proverbs 5,3 and five other verses of that book; more tolerantly Rahab in Jos 5,5. Homosexuality as a disease is focused in some recent biblical researches (Schrijvers 1985); its prohibition in Lev 18,22 is held valid today (Gilbert 1986; Winter 1986, p.155 against Bailey 1955).

The not necessarily medical importance of circumcision is prominent in the Bible (Gen 17,23; Jos 5,3), and was shared with Semitic and other neighboring peoples. We can still see *in situ* the famous Memphis depiction of a circumcision (Kornfeld 1991; Hyatt *IDB* 1,629). "The uncircumcised" was a common term of reproach for enemies unrelated to Israel, especially the Philistines (1 Sam 17,26). When forced to live in the midst of a Greek ("gymnasium") culture, many Jews made efforts to "uncircumcise" themselves (1 Mcb 1,15).

Epilogue on sicknesses

As a final word about sicknesses in the Bible we may well mention what is said in several researches. The main cause of death was war. But despite the terrific decimation of youth caused by war and infant mortality, there are many Old Testament references to aged people; and the life-span went on slowly but steadily increasing (Adamson p. 11). Actually however the normal life-span clearly stated in Psalm 90,10 as between 70 and 80 years (men some 8 years less than women, Andouche 1995) is pretty much the same today, despite our vaunted prolongation of life. Death much before 70, though still considered "premature", is quite frequent; and life after 80 is still "replete with ills" whatever be our high-powered medicines and health-insurance.

There is a sense also in which "the main cause of death is life itself": notmerely overindulgence and accident-prone headstrong youth. From the very moment of birth the physical powers start "using themselves up"; the sicknesses which come along the way render known not only to ourselves but also to the medical profession the recuperative and creative powers of life; and death whenever it comes is a "completeness" rather than an interruption.

III. Remedies in the biblical background

We now turn to interrogate the Bible as to what it has to say about the remedies by which people sought to alleviate or heal their ills. It will not surprise us that most such references are to God as the giver and only remover of disease. This reaction is studied at length in several of the treatises purportedly on medicine in the Bible, though not many conclude as relentlessly as Kee and Seybold that it leaves no place for human resources whatever. In any case it is our business, like Asaph's (Newmyer 1993), to detail what little the Bible really does say on the subject of natural remedies, even if only to condemn them.

1. Ointments and potions

Jeremiah speaks three times of liniment, called balm or balsam (51,8, šerî), of which Gilead across the Jordan was a special supplier (8,22). At 'En Gedi was recently excavated a tub claimed to have been used for processing balsam (Hirschfeld 1996). A sample of balsam has been identified at Qumran (Patrich 1989; Crocker 1989). (An alleged "Therapy" scroll from Cave 4 has been reassessed: Charlesworth 1989; Naveh 1986). Jeremiah 46,11 speaks also of "many (other) remedies", rᵉpû'ôt.

The Greek-era Tobit 8,3 is quite detailed in describing how an eye-remedy can be got from the interior of a fish (Kollmann 1994). Scharbert mentions also "powders" but cites no example; and anyway warns that the healing is really done by "time itself", i.e. Mother Nature, the marvelous recuperative power of our own body (TRE 19,681). The doctor mostly just clears away the obstacles. The remedies mentioned in the Bible were chiefly palliatives and seldom conduced to any real healing. The exception in Tobit 11,12 is so dramatic as to suggest an intervention of God and/or "his angel" ("presence", North 1967,446). The very name Raphael (5,4) means "God heals".

When Hezekiah became mortally sick, Isaiah told him that he would be healed by God because of his penitent prayer; but nevertheless Isaiah himself directs the application of "a poultice of figs on the eruption", 2 Kgs 20,7. Neither here nor in 2 Chr 32,24 is anything said about a "book of remedies hidden away", as in the Rashi and Maimonides comments on Pesahim 56 (Rosner 1985; Greenblatt 1985). In Isaiah 1,6 for festering sores is mentioned *šemen*, "oil"; Walter adds that vinegar even if not curative at least gives ritual purity.

Ezekiel's promised wondrous river (47,12) is described in terms which show he is familiar with liquid medicines. The Greek-era Wisdom of Solomon 7,20 has a very discreet allusion to "special powers of certain plants and roots" not specifically medicinal (more specialized Greek in Rippinger). But we are justified in assuming that the Hebrews had some knowledge of the immense number of medicinal herbs catalogued by the Egyptians (Grapow 1959, vol.6; Riddle 1992). These amount to some 500, but include also products from minerals and 30 different animals (Wiseman 1986, p.38; Mariani Canova 1989). But *t3-mah* as "crocodile-dung" is to be rendered rather "fayence" (Kurth 1989). There is a more specifically biblical focus in Duke (1983; also de Waal 1984).

2. *Wounds and surgical instruments*

The treatment of wounds, considered frequent in the Bible (Hempel 1958 as cited in IV below, p.33), is perhaps specially noticeable just as wound itself is among the most noticeable forms of sickness. The term *habaš*, "bind, tie" is used in Hosea 6,1 (predictively) for bandaging. In Ezekiel 34,4 there is blame for "not binding up" the "fracture(d)" (Nifal/passive of *šeber* "break", used also for cripples).

In citing the celebrated passage of Isaiah 61,1, Jesus in his home-town synagogue (Lk 4,18) omits precisely the term which interests us here, "to bind up those broken *of heart*"; in Isaiah we note especially the use of *lēb* as a general term for (suffering) internal organs. The wounds of war, which were so frequent, are surprisingly seldom mentioned as being washed or treated. But we are told in detail how the blood of Ahab wounded in battle spilled into his chariot, which was thereafter brought back to his capital and washed (1 Kgs 22,35.38).

In the Egyptian (especially Smith) papyri, on the contrary, a very large number of treatments for different wounds are indicated (Breasted 1930; Ebbell 1939). Perhaps the most usable concise summary of the remedies mentioned in Egypt is that given by Gelin (*SDB* 1956). But he says "we will not be surprised to find in the Bible medical knowledge and healing-procedures". It would have been safer to say "we *would not* be surprised if we *did* find more such data in the Bible". The simple fact is that he and most other experts *suppose* the biblical people to have used Egyptian techniques of which the Bible itself shows hardly a trace.

Assyro-Babylonian medicine is much less well known, and presumably had less influence in Israel. But this brief summary of it seems impressively modern: "The standard therapeutic medical texts include the purpose of the treatment, a list of ingredients, the method of preparing them, and instructions for administering the treatment", sometimes with prognosis, usually "he will recover" (Biggs *RLA* 7,624).

Though the above treatment of wounds would be classed with surgery, and we earlier noticed examples of trepaning the skull, still Gelin states that the actual sawing of bones or incisions in the flesh were excluded by the tremendous biblical reverence for blood and regulations regarding its shedding. This was noticed above in relation to the leech in Pvb 30,15.

Gelin also holds that all progressive embryology was blocked because God wishes the formation of the fetus in the womb to be his own exclusive domain shrouded in mystery (Ps 139,13; Job 10,11). Such interpretations push too far some poetic allusions stressing the fact that the complexity of the functions of blood and womb are far beyond our ken. As for a surgical knowledge of anatomy to be gained from post-mortem dissection, it may be admitted that any such practice of the biblical people fell under the stigma (at least ritual, where necessary) of contact with cadavers. But there is recorded a famous breakthrough of one Rabbi Ishmael in securing for medical dissection the body of an executed criminal (Bekorot 45a; *SDB* 5,962).

Silence of the Bible about surgical operations is somewhat compensated by the archeological discovery of numerous varied surgical instruments, though from a date near the closing of the biblical record (Künzl 1983, drawings reproduced in North 1995; Künzl 1986; Goerke; Matthäus; Snyder). Gadara in the Decapolis is the most prominent biblical city to have yielded such finds (Weber 1991).

From the famed site of Jewish resistance at Masada beside the Dead Sea has come a Roman cucurbitula (Hershkovitz 1989). Also in Palestine were found the eye-treatment spatulas noticed above. At Pompeii in 1771 near the Herculaneum-Gate was found a whole "Surgeon's House"; and eleven tools were found in 1940 in an Etruscan tomb near Volterra (Tabanelli 1958,36; pl VI).

Especially from shipwrecks medical tools have been rescued; thus from a Roman wreck 15 miles south of Siracusa in Sicily (Gibbins 1988; 1989). Notable discoveries were made in Spain and at south Egyptian Kom Ombo (Hibbs 1991. Stettler 1982). At Paphos in Cyprus has been excavated a Roman surgeon's tomb, giving rise to the claim that ancient medicine was a by-product of copper mining (Foster 1985).

Some of the recent surveys of ancient medicine give remarkably vivid photos of single instruments or collections (Penso, Krug). A collection of coins relating to medicine (Holzmair 1989) is rather extraneous to our concerns here (but see Penn 1994; Hart, Kraay, Storen). From the Antibes congress of 1986 the presentation of surgical instruments has been singled out for special praise by a reviewer who was otherwise quite severe on the articles about sex and its deviations (Byl on Marganne-Mellard).

IV. The doctor

And so at long last we turn to the person of the physician, who as already mentioned is the very first thing most people think of when they are sick (Kölbing 1977). It must be recognized that in the Old Testament medicine, "primitive and very inferior to that of the great ancient civilizations", the doctor is rarely mentioned and is of low social rank (Humbert 1964, p. 24 & 11). As against this, Hempel begins his 1958 survey with "Status of early-Israel medicine: The activity of the doctor as carried out in the practical reality of early Israel, was in Hebrew expressed by two verbs" which are not really named, but are shown by an example to be the binding up of wounds as the common and frequent chore of the doctor though he is not mentioned in the texts.

At any rate toward the end of the biblical period, our point of departure can be the praise of the doctor in Sirach 38,1-15. Though this book was written under strong Greek cultural influence, and was long thought to have been transmitted only in Greek, we now have from the Cairo Geniza and the Dead Sea caves a substantial portion of what is generally admitted to be the original Hebrew.

1. Sirach's portrayal of the physician

This lengthy passage emphasizes several quite different aspects of the physician's prized services, as has been well set forth by Lührmann (1979). Since very much stress is laid on the *honor* due to him, "and in the presence of great men he is admired" (verse 1 and 3), his "skill" is recognized to be a genuine wisdom, and not just a trade (Nutton 1988; 1991). But Greek medicine is recognized as *both* science and craft (Temkin 1971; Edelstein 1987).

Part of the doctor's wisdom is seen to lie in what is called by the Greek word diagnosis; but it is interesting to note that this term in recent translations professional status of the physician is claimed to show also his "independence" as not being a slave, nor a functionary of the State (Kudlien 1979 p.112). But a certain dependence on the state (Deichgräber) may sometimes have been possible. And to judge by the high and confidential positions entrusted to some unusually intelligent slaves (*paidagogós*, accountant-scribe) it does not seem unlikely that some may have been trained and allowed to practise medicine.

Strictly speaking we should admit that the chief skill attributed by Sirach to the physician is that of pharmacist (*myrepsós* verse 8). And interwoven into all the praises of the doctor is the fact that his healing-power ultimately comes from God (verse 2); the patient must first of all have recourse to prayer and sacrifice as fully as he can, and only then "give the proper place also to the physician" (verse 12), who also prays for success in his work, and recognizes his dependence upon God (Noorda 1979, Amundsen, Constantelos).

In all this there is no hint of magic or even of miraculous healing. To the priest are attributed no healing powers (nor to the King, adds Hempel 1988,292), though the priest has competence to pronounce that "leprosy" has been healed (p.20 above). Our dependence upon God in the healing of sickness is just as in all the other areas of our existence. We must also recognize that these praises of the physician come from a devout and fully Jewish author, but the attitudes here rendered explicit are nowhere so formally expressed within the Hebrew Testament (Baruch 1964a). At the same time this passage is an expression of Greek culture, to which we may justly turn in order to piece out its significance.

2. Social status and training of the physician

There are numerous specialized studies of the professional physician's academic and social status in Rome (Scarborough 1969, p.122-133; Muri; Sabbah). Actually most of the doctors in Rome were from Greece (Archagathos as early as 219 BC says Pliny NH 29,12, or more probably specialists from the Greek city of Alexandria in Egypt: André 1987, p.16 & 59).

An interesting question is the *age* of the practising doctors. A quite recent study claims that most of them were boys in their teens: under 20 in ten epitaphs, 17 to 20 in census or army lists; their training was from age 14 to 17 (Kleijwegt 1991, p.157). But a different admittedly small sampling shows a normal distribution: one under 20, two over 80, four each 20-30 or 40-50 (Korpela 1987 p. 83).

Not much is known about the course of studies which they had to undergo (Mudry 1991). But we do have the title of a Greco-Arabic work, Examinations by which the best physicians are recognized (Iskander 1988). There are indications of medical schools in Egypt (Schäfer 1899; denied by Lefebvre 1956, p.17). Many Egyptian doctors were also (the cream of the) scribes (De Meulenaere, LexÄg 1,457).

There has been specialized research in army physicians (Davies 1989, p. 209 & 290). Rome's great contribution was the invention of the military hospital (Majno 1975, p. 393; Gabriel 1992). The lofty and versatile academic standing of the Ancient Near East physician may perhaps be suggested by the recorded fact that the Kassite royal doctors Imgurru and Mukallim had to maintain a singing-school as part of their duties (Ebeling RLA 1,164).

3. Punishments for alleged malpractice

In the Near East contemporary with the earliest biblical record we know that physicians were often severely punished (Remus 1985). For instance, cutting off an arm if the operation failed was the fate allotted by Hammurabi even for loss of sight in an eye-operation (and a nurse whose ward has died is to have her breast cut off). But the same sections of Hammurabi specify in detail the payment to be given to the physician for a successful operation (Pritchard, ANET[2], §218 & 194, p.175). Curiously ANET gives no special category of medical texts; p. 495 mentions briefly the Ebers papyrus only for its claim of "transmitting old tradition".

In the "(medically) classical" Greek theory and practice, liability of the physician was more detailed (Amundsen 1977a; Gómez Royo 1990; Krug[2] p.267).

4. Imhotep and Hippocrates as ideal image of the doctor

From the dawn of antiquity in Egypt, the name of Imhotep was venerated as the founder of the medical profession, from whom all later practices are claimed to derive their authority. This is strange, because he was known to have been a vizier (of Djoser c. 2700) or highly-placed statesman; and indeed all researches aimed to clarify what he really contributed to medicine have so far failed (Wildung 1977AB; Estes 1989 starts with Imhotep "though we don't know why"; Jonckheere 1958, frontispiece).

The case of Hippocrates is somewhat clearer, though also muddled (see II. above, p. 11; & Beckmann-Hueber 1994; Kudlien 1967). He as well as the

equally normative Galen (Nutton 1987; Gelpke; Fortuna) and other real founders
of Greek-style medicine worked on the island of Cnidus off the southwest tip of
Turkey (Grensemann 1987; Santana Henríquez 1991; Ilberg 1924). But their real
influence was most monumental in Alexandria, where however the active leader
was Hierophilus (von Staden 1989).

Nevertheless the studies and practice flourishing there came to be known
as "the Hippocratic corpus", which we now possess and call by that name,
though the proportion of it actually due to Hippocrates is quite limited (Jouanna
1989; 1990; Lloyd 1987; Maloney 1982; 1989; Potter; Di Benedetto). Even the
famed "oath of Hippocrates" normative even today (with reserves) is of contested
authenticity (Bauer 1995; Lichtenthaeler 1984; Deichgräber). But these great
names, like the patron saints of Christianity and Judaism and Islam, have
doubtless contributed to the honor and seriousness of the profession (Dagen
1990). It was this "Hippocratic medicine" which was moved en masse to
imperial Rome, and which in II,2 p.17 above we have considered to be somehow
related to terracottas of the nearby Etruscans.

5. *Hospitals; public and preventive medicine*

Apart from the above-mentioned Roman army innovation. the hospital
seems to be scarcely represented in the early medical record. What is called in
modern Hebrew *bêt hôlîm*, "house of the sick", seems to be known in the Bible
only by the euphemism *bêt ha-hopšît*, "house of freedom" meaning really "of
confinement" (for dangerous or contagious cases, 2 Kgs 15,5; Zilber 1985; on
"public doctors", Roesch 1987).

Efforts have been made to find in the Bible traces of "preventive
medicine", such as teaching of the Mosaic law that fatty foods are to be avoided;
or circumcision as a measure for the prevention of cancer (Fawver 1990).
"Medical science" (Hasel 1983 p.194 without source) shows that those who get
less than one rest day every seven function under par and are vulnerable to
breakdown.

The antiquated but quite orderly "Medicine in the Old Testament" by
Ebstein takes as its very point of departure a sixty-page survey of the healthiness
of the living conditions: dwellings, clothes, nourishment; and the variations for
the various age-groups. Among health-preservatives an archeology review
mentions smoke as insecticide (Neufeld 1971,60). Sirach 37,30 against gluttony
and overeating has been taken to show that the medical ideal was overall good
health. not just emergencies (Lührmann 1979, p.67; Klopfenstein 1978).

A promise of information from antiquity about "socialized medicine"

[Fuchs 1998], "new hygiene, health laws", house-doctors, specialists (including women, who here turn out to be largely midwives; but see Nickel 1979), "unions", and a "cosmetic industry" (not apparently referring to aesthetic surgery), is in fact mainly concerned with a free hand and unimpeded fees for the doctor: as a genuine payment and not just "honorarium" despite his professional loftiness (Kudlien 1979).

6. "YHWH *your doctor" (Ex 15,26)*

The rendition "your healer" would be just as appropriate or more so. The Hebrew *rôpē'* is more cautiously rendered "the healing one" (*iōmenos*) by the Septuagint, to avoid giving the impression that God is an *iatrós* with its Asclepius and Epidaurus overtones. But a fair number of recent titles have "doctor, *Arzt*" (Stöhr 1990; Deselaers 1982) -- even for Jesus, though this is not explicit in the New Testament (Sauser 1992). And even in the Hebrew Bible this is a unique brief statement which has called forth ample explanation.

As title of Hempel's now aging but witty survey (1957) it is merely a motto, as Lohfink points out in his own similarly titled research. For Lohfink it is not a mere motto, but the whole essence of a lengthy and profound work of literary criticism. He concludes that this unusual phrase can have come into our Bible only at the very end of a long period not merely of development (the JEPD sources) but even of later redaction or even interpolation.

But along the way Lohfink makes much of his incidental observation that though individual Israelites undoubtedly turned to God to heal them, still God is presented as "healer of Israel" rather than of individuals. Lohfink's subsection, "The health of Israel in the Deuteronomic tradition" shows that among the blessings promised, only the *second* and *part* of the 3d-4th refer to *physical* health as merely one aspect of the well-being which God's healing mercy provides (p. 49-57; so Halbe 1975, p.484-494 on the parallel Ex 23,25).

Under the title "YHWH as Physician" (1991), Niehr concludes that our knowledge of medicine is too skimpy to warrant the claim of Seybold (1978, p.39-48; 1973) and others that YHWH's role left no room for human physicians. I would add that the biblical people do indeed turn to God and to God alone for healing as for all other needs and blessings: but not to the exclusion of the intermediate agents with which his goodness has surrounded us (Russell 1982; Marsch 1984). They pray to God for harvest; but they also sow and plow diligently.

At this point it would be well to acknowledge that we have above sometimes cited reputable physicians or encylopedias seeming to explain away as a purely natural or medical phenomenon something which is presented in Scripture as a divine intervention.   Thus for example the "men like trees walking" in Mt 8,24 on p.15; or some of the Plagues of Egypt in Ex 7-11 on p. 16.   Doubtless even many believing exegetes have gone to extremes in citing some recorded experience as similar to the biblical narrative.   But their intention often has been to show that God's way of intervention tends rather to conform as far as possible to procedures which are normally human or attested.   In many cases the "medical explanations" offered for sicknesses or healings whether or not noted in the Bible are just "interesting possibilities" often not accepted even by colleagues.

Unless we change the vowels to read *El Rôpē'* in Numbers 12,13 (Rouillard 1987), God himself is called a physician or rather healer only in Ex 15,26.   And in the whole New Testament neither God nor Jesus is ever called "physician"'.   Moreover the three rather negative judgments on physicians in the New Testament all come from the Gospel of Luke -- "the physician" (Col 4,14; Lk 5,31; 8,43; 4,23; Hempel 1957 p. 250).   This title is indeed used for Jesus in early Christian literature, and may be said with an 1892 work of Harnack to be "rooted" in the NT, but the only case cited is Mt 9,12, where in no relation to any of his healings Jesus says that the (morally) sick need the physician (Dumeige p. 117).   It is also true that early Christian art borrowed the image of Asclepius for Jesus (Dinkler 1980).

In conclusion, however, we must not fail to take into account one further biblical testimony: the prominence of proper names compounded with the name of God and a word for healing, like Raphael (Stendahl 1950).   And at Uza in Israel was recently found *mrp(t/')m* (Misgav 1990).   Theophoric RP'-names are found very often in the Semitic background outside the Bible. Niehr mentions even a "healing Sun-God" from Hatra (1991,p.8; Vattioni 1981, N.107;138;218).

These will be of need in trying to explain the frequent biblical Rephaim, which linguistically (as in fact in LXX Isa 26,14; Ps 88,11: Hogan 1985, 107-112)) might be taken as a variant for "physicians", but for which in the Bible are attested the two incompatible meanings "giants" / "shades of the dead" (Liwak TWAT; de Moor).   The Ugaritic "Ba'al *Rpw*" has the appearance of a parallel to YHWH-*rôpē'* (Dietrich 1980).   But we are here within the realm of Northwest Semitic which almost daily adds to our knowledge of the whole biblical background, including hopefully "God our healer".

S u m m a r y

Here are some chief results of our research:

1) The commonest sicknesses like headache, colds, stomach-ache pass virtually unnoticed in the Bible.

2) There is absolutely no word for brain in biblical Hebrew, nor really for nerve either; neural disorders are experienced chiefly as a demonic attack.

3) The Hebrew word generally translated "heart" does not mean this specific organ (which we now know serves chiefly for regulating the blood) in a single one of its 850 biblical occurrences; it is rather the center of "understanding", but also of will, emotion, and body-control, located amid the jumble of organs in the torso as in the Madrid Etruscan votive statuette.

4) The commonest disease in the Bible, called sara'at, means "dreaded discoloration of the surface" not only of human skin but also of cloth or walls; probably never what is today called "leprosy", unattested in the Middle East before 500 A.D.

5) Such skin-diseases and others are not in the Bible specifically related to sins especially of sex.

6) Sickness bewailed in the "Complaint Psalms" cannot well be reduced to any specific symptoms, but may have been regarded as effect of an enemy magic.

7) Any actual ointment or potion is very rarely attested either in the Bible or in relevant excavations.

8) Though only a few (ophthalmic) surgical tools were actually found in Palestine (and recently at Gadara), there is doubtless relevance to biblical conditions in the assortments of Roman instruments visible in museums.

9) Even closer to the biblical situation are the case-studies of treatment of broken bones in the Egyptian Smith and Ebers papyri.

10) Sirach 38 praises the doctor in terms that reflect Greco-Roman experience.

11) The claim that most practising physicians were teen-agers has been countered by other statistics equally sparse.

12) God is the only healer ("of Israel" rather than of individuals in the late or interpolated Ex 15,26) but by ordinary governance, not excluding physicians.

Bibliography

To find where these authors are mentioned in above text, → p.177

♦ Outer Organs; ♥ Inner Organs; ¶ Remedies; † Religion; * Archaeology; ‡ Egypt; ° Greece-Rome

° ADAMS   James N., PELAGONIUS *and Latin Veterinary Terminology in the Roman Empire*: Studies in Ancient Medicine 11. Leiden 1995, Brill. viii-695 p.

ADAMSON[82]   P.B., "Human Diseases and Death in the Ancient Near East", *Welt des Orients* 13 (1982) 5-14.

* ADAMSON[93]   P.B., "An Assessment of Some Akkadian Medical Terms", *Revue d'Assyriologie* 87 (1993) 153-159.

♥ ADINOLFI Marco, con GERACI Paola, *Bibbia e ginecologia a confronto.* Casale Monferrato 1989, Piemme. 176 p.

* AGALARAKIS   Anagnostis, *The Paleopathological Indicators of Stress; Neolithic Skeletal Collections*: diss. NY 1990, Columbia.

♦ AIGNER   Heribert, "Zur gesellschaftlichen Stellung von Henkern, Gladiatoren und Berufsathleten", in WEILER Ingomar., ed., *Soziale Randgruppen und Aussenseiter*: Symposium Graz, 21.-28. Sept. 1987 (Graz 1988, Leykam), p. 201-220.

† ALLAN Nigel, "Christian Mesopotamia and Greek Medicine", *Hermathena* 145 (1988) 39-58.

° ALLBUTT T. Clifford, *Greek Medicine in Rome.* London 1921. P. 13: to Egypt was due chiefly an accumulation of drugs.

♦ AMITAI Pinchas, "Scorpion Ash Saves Woman's Eyesight", *Bible Review* 11,2 (1995) 36-37.

† AMUNDSEN[96] Darrel W., *Medicine, Society, and Faith in the Ancient and Medieval Worlds.* Baltimore 1996, Johns Hopkins Univ.

° AMUNDSEN[97A]   D., "The Liability of the Physician in Classical Greek Theory and Practice", *Journal of the History of Medicine* 32 (1977) 172f.

† AMUNDSEN[97B] D.W., "Medicine and Religion in Western Traditions", in ELIADE Mircea, ed., *Encyclopedia of Religion* 9 (NY 1987, Macmillan) p.319-324; Bible p. 320.

ANDOUCHE Iris & SIMELON Paul, "STACE et la mortalité masculine" [65 ans normal]: *Latomus* 54 (1995) 319-323.

° ANDRÉ[87] Jacques, *Être médecin à Rome*: Realia 9. Paris 1987, Belles Lettres.

° ANDRÉ[90] Jacques, *Le vocabulaire latin de l'anatomie:* Collection des Études Anciennes 59. Paris 1990, Belles Lettres. 282 p.

♥ ♦ ARENSBURG[85A] B., *al.,* "What Jewish Skeletal Remains Tell us about Health in Biblical and Talmudic Times", *Koroth* 9/1 (1984/5) 73-83.

* ARENSBURG[85B] B. & RAK Y., "Jewish Skeletal Remains from the Period of the Kings of Judaea", *Palestine Exploration Quarterly* 117 (1985) 30-34.

* ARMELAGOS G.J., *al., Bibliography of Human Paleopathology.* Amherst 1971.

♦ ARTHUR-KATZ Marilyn, "Sexuality and the Body in Ancient Greece", *Métis* 4 (1989) 155-179.

♥ † ASHBROOK James B. & ALBRIGHT Carol R., *The Humanizing Brain; Where Religion and Neuroscience Meet.* Cleveland 1997, Pilgrim. xxiv-233 p.

† AVALOS[91] H.I., *Health and Health Care in Ancient Israel; a Comparative Study on the Role of the Temple*: diss. Harvard 1991.

† AVALOS[95A] Hector, *Illness and Health Care in the Ancient Near East: the Role of the Temple in Greece, Mesopotamia, and Israel*: Harvard Semitic Monographs 54. Atlanta 1995, Scholars.

AVALOS[95B] Hector, "Ancient Medicine": *Bible Review* 11,2 (1995) 26-34.48.

° AYACHE Laurent, HIPPOCRATE: Que sais-je ? 2660. Paris 1992, Presses Universitaires. 128 p.

° BAADER Gerhard & WINAU Rolf, eds., *Die hippokratischen Epidemien*, V[e] colloque international hippocratique, Berlin 10.-15.IX.1984. Stuttgart 1990, Steiner.

† BACCHIOCCHI Samuele, *Immortality or Resurrection: a Biblical Study on Human Nature [body-soul relation] and Destiny:* Biblical Perspectives 13. Berrien Springs 1987.

♥ * BAGGIERI Gaspare, *al., 'Speranza e sofferenza' nei votivi anatomici dell'antichità.* Roma 1996, Complesso Monumentale S. Michele. 80 p.; 82 fig.

† BAILEY D. Sherwin, *Homosexuality and the Western Christian Tradition.* London 1955, Longmans.

♥ ♦ BARCÍA GOYANES Juan José, "La anatomía en la Biblia" [with little help more recent than KATZNELSON, treats stiff neck Ex 32,9; parched throat Ps 69,4]: *Escritos del Vedat* 17 (1987) 61-74; further 18 (1988) 33-42; 19 (1989) 127-132; 20 (1990) 227-235.

♦ BARDINET Thierry, *Dents et mâchoires dans les représentations religi- euses et la pratique médicale de l'Égypte ancienne*: Studia Pohl 15 (Rome 1990, Pontificio Istituto Biblico). xxii-280 p. Review in *Bibliotheca Orientalis* 52 (1995) 65-68 (W. WESTENDORF).

♥ BARKAI Ron, *Les infortunes de Dinah ou la gynécologie juive au Moyen Âge* (Sefer ha-toledet, tr. GAREL Michel). Paris 1991, Cerf. 300 p.

♦ BARNETT R.D., "Six Fingers in Art and Archaeology", *Bulletin of the Anglo-Israel Archaeological Society* 6 (1986-7) 5-12; 3 fig.

BARRAS Gabriel, "Notre corps et nous", *Échos de Saint-Maurice* 22,2 (Valais 1992), also p. 22; and p.18-37.

† BARRETT-LENNARD R.J.S., *Christian Healing after the New Testament; Some Approaches to Illness in the Second, Third and Fourth centuries* [diss. Macquarie 1988, dir.JUDGE E.]. Lanham MD 1994, UPA. xi-419 p.

BARUCH⁶⁴ᴬ J.Z., "The Social Position of the Physician in Ancient Israel", *Janus* 51 (1964) 161-8.

† BARUCH⁶⁴ᴮ J.Z., "The Relation between Sin and Disease in the Old Testament", *Janus* 51 (1964) 295-302.

° BATTON Tamsyn S., *Power and Knowledge; Astrology, Physiognomics, and Medicine under the Roman Empire*: The Body in Theory. Ann Arbor 1994, Univ. Michigan. xiv-254 p.

° BAUER Axel W., "Der Hippokratische Eid. Medizinhistorische Neu-interpretation eines (un)bekannten Textes im Kontext der Pro-fessionalisierung des griechischen Arztes": *Zeitschrift für medizinische Ethik* 41 (1995) 141-5.

♦ BAUMGARTNER Joseph M., "The 4Q Zadokite fragments on Skin Diseases", *Journal of Jewish Studies* 41 (1990) 153-163; 2 pl.

° BECKMANN-HUEBER Dorothee, *Hippokratisches Ethos und ärztliche Verantwortung. Zur Genese eines anthropologischen Selbstverständ-nisses griechischer Heilkunst* [kath. Diss. dir. HUNOLD]. Tübingen 1994.

° BÉGUIN Daniel, "Le problème de la connaissance dans le De optima doctrina de GALIEN", *Revue des Études Grecques* 108 (1995) 107-127.

BEHRENS H. → LEICHTY.

♥ BEN-NAHUM Y., "What Ailed the Son of Kish ?" [1 Sam 10,10-12; 19,24: diabetes]: *Jewish Bible Quarterly* [=*Dor le-Dor*] 19 (1990-1) 244-9.

♥ BENTON A.L., "A Biblical Description of Motor Aphasia" [Ps 137,5f], *Journal of the History of Medicine* 26 (1971) 442-444, approved in *AnchorBD* 6 (1992) 14.

* BIGGS⁶⁹ Robert, "Medicine in Ancient Mesopotamia", *History of Science* 8 (1969) 96-97.

* BIGGS⁹⁰ R.D., "Medizin", *Reallexikon der Assyriologie* 7/7s (Berlin 1990, de Gruyter) 623-9 (-631, "Hethiter", BECKMAN G.).

¶ ° BLIQUEZ L.J., *Roman Surgical Instruments and Minor Objects in the University of Mississippi*: Studies in Mediterranean Archaeology Pocketbook 58. Göteborg 1988, Åström.

♦† BLOCHER C.J., *L'œil et l'oreille; leur signification religieuse*: Sacred Bridge, Numen supp. 7. Leiden 1963, Brill.

♥ BLONDHEIM S.H. & M., "The Obstetrical Complication of Benjamin's Birth: Breech Delivery" [Gen 35,16-19], *Koroth* 8 (1982) 29-34.

† BONNER Gerald, "Sickness, Death and Sin in the Early Church", *Milltown Studies* 27 (1991) 38-61.

† BONO James J., *The Word of God and the Languages of Men; Interpreting Nature in Early Modern Science and Medicine, I. Ficino to Descartes*: Science and Literature. Madison 1995, Univ. Wisconsin. xi-317 p.

BONSOR Jack A., "Homosexual Orientation and Anthropology: Reflections on the Category 'Objective Disorder'", *Theological Studies* 59 (1998) 60-83.

° BOROBIA MELENDO[92] E.L., "Instrumentos médicos hispanorromanos. El espéculo y los ginecólogos romanos", *Revista de Arqueología* 13/140 (1992) 6-7.

° BOROBIA MELENDO[93] E.L., "La specilla en la práctica médica romana", *Revista de Arqueología* 13/142 (1993) 46-49.

BORZA Eugene N., "Malaria in Alexander's Army", *Ancient History Bulletin* 1 (Calgary 1987) 36-38

BOWMAN Sheridan, ed., *Science and the Past*. London 1991, British Museum. 192 p.; ill.

° BRAIN Peter, GALEN *on Bloodletting*. Cambridge 1986, Univ. 189 p.

BRANDENBURG Dietrich, *Medizinisches bei* HERODOT: Medizingeschichtliche Miniaturen 2 (3. in press: *Das ärztliche Rezept*). Berlin 1976, Hessling.

‡ BREASTED J.H., *The Edwin Smith Surgical Papyrus*: Oriental Institute Publications 3. Chicago 1930, Univ.

† BRESLAUER S. Daniel, *Toward a Jewish (M)Orality: Speaking of a Postmodern Jewish Ethics*: Contributions to the Study of Religion 53. Westport CT 1988, Greenwood. From the chapter-headings one might be led to suppose that the "M(O)" of the title implies that modern "orality" research is a way of playing with words or texts.

BROTHWELL[59] D.R., "Teeth in Earlier Human Populations", *Proceedings of the Nutrition Society* 18 (1959) 59-65.

BROTHWELL[67] D. & SANDISON A.T., *Diseases in Antiquity*. Springfield IL 1967, Thomas; p. 206 on *saharšubbu* and *epqu*. → DAWSON.

BROWN[90] M.L., "*Rāpā'*", *Theologisches Wörterbuch zum AT,* ed. FABRY H.-J., RINGGREN H. (Stuttgart 1990, Kohlhammer) 7, 617-625.

† BROWN[95] Michael L., *Israel's Divine Healer*: StOTbT. Grand Rapids 1995, Zondervan. 462 p.; bibliog. 423-441.

♦ BROWNE Stanley G., "Leprosy in the Bible" → PALMER Bernard, *Medicine and the Bible* (Exeter 1986, Paternoster) p. 101-125.

♥ BRUEGGEMANN Walter, "Tongue", *Interpreter's Dictionary of the Bible* 4 (Nashville 1962, Abingdon) p. 670.

♥ BRUNNER Hellmut, "Herz", *Lexikon für Ägyptologie* 2 (1977) 1158-1168.

* BRYANT V.M.jr., "The Role of Coprolite Analysis in Archaeology": *Bulletin of the Texas Archaeological Society* 45 (1974) 1-28 [*AnchorDB* 5,63: efforts so far not very helpful along the desired lines].

‡ BUCAILLE Maurice, *Mummies of the Pharaohs: Modern Medical Investigations.* NY 1990, St. Martin's.

¶ BUCKLER W.H. & CATON R., "Account of a Group of Medical and Surgical Instruments Found at Kolophon", *Proceedings of the Royal Society of Medicine* 7,6 (1914) 335-342.

° BURGUIÈRE Paul, *al.*, ed., SORANOS *d'Éphèse, Maladies des Femmes I*: Collection Budé. Paris 1988, Belles Lettres.

* BUSH Helen & ZVELEBIL Marek, ed., *Health in Past Societies: biocultural interpretations of human skeletal remains in archaeological contexts*: British Archaeological Reports International S-567. Oxford 1991. viii-145 p.; 40 fig.; 22 pl.

° BYL[89] Simon, "L'odeur végétale dans la thérapeutique gynécologique du Corpus hippocratique", *Revue Belge de Philologie* 67 (1989) 53-64.

BYL[95] Simon, "MOLIÈRE et la médecine antique", *Études Classiques* 63 (1995) 55-66.

CAMERON[70] J.M., "The Bible and Legal Medicine", *Medicine, Science and Law* (Jan. 1970) 7-13 [< *AnchorBD* 6,14].

CAMERON[91] Nigel M., *Life and Death after [medicine's abandonment of the Oath of] Hippocrates.* Wheaton IL 1991, Crossway. 187 p.

† CAMPBELL Alastair V., *Health as Liberation: Medicine, Theology, and the Quest for Justice.* Cleveland 1995, Pilgrim. 168 p.

¶ ° CAPASSO[89] L., "I Romani in Farmacia", *Archeo* 57 (1989) 55-99.

¶ ° CAPASSO[93] Luigi, *Le origini della chirurgia italiana.* Rome 1993, Ministero della Cultura. 135 p.

♥ CARASIK Michael A., *Theologies of the Mind in Biblical Israel*: diss. Brandeis 1997, dir. BRETTLER M. *Diss. Abstracts* 57,9 (1997) p.3981.

† CARROLL John T., "Sickness and Healing in the New Testament Gospels", *Interpretation* 49 (1995) 130-142.

CASTRÉN Paavo, ed., *Ancient and Popular Healing:* symposium on ancient medicine, Athens 9-10 Oct. 1986. Helsinki 1989, Finnish Institute at Athens. 125 p.

♥ CASWELL Caroline P., *A Study of Thumos in Early Greek Epic*: Mnemosyne 114. Leiden 1990, Brill. ix-85 p.

CHARLESWORTH James H., "A Misunderstood Recently Published Dead Sea Scroll", *Explorations* 1,2 (1989) 2, retracting his "The Discovery of a Dead Sea Scroll (4Q Therapeia}; its Importance in the History of Medicine and Jesus Research", *International Center for Arid and Semi-Arid Land Studies* (1985 meeting at Lubbock TX); so also NAVEH 1986.

♥ CHEN XU, "Hittite *keer/kart*, functional and ritual aspects", *Journal of Ancient Civilisations* 10 (1995) 33-40.

† CHETWYND, "A Seven Year Famine in the Reign of King Djoser with Other Parallels between Imhotep and Joseph", *Catastrophism* 9 (1987) 49-56.

° CHEVALLIER Raymond, *Sciences et techniques à Rome*: Que sais-je? 1763. Paris 1993, Presses Universitaires. 128p.

♥ CHIESA Bruno, "Sangue e anima nell'esegesi giudeo-araba medievale di Lv 17 e Nm 6", *Sangue e antropologia nel Medioevo* (Roma 25-30 novembre 1991) N° 8 in the series edited by VATTIONI Francesco [1. Sangue e antropologia biblica, 10-15 marzo 1980; 48 art.); 2. Sangue e antropologia biblica nella Patristica (23-28 nov. 1981; 44 art: Roma 1981s, Pia Unione Prez. Sangue].

° CILLIERS Louise, "Public Health in Roman Legislation", *Acta Classica* 36 (S.Africa 1993) 1-10.

* CIVIL M., "Prescriptions médicales sumériennes", *Revue d'Assyriologie* 54 (1960) 52-72; 55 (1961) 91-94.

‡ CLAGETT M., *Ancient Egyptian Science: a Source-Book.* Philadelphia 1989, American Philosophical Society. xv-863 p.

† COAKLEY Sarah, ed., *Religion [largely Eastern] and the Body: Cambridge Studies in Religious Traditions* 8. NY 1997, Cambridge Univ. Press. xvii-312.

COCKBURN Aidan & Eve, *Mummies, Disease and Ancient Cultures.* Cambridge 1980, Univ.

° COHN-HAFT L., *The Public Physician in Ancient Greece.* Northampton 1956.

¶ ° COMO J., "Das Grab eines römischen Arztes in Bingen", *Germania* 9 (1925) 152-162.

† CONSTANTELOS Demetrios J., "The Interface of Medicine and Religion in the Greek and the Christian Greek Orthodox Tradition", *Greek Orthodox Theological Review* 33 (1988) 1-17.

* CONTENAU Georges,*La médecine en Assyrie et en Babylonie*².Paris 1938.

° COOTJANS Gerrit, *La stomatologie [noms des dents] dans le Corpus aristotélicien*: Mémoire 69/3. Brussels 1991, Academy. 242 p.; 1 fig.

° CORDES Peter, *Iatros; das Bild des Arztes in der griechischen Literatur von Homer bis Aristoteles*: Palingenesia 39.Stuttgart 1994,Steiner.208 p.

° CORVISIER Jean-Nicolas, "Médecine et biographie. L'exemple de PLUTARQUE", *Revue des Études Grecques* 107 (1994) 129-157.

° CRAIK Elizabeth, "Hippokratic diaita", in WILKINS John, ed., *Food in Antiquity* [meeting 1992; Exeter 1995, Univ.] 343-350.

* CROCKER P.T., "Apothecaries, Confectionaries, and a New Discovery at Qumran", *Buried History* 25 (1989) 36-46.

° CUBBEDU P.T.I., *Assonanze e dissonanze fra l'opera ippocratica e il Talmud ebraico*, VIIe colloque international hippocratique, Madrid 24-29.IX.1990 [< *Gnomon* 63 (1990) 90-91].

‡ CURTO Silvio, *Medicina e medici nell'antico Egitto.* Torino 1970.

° DAGEN Rainer, "Das Verzeichnis der Schriften des Hippokrates in der Überlieferung des Barhebraeus. Ein kritischer Bericht", in Festschrift ASSFALG J., *Lingua Restituta Orientalis*: Agypten und Altes Testament 20 (Wiesbaden 1990, Harrassowitz) p. 79-88.

‡ DASEN[88] Véronique, "Dwarfism in Ancient Egypt and Classical Antiquity: Iconography and Medical History", *Medical History* 32 (London 1988) 253-276.

° DASEN[90] Véronique, "Dwarfs in Athens", *Oxford Journal of Archaeology* 9 (1990) 197-207; 6 fig.

‡ DASEN[93] Véronique, *Dwarfs in Ancient Egypt and Greece* (diss. Oxford 1988): Monographs in Classical Archaeology. Oxford 1993, Clarendon. xxix-334 p.; 80 pl.

‡ DAVID[84] A.R., *Evidence Embalmed: Modern Medicine and the Mummies of Egypt.* Manchester 1984, Univ.

‡ DAVID[86] A.R., *Science in Egyptology.* Manchester 1986.

‡ DAVID[92] A.R. & TAPP E., ed., *The Mummy's Tale: the Scientific and Medical Investigation of Natsef-Amun, Priest in the Temple of Karnak.* London 1992, O'Mara. 176 p.

° DAVIES R.W.,*Service in the Roman Army.* Edinburgh 1989,Univ. xxi-336p.

† DAVIES Stevan L., *Jesus the Healer: Possession, Trance, and the Origins of Christianity.* London 1995, SCN. → LLOYD DAVIES.

‡ DAVIES W.Vivian & WALKER Roxie, ed., *Biological Anthropology and the Study of Ancient Egypt.* London 1993, British Museum. xi-197 p.; 18 pl.

♥ DAVIS[82] E., "Raynaud Phenomenon in Moses" [Ex 4,6f], *Advances in Microcirculation* 10 (1982) 110f [*AnchorBD* 6,11: dubious].

DAVIS[85] E., "Aspects of Medicine in the Hebrew Bible", *Koroth* 9 (1985) 265-268.

DAVIS[95] Eli & FRENKEL David A., *The Hebrew Amulet, Biblical-Medical-General* [from Jerusalem Medical School collections]. Jerusalem 1995, Institute for Jewish Studies. 212 p.

DAWSON W.R., in BROTHWELL & SANDISON p. 98-111.

° DEAN-JONES[89] Lesley, "Menstrual Bleeding according to the Hippocratics and Aristotle", *American Philological Transactions* 119 (1989) 177-191.

° DEAN-JONES[94] Lesley A., *Women's Bodies in Classical Greek Science*. Oxford 1994, Univ. xiii-293 p.

† DEBARGE Louis, "Le religieux et le médical" [... le problème; l'Antiquité], *Esprit et Vie* 99 (1989) 509-511.

♥ DECOUFLÉ P., *La notion d'ex-voto anatomique chez les Étrusco-Romains. Analyse et synthèse*: Collection Latomus 72. Brussels 1964.

† DE FILIPPIS CAPPAI[91] Chiara, "Il culto de Asclepio da Epidauro a Roma. Medicina del Tempio e medicina scientifica", *Civiltà Classica e Cristiana* 12 (1991) 271-284.

° DE FILIPPIS CAPPAI[93] Chiara, *Medici e medicina in Roma antica*. Torino 1993, Tirrenia. x-246 p.

° DEICHGRÄBER K., *Das hippokratische Eid*[4]. Stuttgart 1983, Hippokrates-V. → FLASHAR 1971.

° DE LACY Phillip, GALEN, *On Semen*: Corpus Medicorum Graecorum 5/3/1. Berlin 1992, Akademie. 291 p.

° DE LAET S., & DESITTERE M., "Ex voto anatomici di Palestrina nel Museo Archeologico dell' Università di Gand", *L'Antiquité Classique* 38 (1969) 16-27.

‡ DE MEULENAERE H., "Arzt" (en français), *Lexikon der Ägyptologie* 1 (Wiesbaden 1975, Harrassowitz) 455-9.

DE NOOR J.C., "*Rapi'uma* -- Rephaim", *ZAW* 88 (1976) 323-345.

† DESELAERS P., "Jahwe -- der Arzt seines Volkes. Das Buch Tobit als Beispiel biblischer Heilslehre", *Geist und Leben* 55 (1982) 294-303.

♥ DE SOUZA SCHULZ Eduardo, "O coração no AT como realidad parcial e total do homem", *Revista de Cultura Biblica* 14,55s (1990) 74-80.

DEVRIES A. & WEINBERGER A., "King Asa's Presumed Gout [1 Kgs 15,23f]: Twentieth Century A.D. Discussion of Ninth Century B.C. Biblical Patient': *New York State Medical Journal* 75 (1975) 452-455.

DHORME E., *L'emploi métaphorique des noms de parties du corps en hébreu et en akkadien*. Paris 1963, Geuthner.

° DI BENEDETTO Vincenzo, *Il medico e la malattia. La scienza di Ippocrate*. Turin 1986, Einaudi. 302 p.

DIEPGEN Paul, *Geschichte der Medizin I. Altertum.* Berlin 1913, Göschen. (II. 1914, Mittelalter; III. 1919, Neuzeit).

* DIETRICH M. & LORETZ O., "Baal *rpu* in KTU 1,108; 1,123 und nach 1,247.VI.25-33", *Ugarit-Forschungen* 12 (1980) 171-182.

* DINKLER Erich, *Christus und Asklepios. Zum Christustypus der polychromen Platten im Museo Nazionale Romano*: Sitzungsberichte Heidelberg ph/h 1980/2. Heidelberg 1980, Winter. 40 p.; XX pl. My review in *Zeitschrift für Kirchengeschichte* 94 (1983) 119-120.

¶ DUKE James A., *Medicinal Plants of the Bible* NY 1983, Trado-Medic.

† DUMEIGE Gervais, "Le Christ médecin dans la littérature chrétienne des premiers siècles", *Rivista di Archeologia Cristiana* 48 (1972) 115-141.

* DURAND J.-M., "Maladies et médecines", *Archives Épistolaires de Mari* 1/1 (1988) 541-584.

¶ ° DURLING[92] Richard J., "The Language of Galenic Pharmacy", *Glotta* 70 (1992) 62-70.

° DURLING[93A] R.J., *A Dictionary of Medical Terms in* GALEN: StAncMed 5. Leiden 1993, Brill. xiii-344 p.

DURLING[93B] Richard J., "A Guide to the Medical Manuscripts Mentioned in [1990 Paul O.] KRISTELLER's *Iter italicum* V-VI", *Traditio* 48 (1993) 253-316.

¶ DVORJETSKI Esti, "Medicinal Hot Springs in Eretz-Israel and the Decapolis during the Hellenistic, Roman and Byzantine Periods", ARAM 4,2 (Oxford 1992) 415-449; 7 fig.

‡ EBBELL[37] B., *The Papyrus Ebers, the Greatest Egyptian Medical Document.* Copenhagen 1937, Munksgaard.

‡ EBBELL[39] B., *Die alt-ägyptische Chirurgie. Die chirurgischen Abschnitte Smith und Ebers*: Norsk Videnskaps Akademie 1939/2. Oslo 1939, Dybwad.

* EBELING Erich, "Anatomie", *Reallexikon der Assyriologie* (Berlin 1932, de Gruyter) 1,105.

EBSTEIN[01] Wilhelm, *Die Medizin im Alten Testament.* Stuttgart 1901, Enke.

EBSTEIN[03] W.,*Die Medizin im Neuen Testament und im Talmud.*Stuttgart 1903

‡ EDEL[76] Elmar, *Ägyptische Ärzte und ägyptische Medizin am hethitischen Königshof.* Göttingen 1976.

EDELSTEIN Ludwig, *Ancient Medicine*, ed. TEMKIN O. & C. Baltimore 1987, Johns Hopkins Univ.

‡ ENGELMANN Heinz & HALLOF Jochen, "Zur medizinischen Nothilfe und Unfallversorgung auf staatlichen Arbeitsplätzen im Alten Ägypten", *Zeitschrift für Ägyptologie* 122 (1995) 104-136; 3 fig.

‡ ESTES J. Worth, *The Medical Skills of Ancient Egypt.* Canton MA 1989, Watson. 196 p.

♥ FABRY Heinz-Josef, *"Lēb", Theologisches Wörterbuch zum Alten Testament* 4 (Stuttgart 1982, Kohlhammer) 413-451.

FARAONE C.A. & OBBINK D., *Magika Hiera.* NY 1991, Oxford. → SCARBOROUGH J.

FAWVER Jay D. & OVERSTREET R. Larry, "Moses and Preventive Medicine", *Bibliotheca Sacra* 147 (1990) 270-285.

FENELLI[75A] N., "Contributo per lo studio del votivo anatomico. I votivi anatomici di Lavinio", *Archeologia Classica* 27 (1975)

FENELLI[75B] N., "Votivi anatomici in Le Tredici Are", *Lavinium* 2 (1975) 253-255.

† FENNER F., *Die Krankheit im Neuen Testament. Eine religions- und medizingeschichtliche Untersuchung*: Untersuchungen zum NT 18. Leipzig 1930.

° FESTUGIÈRE A.J., *Hippocrate. L'ancienne médecine.* Paris 1948.

† FICHTNER G., "Christus als Arzt. Ursprünge und Wirkungen eines Motivs", *Frühmittelalterliche Studien* 15 (1982) 1-18.

‡ FILER Joyce, *Disease*: Egyptian Bookshelf. London 1995, British Museum. 112 p.; 68 fig.; VIII colour pl.

FINET A., "Les médecins au royaume de Mari", *Annuaire de l'Institut de Philologie et d'Histoire Orientales et Slaves* 14 (1954-7) 122-144.

† FINKEL Avraham Y., *In my Flesh I See God; a Treasury of Rabbinic Insights about the Human Anatomy.* Northvale NJ 1995, Aronson. xxviii-356 p.

° FISCHER Klaus-Dietrich, "Ein neuer Textzeuge der altlateinischen Übersetzung der hippokratischen Schrift Über die Umwelt", *Latomus* 54 (1995) 50-57; 1 pl.

* FISCHER Peter M., *Prehistoric Cypriot Skulls*: Studies in Mediterranean Archaeology 75. Göteborg 1986, Åström.

FLASHAR H., ed., *Antike Medizin:* Wege der Forschung 221. Darmstadt 1971, Wiss.-B. -- p. 94-120, DEICHGRÄBER K. (→), "Die ärztliche Standesethik des hippokratischen Eides".

FOHRER Georg, "Krankheit im Lichte des Alten Testaments", in his *Studien zu alttestamentlichen Texten und Themen*: BZAW 155 (Berlin 1981, de Gruyter) p. 172-187.

° FORTUNA Stefania, "La tradizione del De constitutione artis medicae di Galeno", *Accademia dei Lincei Bollettino dei Classici* 3/11 (1990) 48-77.

¶ ° FOSTER G.V., *al.*, "A Roman Surgeon's Tomb from Nea Paphos", *Report of the Department of Antiquities of Cyprus* [(1985) 315-332, I. by MICHAELIDES D.] II. (1988,2) 229-234 (powder/salt remedies); 1 fig.; pl. LXX-LXXI.

♦ FRASER H., "The Gospel According to Saint Mark, Chapter Eight Verses 22 to 26": *Medical Journal of Australia* 2 (1973) 657-658.

FRIEDENWALD H., *The Jews and Medicine.* Baltimore 1994. 2 vol.

FRINGS J.J., *Medizin und Arzt bei den griechen Kirchenvätern bis Chrysostomos*: diss. Bonn 1959.

FUCHS Éric, "Social Justice snd Health Care" ["La justice sociale et les coûts de la santé", *Église et Théologie* 28 (1997) 5-17], summarized by Rosemary JERMANN, *Theology Digest* 45 (1998) 213-8.

FULTON J.F., *The Great Medical Bibliographies.* Philadelphia 1952.

GABRIEL Richard A. & METZ Karen S., *A History of Military Medicine I. From Ancient Times to the Middle Ages*: Military Studies 124. NY 1992, Greenwood. xxi-247 p.

° GAROFALO Ivan, GALENO, *Procedimenti anatomici; testo greco a fronte.* Milan 1991, Rizzoli. 1145 p.

GARRISON Fielding H., *An Introduction to the History of Medicine.* Philadelphia 1929. Egypt p. 57.

♦ GASTI Fabio, "I pupilli senza occhi; una noterella isidoriana (Etym. 11.2.12)", *Athenaeum* 83 (1995) 264-270.

GATTI LO GUZZO, *Il deposito votivo dell'Esquilino detto di Minerva Medica*: Studi e Materiali di Etruscologia e Antichità Italiche 17. Florence 1978, Sansoni.

GELIN Albert, "Médecine dans la Bible", *Dictionnaire de la Bible, Supplément*, vol. 5 (Paris 1953, Letouzey et Ané) 957-961.

° GELPKE Almuth, *Das Konzept des erkränkten Ortes in GALENS 'De locis affectis'*: Medizingeschichtliche Abh. 190. Zurich 1987, Juris. 129 p.

* GERMER Renate, *al.*, "Die Wiederentdeckung der Lübecker Apotheken-Mumie", *Antike Welt* 26 (1995) 17-40; 38 fig.

° GEROULANOS Stephanos & BRIDLER René, *Trauma. Wund-Entstehung und Wund-Pflege im antiken Griechenland*: Kulturgeschichte der Alten Welt 56. Mainz 1994, von Zabern. 172 p.; ill.

‡ GHALIOUNGUI Paul, *The Physicians of Pharaonic Egypt*: Sonderschrift 18. Cairo 1983, Al-Ahram Center.

¶ ° GIBBINS[88] David, "Surgical Instruments from a Roman Shipwreck off Sicily", *Antiquity* 62 (1988) 294-7; 3 fig.

GIBBINS[89] David, "The Roman Wreck of c. AD 200 at Plemmirio, near Siracusa (Sicily): Second Interim Report, the Domestic Assemblage 1.

Medical Equipment and Pottery Lamps", *International Journal of Nautical Archaeology* 18 (1989) 1-25; 16 fig.

GIL MODREGO A., *Estudio de lēb/āb en el Antiguo Testamento. Análisis sintagmático e paradigmático*: Diss. Univ. Complutense. Madrid 1992.

GILBERT   Maurice, "La Bible et l'homosexualité", *Nouvelle Revue Théologique* 109 (1986) 78-95

° GINOUVÈS R., al., *L'eau, la santé et la maladie dans le monde grec. Actes du colloque de Paris (25-27 novembre 1992)*:   Bulletin de Correspondance Hellénique supp. 28. Paris 1994, de Boccard.

GIORDANO Lisania, "Morbus acediae. Da Giovanni Cassiano e Gregorio Magno alla elaborazione medievale", *Vetera Christianorum* 26 (1989) 221-245.

GLENN J.E., *The Bible and Modern Medicine.* NY 1959.

GOERKE Hans, *Arzt und Heilkunde. Vom Asklepiospriester zum Klinikarzt, 3000 Jahre Medizin.* Munich 1984, Callwey. 286p.; p. 87, tools from a Bingen physician's grave; p. 225, eye-ills.

GOLTZ Dietlinde, *Studien zur altorientalischen und griechischen Heilkunde. Therapie -- Arzneibereitung -- Rezeptstruktur*: Beiheft 16. Wiesbaden 1974, Sudholfs Archiv.

GÓMEZ ROYO E., "Die Haftung der Ärzte", *Revue Internationale des Droits de l'Antiquité* 37 (1990) 167s.

GORDIS L., "An Early Commentary on Medical Care": *New England Journal of Medicine* 292 (1975) 44-45 [< AnchorBD 6,14].

♦ GORDON B.L., "Ophthalmology in the Bible and in the Talmud", *Archives of Ophthalmology* 9 (1933) 751-3.

° GOURÉVITCH[84A] Danielle, *Le mal d'être femme. La femme et la médecine dans la Rome antique.* Paris 1984, Belles Lettres.

° GOURÉVITCH[84B] Danielle, *Le triangle hippocratique dans le monde gréco-romain. Le malade, sa maladie et son médecin.* Rome 1984, École Française.

GOURÉVITCH[94] Danielle, "Correction d'une correction" [Oroz Reta 1982], *Traditio* 40 (1994) 317-9.

‡ GRAPOW[35] Hermann, "Die ägyptischen medizinischen Papyri und was sie enthalten", *Münchener Medizinische Wochenschrift* 82/24 (14. Juni 1935) 958-962 . 1003-5.

‡ GRAPOW[54] Hermann, *Grundriss der Medizin der alten Ägypter.* Berlin 1954.

‡ GRAPOW[58] H., *Die medizinischen Texte in hieroglyphischer Umschreibung autographiert.* Berlin 1958, Akademie.

¶ ‡ GRAPOW[59] H., with VON DEINES Hildegard. *Grundriss vol. 6, Wörterbuch der ägyptischen Drogennamen*. Berlin 1959, Akademie.

GREENBLATT Robert B., *Search the Scriptures: Modern Medicine and Biblical Personages*. Totowa NJ 1985, Barnes & Noble. 223 p.

GRENSEMANN H., *Knidische Medizin:* I. Ars Medica II 4,1, Berlin/NY 1975. -- II. HermesEinz 51. Stuttgart 1987. 91 p.

GRIFFITHS John G., "Love as a Disease", in Festschrift LICHTHEIM Miriam, *Studies in Egyptology*, ed. ISRAELIT-GROLL Sarah (Jerusalem 1990, Hebrew Univ.), p. 349-364, citing Lichtheim's *Ancient Egyptian Literature 2. Papyrus Beatty I* (1976) p. 185.

° GRMEK Mirko D., *Diseases in the Ancient Greek World* [= *Les maladies à l'aube de la civilisation occidentale*. Paris 1983, Payot]. tr. MUELLNER M. & L. Baltimore 1988, Johns Hopkins Univ.   458 p.

‡ GUILHOU Nadine, "Un texte de guérison [BM 10059,38]", *Chronique d'Égypte* 70 (1995) 52-64.

* GUILLERMAND Jean, al.., *Archéologie et médecine*, VIIe rencontres internationales d'archéologie et d'histoire d'Antibes, 23-25 oct. 1986. Juan les Pins 1987, APDCA.

* HAAS N. & NATHAN H., "Anthropological Survey of the Human Skeletal Remains from Qumran": *Revue de Qumran* 6 (1967-9) 345-352 [323-336, STECKOLL S.H.].

‡ HABRICH Christa, al., *Ein Leib für Leben und Ewigkeit. Medizin im alten Ägypten*: Ausstellung Ingolstadt Medizinhistorisches Museum 1985. 54 p.

HALBE Jörn, *Das Privilegrecht Jahwes, Ex 34.10-26*: FRLANT 114. Göttingen 1975, Vandenhoeck & Ruprecht.

HALPERIN D.J., "The *Book of Remedies*, the Canonization of the Solomonic Writings, and the Riddle of Pseudo-Eusebius", *Jewish Quarterly Review* 72 (1981-2) 269-292.

HANKINSON[88] R.I., ed., *Method, Medicine and Metaphysics; Studies in the Philosophy of Ancient Science* [Montreal McGill Univ. Oct.2-3, 1986]: Apeiron 21. Alberta 1988. 194 p.

° HANKINSON[91] R.J., tr., ed., GALEN, *On the Therapeutic Method, Books I-II*: Later Ancient Philosophers. Oxford 1991, Clarendon. xxxix-269 p.

‡ HARER W.Benson, "Implications of Molecular Biology for Egyptology," *Bulletin of the American Research Center in Egypt* 32 (1995) 67-70.

‡ HARRIS James E. & PONITZ Paul V., "Dental Health in Ancient Egypt" in COCKBURN A. & E., *Mummies* (Cambridge 1980, Univ). 45-51.

* HARRISON[53] R., "Disease, Bible, and Spade", *Biblical Archaeologist* 16 (1953) 88-92.

HARRISON[62] 1962 R.K., "Disease" in *Interpreter's Dictionary of the Bible* 1 (Nashville 1962, Abingdon) 847-854 (nothing in the 1975 update-volume) & "Blindness" 1,448-9; "Fever" 2,266; "Leprosy" 3,111-3.

* HART[73] G., "The Diagnosis of Disease from Ancient Coins", *Archaeology* 26,2 (1973) 123-7.

HART[83] Gerald D., ed., *Disease in Ancient Man* [London-Toronto conference 1979]. Toronto 1983, Clarke Irwin. 297 p.   `

HARTMAN Louis, also ed., (VAN DEN BORN A.), "Finger", *Encyclopedic Dictionary of the Bible* (NY 1963, McGraw-Hill) 773s.

HASEL Gerhard F., "Health and Healing in the Old Testament", *Andrews University Seminary Studies* 21 (1983) 191-202.

† HAUERWAS Stanley, *Naming the Silences; God, Medicine, and the Problem of Suffering.* Edinburgh 1993, Clark [= Eerdmans 1990]. xiv-154 p.

¶ ‡ HELBING M., *Der altägyptische Augenkranke, sein Arzt und seine Götter.* Zurich 1980, Medizingeschichtliche Abhandlungen.

‡ HELLWEG Rainer, *Stilistische Untersuchungen zu den Krankengeschichten der Epidemienbücher I und III des Corpus Hippocraticum*: diss. Bonn 1985, Habelt. 252 p.

HEMER C.J., "Medicine in the New Testament World", in PALMER 43-83.

† HEMPEL[57] Johannes, "Ich bin der Herr, dein Arzt" (Ex 15,26)", *Theologische Literaturzeitung* 82 (1957) 809-826.

HEMPEL[58] J., "Heilung als Symbol und Wirklichkeit im biblischen Schrifttum", *Nachrichten der Göttinger Akademie* 1958/3 (Göttingen 1958) 239-314.

* HERBERO Pablo, *La thérapeutique mésopotamienne*: Mémoire 48. Paris 1984, Recherche sur les Grandes Civilisations. 139 p.

° HERSANT Yves, ed., HIPPOCRATÈS, *Sur le rire et la folie.* P 1989, Rivages. 129 p.

° HERSHKOVITZ Malka, "A Roman Cupping Vessel from Masada" (in Hebrew), *Eretz Israel* 20 (Y. YADIN memorial, 1989) 275-7; 8 fig.; Eng. 204*.

† HERZOG Markwart, "Christus medicus, apothecarius, samaritanus, balneator. Motive einer medizinisch-pharmaceutischen Soteriologie", *Geist und Leben* 67 (1994) 414-434; 2 pl.

♦ HEYMER Armin, "Der ethno-kulturelle Werdegang apotropäischer Verflechtungen von Pygmäen, Chondrodystrophen und Zwergenfiguren", *Saeculum* 44 (1993) 116-178.

¶ ° HIBBS V.A., "Roman Surgical and Medical Instruments from La Cañada Hondá (Gandul)", *Archivo Español de Arqueología* 64 (1991) 111-134.

HILLERT A., *Antike Ärztedarstellungen:* Marburger Schriften zur Medizingeschichte 25. Frankfurt 1990, Lang.

¶ HIRSCHFELD Yizhar, "The Balm of Gilead", *Biblical Archaeology Review* 12,5 (1996) 19-20 & 24.

HIRT Marguerite, "Le statut social du médecin" → GUILLERMAND, Antibes VII (1986-7) 95-107.

HOFFMEIER James K.,"Egypt, plagues in", *Anchor Bible Dictionary* 2 (1992) 374-8.

* HOFFNER H.A. jr., "From Head to Toe in Hittite; the Language of the Human Body", in Festschrift YOUNG Dwight W., *"Go to the Land I will Show you"* ed. GIBSON Joseph E., MATTHEWS Victor A. (Winona Lake 1996, Eisenbrauns) 247-259.

HOGAN[85] Larry, "Healing and Ignorance in the Bible", *Koroth* 9 (1984/5) 107-112.

HOGAN[92] L.P., *Healing in the Second Temple Period*: Novum Testamentum et Orbis Antiquus 21. Fribourg/Göttingen 1992, Univ./Vandenhoeck & Ruprecht. [xiv-] 337 p.

† HOHEISEL K. & KLIMKEIT H.J., ed., *Heil und Heilung in den Weltreligionen.* Wiesbaden 1995, Harrassowitz. x-188 p.;p.99-116, BALZ H., NT.

HOLOUBEK Joe E. M.D. & Alice B. M.D., "A Study of Death by Crucifixion with Attempted Explanation of the Death of Jesus Christ", *Linacre Quarterly* (1994) 10-19.

* HOLZMAIR Eduard, *Medicina in nummis*, Sammlung Dr. Joseph Brettauer [Trieste ophthalmologist's gift to Vienna Univ.], Katalog 1928; [2]1989 ed. GÖBL Robert; Veröffentlichung der Numismatischen Kommission 22.

♦ HORSFALL Nicholas, "Rome without Spectacles [eye-glasses]", *Greece and Rome* 42 (1995) 49-56.

° HORSTMANSHOFF[89] Herman F.J., *De pijlen van de pest; pestilenties in de Griekse wereld, 800-400 v.C.*; diss. Leiden. Amsterdam 1989. 289 p.

HORSTMANSHOFF[91] H.F.J. [announced as organizer in *Études Classiques* 59 (1991) 52], *La médecine ancienne dans son contexte socio-cultural,* Leiden 13-15 apr. 1992.

HÜBNER Jürgen, "Gesundheit und Krankheit", *Evangelisches Kirchenlexikon* 12 (Göttingen 1989, Vandenhoeck & Ruprecht) 158-161 (AT 159).

* HULSE[71] E.V., "Joshua's Curse and the Abandonment of Ancient Jericho": *Medical History* 15 (1971) 376-386 [*AnchorBD* 6,10: the water from which its (Bronze Age) mud bricks were made contained causes of schistosomiasis].

♦ HULSE[75] E.V., "The Nature of the Biblical 'Leprosy' and the Use of Alternative Medical Terms in Modern Translations of the Bible", *Palestine Exploration Quarterly* 107 (1975) 87-105.

HUMBERT Paul, "Maladie et médecine dans l'AT", *Revue d'Histoire et de Philosophie Religieuses* 44 (1964) 1-29.

HYATT J.P., "Circumcision", *Interpreter'sDB* 1,629-631 with drawing.

ILBERG J., *Die Ärzteschule von Knidos*. Sitzungsberichte Leipzig 1924.

IN DER SMITTEN Wilhelm T., "Die Welt der Kranken im Alten Testament", *Janus* 61 (1974) 103-129 (295-302 there, BARUCH J.).

* ISAACS Haskell D., (BAKER Colin F.), [1616 Judeo-Arabic] *Medical and Para-Medical Manuscripts in the Cambridge Genizah Collections*: Genizah Series 11. Cambridge 1994, Univ. xxi-144 p.; 20 pl.

° ISKANDAR Albert Z., *On Examinations by which the Best Physicians are Recognized* [Arabic with translation]: Corpus Medicorum Graecorum, Supp. orientale 4. Berlin 1988, Akademie.

* JACK J.W., "The Trephined Skulls from Lachish", *Palestine Exploration Quarterly* 69 (1937) 62-66; photo in IDB 1,848; → TUFNELL.

¶ JACKSON[86] Ralph, "A Set of Roman Medical Instruments from Italy [antiquities dealer: rare types; three catheters]: *Britannia* 17 (1986) 119-167.

JACKSON[88] Ralph, *Doctors and Diseases in the Roman Empire*. London 1988, British Museum; p.32, "Fitness, food and hygiene".

¶ JACOB Irene & Walter, ed., *The Healing Past: Pharmaceuticals in the Biblical and Rabbinic World* [1989 symposium]: Studies in Ancient Medicine 7. Leiden 1993, Brill. xvi-126 p.

JACOBSEN T. → LEICHTY.

JACOBY M.G., "The Fifth Plague of Egypt" [Ex 9,3-6, next after flies]: *Journal of the American Medical Association* 249 (1963) 2779-2780 [AnchorBD 6,9 objects with Shimshony that foot/mouth does not affect many animals involved].

† JEKEL James F., "Biblical Foundations for Health and Healing", *Perspectives in Science and Christian Faith* 47 (1995) 150-158.

° JENNER K.A., *A Study of GALEN's "Commentary" on the "Prognostikon" of HIPPOCRATES I, 1-26*: diss. Oxford 1989. 406 p.

JOHNSON Aubrey, *The Vitality of the Individual in the Thought of Ancient Israel*. Cardiff 1949, Univ. Wales.

° JOHNSON Fiona, *The Hippocratics and Women; a Whole Sex of Patients*: M.A. diss. King's College London.

‡ JONCKHEERE[47] Frans, *Le papyrus médical Chester Beatty*. Brussels 1947, Fondation Reine Élisabeth.

‡ JONCKHEERE[58] Frans, *Les médecins de l'Égypte pharaonique. Essai de prosopographie*: La Médecine égyptienne 3. Brussels 1958, Fondation Reine Élisabeth.

JONES Richard N., "Paleopathology": *Anchor Bible Dictionary* (NY 1992, Doubleday) 5, 60-69.

JONES 1938 W.H.S., Loeb HIPPOCRATES → POTTER.

° JOUANNA[74] Jacques, *Hippocrate. Pour une archéologie [étymologiquement] de l'école de Cnide*: Collection Études Anciennes. Paris 1974, Belles Lettres.

† ° JOUANNA[89] Jacques, "Hippocrate de Cos et le sacré", *Journal des Savants* (1989) 3-22.

° JOUANNA[90] Jacques, *Hippocratès. De l'ancienne médecine*: Coll. Budé. Paris 1990, Belles Lettres. 237 (double) p.

° JOUANNA[92] Jacques, *Hippocrate.* Paris 1992, Fayard. 652 p.

° JOUANNA[93] Jacques, "HIPPOCRATE et la Collection hippocratique dans l'Ars Medicinae", *Revue de l'Histoire des Textes* 23 (1993) 95-112; Eng. 353.

° JOUANNA[95] Jacques, "L'HIPPOCRATE de Modène", *Scriptorium* 49 (Brussels 1995) 273-283.

JÜTTNER Guido → KUDLIEN[88].

* KAMMERER T., "Die erste Pockendiagnose stammt aus Babylonien", *Ugarit-Forschungen* 27 (1995) 129-168.

KATZNELSON J.L., *Die normale und pathologische Anatomie des Talmud*: Virchows Archiv 144 (1896).

KEE[86] Howard G., *Medicine, Miracle, and Magic in the New Testament.* Cambridge 1986.

KEE[92] Howard C., "Medicine and Healing", in *AnchorBD* 4 (1962) 659-666; → SUSSMAN.

KELLERMANN Diether, "Die Geschichte von David und Goliath im Lichte der Endokrinologie," *Zeitschrift für die alttestamentliche Wissenschaft* 102 (1990) 344-357.

KERNER D., "Medizin und Magie im babylonischen Talmud", *Münchener Medizinische Wochenschrift* (1963) 464-9.

† KILNER John F., ed., *Bioethics and the Future of Medicine; a Christian Appraisal.* Grand Rapids 1995, Eerdmans.

KINNIER WILSON J.V., "Medicine in the Land and Times of the Old Testament', in ISHIDA T., ed., *Studies in the Period of David and Solomon* (Tokyo 1982) 337-365.

KLEIJWEGT Marc, "The Physician in Ancient Society" in his *Ancient Youth. The Ambiguity of Youth and the Absence of Adolescence in Greco-Roman Society* (Dutch Monographs in History 8; Amsterdam 1991, Gieben) 135-163.

KLOPFENSTEIN Christian, *La Bible et la santé*. Paris 1978.

KOELBING[77] H.M., *Arzt und Patient in der antiken Welt*. Zurich/Munich 1977.

° KOELBING[89] Huldrych M., "Le médecin dans la cité grecque", *Gesnerus* 46 (Aarau, Société suisse de l'histoire de la médecine 1989) 29-43 (p.11-28, KOLLESCH J.).

¶ ° KÖNIG Roderich & HOPP Joachim, PLINIUS DER ÄLTERE, *Naturkunde lat.-deutsch, XXIXf. Medizin und Pharmakologie / Heilsmittel aus dem Tierreich [XXXI ... aus dem Wasser).* Darmstadt 1991 [/4], Wissenschaftliche Buchg. 335 p. [176 p.]

KOLLESCH[91] Jutta, "Darstellungsformen der medizinischen Literatur im 5. und 4. Jahrhundert v.Chr.", *Philologus* 135 (1991) 177-183.

‡ KOLLESCH[93] Jutta & NICKEL D., GALEN *und das hellenistische Erbe* [Symposium Berlin Univ. 18-20 Sept. 1989]: Sudhoff 32. Tübingen 1993, Steiner. 214 p.

° KOLLESCH[94] Jutta, "Die Sprache von Ärzten nichtgriechischer Herkunft im Urteil GALENs", *Philologus* 138 (1994) 160-263.

KOLLMANN[94]   B., "Göttliche Offenbarung magisch-pharmakologischer Heilkunst im Buch Tobit", ZAW 106 (1994) 289-299.

KOLLMANN[96] Bernd, *Jesus und die Christen als Wundertäter. Studien zu Magie, Medizin und Schamanismus in Antike und Christentum*; FRLANT 170. Göttingen 1996, Vandenhoeck & Ruprecht. 438 p. 118-127 Tobit, Sirach; 33 & 363-8, Jesus der Arzt.

KONSTAN David, ed., *Women and Ancient Medicine*: Brown Univ, 28-29 Oct. 1988: *Helios* 19,1 (1992).

KORNFELD W., "Beschneidung", in GÖRG Manfred, ed., *Neues Bibel-Lexikon* (Zurich 1991) 1.277, enlarged fig.6.

° KORPELA Jukka, *Das Medizinalpersonal im antiken Rom*: Annales Ac.Finn. hum. 45. Helsinki 1987. 235 p.

* KOTTEK[83]   S., "The Essenes and Medicine; a Comparative Study of Medical and Para-medical Items with Reference to Ancient Jewish Lore", *Clio Medica* 18 (1983) 81-99.

KOTTEK[85]   Samuel S., ed., "Proceedings of the Second International Symposium on Medicine in Bible and Talmud, Jerusalem 18-20.XII.1984" [first was 1981] = Koroth 9 (Israel Institute of Medical History, 1985). 264 p.; p. 7-33, "Concepts of Disease in the Talmud"; p. 34-57, NEWMYER Stephen, "Talmudic Medicine and Greek Sources".

KOTTEK[86] Samuel S., "Hygiene and Public Health", *Koroth* 9.1f (1986) 316-344, updated in his *Medicine in Josephus* 1994, 56-80.

KOTTEK[94] Samuel S., *Medicine and Hygiene in the Works of* FLAVIUS JOSEPHUS: Studies in Ancient Medicine 9. Leiden 1994, Brill. xii-217 p.

° KRAAY P.C., *Greek Coins.* London 1956,Thames & Hudson. p.31, N° 96B.

KRONHOLM Tryggve, "Abraham, the Physician; the Image of Abraham the Patriarch [curing various patients 'by medical activity' 'in the word of truth' p.107] in the Genuine Hymns of Ephraem Syrus": Festschrift for Jonas C. GREENFIELD, *Solving Riddles and Untying Knots; Biblical, Epigraphic, and Semitic Studies,* ed. Ziony ZEVIT, *al.* (Winona Lake 1995, Eisenbrauns) 107-115.

KRUG Antje, *Heilkunst und Heilkult, Medizin in der Antike*[2rev]. Munich 1993, Beck. 248 p.; 96 fig.

KRUSE Torsten, "Ars moriendi; Aufgabe und Möglichkeiten der Medizin" [i. Geschichtlich: Heilkunst/Religion] in *Ars moriendi. Erwägungen zur Kunst des Sterbens,* ed. WAGNER Harald: Quaestiones Disputatae 118. Freiburg 1989, Herder (198 p.), p. 99-116.

° KUDLIEN[67] Fridolf, "Hippokrates", *Der kleine Pauly* 2 (Stuttgart 1967, Druckenmüller) 1169-1171. This valuable reference-work has no article Medizin, and under Ärzte only "see specific articles".

° KUDLIEN[79] Fridolf, "Der griechische Arzt im Zeitalter des Hellenismus. Seine Stellung in Staat und Gesellschaft", *Abhandlungen Mainz geist./soz. 1979/6.* Wiesbaden 1979, Steiner.

° KUDLIEN[86] Fridolf, *Die Stellung des Arztes in der römischen Gesellschaft.* Stuttgart 1986, Steiner.

KUDLIEN[88] Fridolf, "Heilkunde", in DASSMANN E., ed., *Reallexikon für Antike und Christentum* (Stuttgart 1988, Hiersemann), vol. 14, p. 223-249; also there p. 249-274, JÜTTNER Guido, "Heilsmittel".

° KUDLIEN[91] Fridolf & DURLING R.J., ed., GALEN*'s Method of Healing* [Symposium Kiel 1982]: Studies in Ancient Medicine 1. Leiden 1991, Brill. viii-205 p.

° KÜHN Josef-Hans, *al., Index Hippocraticus.* Göttingen 1986-9; Vandenhoeck & Ruprecht. 946 p.

¶ ° KÜNZL[83] Ernst (HASSEL F.J., KÜNZL S.), *Medizinische Instrumente aus Sepulkralfunden der römischen Kaiserzeit* (Cologne 1983, Rheinland); = *Bonner Jahrbücher* 182 (1982) 1-131; 98 fig.; Typologie p.15-31; Fabrikanten p.31-35 (Ephesus p. 49-53).

¶ ° KÜNZL[86A] Ernst, "Operationsräume in römischen Thermen. Zu einem chirurgischen Instrumentarium aus der Colonia Ulpia Traiana, mit einem Auswahlkatalog römischer medizinischer Instrumente im römischen Landesmuseum, Bonn", *Bonner Jahrbücher* 186 (1986) 491-509.

* KÜNZL[86B] E. & ANKNER D., "Eine Serie von Fälschungen römischer Instrumentarien", *Archäologisches Korrespondenzblatt* 16 (Mainz 1986) 333-9.

KURTH Dieter, "Zu *t3-mah* in medizinischen Texten", *Göttinger Miszellen* 111 (1989) 81-83.

* LABAT R., *Traité akkadien de diagnostics et prognostics médicaux* I. Paris 1951.

LANÇON B., "Maladie et médecine dans la correspondance de JÉRÔME", in DUVAL Y., ed., *Jérôme entre L'Occident et l'Orient* (colloque de Chantilly sept. 1986; Paris 1988, Études Augustiniennes) p.355-366.

LANGERMANN Y. Tzvi, "MAIMONIDES on the synochous fever" ["continuous"; Maimonides wrote abridgments of some twenty works of GALEN]: *Israel Oriental Studies* 13 (1993) 175-198.

† LANTERNARI Vittorio, ed., *Medicina, magia, religione, valori* [Perugia, apr. 1985]: Anthropos 25. Naples 1994, Liguori. 312 p.

† LARCHET[91] Jean-Claude, *Théologie de la maladie*. Paris 1991, Cerf. 149 p.

♥ LARCHET[92] Jean-Claude, *Thérapeutique des maladies mentales. L'expérience de l'Orient chrétien des premiers siècles*: Théologies. Paris 1992, Cerf. 184 p.

LEATHERMAN Thomas, "Illness as Lifestyle Change", in HUSS-ASHMORE Rebecca, ed., *Health and Lifestyle Change*: Masca 9 (Philadelphia 1992, Museum; 144 p.) p.83-89.

‡ LECA Ange-Pierre, *La médecine égyptienne au temps des Pharaons* [= *La medicina egizia* (1986, Ciba-Geigy)]. Paris 1971, Dacosta. 406 p.

LEE D.I., "The Fiery Serpent and Similar Scourges" [Num 21,6-9]: *Univ. Leeds Review* 16 (1973) 28-41 [*AnchorBD* 6,10: guinea worm, as already T. BARTHOLIN].

‡ LEFEBVRE Gustave, *Essai sur la médecine égyptienne d'époque pharaonique*. Paris 1956.

LEIBOWITZ Yehošua', "*R^epû'â*", *Ensiqlopediya Miqrā'ît* 7 (Encyclopaedia Biblica, Jerusalem 1976) 407-425.

* LEICHTY Erle, ed., Abraham SACHS memorial, *A Scientific Humanist*. Philadelphia 1988, Univ. Museum; p. 261-4, "Guaranteed to Cure"; p.225-232, JACOBSEN Thorkild, "The *Asakku* in Lugal-é"; p. 21-32. BEHRENS Hermann, "Eine Axt für Nergal".

* LEIDERER Rosmarie, *Anatomie der Schafleber in babylonischen Leberorakel*. München 1990, Zuckschwerdt. 198 p.

LEMMELIJN B., "'Zoals het nog nooit was geweest en ook nooit meer zou zijn' (Ex 11,6). De 'plagen van Egypte' volgens Ex 7-11: historiciteit en theologie", *Tijdschrift voor Theologie* 36 (1996) 115-131.

† LEONE S., *La medicina di fronte ai miracoli*. Bologna 1997, Dehoniane. 224 p.

LEVIN S., "Job's Syndrome", *Journal of Pediatrics* 76 (1970) 326 [*AnchorBD* 6,11: poverty-effects rather than yaws].

° LICHTENTHAELER[57] Charles, *La médecine hippocratique*. Neuchâtel 1957.

° LICHTENTHAELER[84] Charles, *Der Eid des Hippocrates. Ursprung und Bedeutung*. Cologne 1984, Deutscher Ärzte-Verlag.

LICHTENTHAELER[88] Charles, *Geschichte der Medizin* I,1[4]. Cologne 1987, Ergänzungsband 1988.

LIWAK R., "*R^e pā'îm*", *ThWAT* 7 (1990) 625-636 → BROWN M.L.

° LLOYD[87] Geoffrey E.R., *The Revolutions of Wisdom: Studies in the Claims and Practice of Ancient Greek Science* (Hippocratic corpus): Sather Lecture 52. Berkeley 1987, Univ. California. 468 p.

LLOYD[94] Geoffrey, "Adversaries and Authorities" [Greek versus Chinese origins of science]: *Proceedings of the Cambridge Philological Society* 40 (1994) 27-48.

LLOYD DAVIES M. & I.A., *The Bible: Medicine and Myth*[2]. Cambridge UK 1993, Silent. x-278 p.

LODS Adolphe, "Les idées des Israélites sur la maladie, ses causes et ses remèdes", *Festschrift K.MARTI*, ed.BUDDE K.: BZAW 34 (1925) 181-193.

† LOHFINK Norbert, "Ich bin Jahwe, dein Arzt" (Ex 15,26), in *"Ich will euer Gott werden". Beispiele biblischen Redens von Gott* (Stuttgarter Bibelstudien 100, 1981, Katholisches Bibelwerk) p. 11-73.

LONGRIGG James, *Greek Rational Medicine: Philosophy and Medicine from Alcmaeon to the Alexandrians*. London/NY 1993, Routledge.

° LÓPEZ FÉREZ[91] Juan Antonio, ed., GALENO, *obra, pensamiento e influencia*: Coloquio internacional, Madrid, 22-25 de marzo 1988. Madrid 1991, Univ. a distancia. 370 p.

° LÓPEZ FÉREZ[92] Juan A., ed., *Tratados hipocráticos (estudios acerca de su contenido, forma e influencia)*: Actas del VII Colloque international hippocratique, Madrid 24-29.IV.1990. Madrid 1992. Univ. a distancia. 751p

LORENZ Günther, *Antike Krankenbehandlung in historisch-vergleichender Sicht*. Heidelberg 1990, Winter.

LÜHRMANN D., "Aber auch dem Arzt gib Raum (Sir 38,1-15)", *Wort und Dienst* 15 (1979) 55-78.

† MCCORMICK Robert A., *Health and Medicine in the Catholic Tradition*. NY 1984.

MCNIELL W.H., *Plagues and People*. Oxford 1976.

MAJNO Guido, *The Healing Hand; Man and Wound in the Ancient World*. Cambridge MA 1975, Harvard Univ. p.313, "Alexandria the Great".

MALONEY[82] Gilles, *Cinq cents ans de bibliographie hippocratique*. Québec 1982, Sphinx. 291 p.

MALONEY[89] Gilles, *Concordantia in corpus hippocraticum*. Hildesheim 1989, Olms.

MARCONI Gilberto, "La malattia come 'punto di vista': esegesi di Giacomo 5,13-20" [mediazioni offerte per la situazione umana di estrema debolezza]: *Rivista Biblica Italiana* 38 (1990) 57-72.

¶ ° MARGANNE-MELLARD[87] Marie-Hélène, "Les instruments chirurgicaux de l'époque gréco-romaine", in [GUILLERMAND] Archéologie et médecine 1986/7.

♦ ° MARGANNE[94] Marie-Hélène, *L'ophtalmologie dans l'Égypte gréco-romaine d'après les papyrus littéraires grecs*: Studies in Ancient Medicine 8. Leiden 1994, Brill. xii-209 p.; 19 fig.

° MARGEL Serge, "Les nourritures de l'âme; essai sur la fonction nutritive et séminale dans la biologie d'ARISTOTE", *Revue des Études Grecques* 108 (1995) 91-106.

¶ MARIANI CANOVA Giordana, "Di sana pianta ... L'uso delle piante ritenute utili alla salute," *Archeologia Viva* 8,3 (1989) 44-49.

† MARTY Martin E., "The Tradition of the Church in Health and Healing", *International Review of Mission* 83 (1994) 227-245.

¶ ° MATTHÄUS Hartmut, *Der Arzt in römischer Zeit. Medizinische Instrumente und Arzneien. Archäologische Hinterlassenschaft in Siedlungen und Gräbern*: Limesmuseum Aalen 43. Stuttgart 1989. 108p.

° MAZZINI Innocenzo, "La medicina nella litteratura latina", *Aufidus* 4 (1988) 45-73; p.53 angina; p. 51 gangrena herpestica en LUCILIO.

MEIER Levi, *Jewish Values in Health and Medicine*. Lanham MD 1991, UPA. xvii-201 p.

MEYER-STEINEG T., "Darstellungen normaler und krankhaft veränderter Körperteile an antiken Weihgaben", *Jenaer medizinhistorische Beiträge* 2 (1912) 22-24.

¶ ° MICHAELIDES D., "A Roman Surgeon's Tomb from Nea Paphos", *Report of the Department of Antiquities of Cyprus* (1984) 315-332 → FOSTER.

MILANESI Claudio, *Mort apparente, mort imparfaite; médecine et mentalités au XVIIIe siècle*: Bibliothèque Scientifique. Paris 1991, Payot. 268 p.

‡ MILLER Robert L. & RITNER Robert K., "*Rwy.t*: 'radiating' symptoms of gallstone disease in ancient Egypt", *Göttinger Miszellen* 141 (1994) 71-76.

* MOODIE R.L., *Palaeopathology; an introduction to the study of ancient evidences of disease.* 1923.

MOWINCKEL Sigmund, *The Psalms in Israel's Worship* [= *Psalmen-Studien 1, Awän und die individuellen Klagepsalmen* (Kristiana 1921, Dybwad; p. 64]: tr. AP-THOMAS D.R. (Oxford 1962, Blackwell), vol. 2, p. 2-5.

° MUDRY Philippe & PIGEAUD Jackie, ed., *Les écoles médicales ä Rome*: Actes du 2ème Colloque International sur les textes médicaux latins antiques, Lausanne (Univ. Nantes) 1986. Genève 1991, Droz. 319 p.

♦ MÜNCHOW W., *Geschichte der Augenheilkunde*, ²VELHAGEN K.: Der Augenarzt IX. Leipzig 1983.

♦ MULL Kenneth V. & Carolyn S., "Biblical Leprosy; is it Really ?", *Bible Review* 8,2 (1992) 22-39 & 62.

MUNTNER Suessman, "Medicine", *Encylopaedia Judaica* 11 (Jerusalem 1972, Keter) 1178-1195; → ROSNER 1977.

° MURI Walter, *Der Arzt im Altertum* [Greek and Latin texts with the German]. Munich 1962 = 1938, Heimeran.

¶ MUSCHE Brigitte, "Zur altorientalischen Rosette [chrysanthemum]. Ihr botanisches Vorbild und dessen pharmaceutische Verwertung", *Mesopotamia* 29 (Turin/Florence 1994) 49-70; Eng. 71.

♦ ° MUSTAKALLIO Kimmo K., "Ancient Greek Medicine and Skin Disease", in → CASTRÉN, *Ancient and Popular Healing* 1986/9, p. 39-42.

♦ NATHAN G.S., "Medicine and Sexual Practice in Late Antiquity", *Epoche* 18 (Los Angeles 1993) 20-32.

* NAVEH J., "A Medical Document or a Writing Exercise? The So-Called 4Q Therapeia", *Israel Exploration Journal* 36 (1986) 52-55.

NEUFELD[71] Edward, "Hygiene Conditions in Ancient Israel (Iron Age)", *Biblical Archaeologist* 34 (1971) 41-66.

* NEUFELD[86] Edward, "The Earliest Document of a Case of Contagious Disease in Mesopotamia (Mari tablet ARM X,129)", JANES 18 (1986) 53-66.

¶ ° NEWMYER[93] S., "Asaph the Jew, an Enlightened Student of Greco-Roman Pharmaceutics", in → JACOB I. & W., The Healing Past (Leiden 1993) 107-120.

° NEWMYER[95] Stephen T., "PLUTARCH on the Moral Grounds for Vegetarianism", *Classical Outlook* 32 (1995) 41-43; → KOTTEK.

NICKEL D., "Berufsvortstellungen über weibliche Medizinalpersonen in der Antike", *Klio* 61 (1979) 5f5s.

NICOLAS Maurice, *La Médecine dans la Bible*. Paris 1977.

† NIEHR Herbert, "YHWH als Arzt. Herkunft und Geschichte einer alttestamentlichen Gottesprädikation", *Biblische Zeitschrift* 35 (1991) 3-17 (p. 17 against SEYBOLD 1973 & 1978).

NOEGEL S.B., "The Significance of the Seventh Plague", *Biblica* 76 (1995) 532-9.

NOLLAND J., "Classical and Rabbinic Parallels to 'Physician, Heal Yourself'" (Lk IV 23): *Novum Testamentum* 21 (1979) 193-209.

† NOORDA Sijbolt, "Illness and Sin, Forgiving and Healing: the connection of Medical Treatment and Religious Beliefs in Ben Sira 38,1-15", in

VERMASEREN M.J., ed., *Studies in Hellenistic Religions*: *ÉPROER* 78 (Leiden 1979, Brill) 215-224.

NORTH[67] Robert, "[Angels:] Separated Spiritual Substances in the Old Testament", *Catholic Biblical Quarterly* 19 (Festschrift HARTMAN Louis, 1967) 419-449.

NORTH[93] R., "Brain and Nerve in the Biblical Outlook", *Biblica* 74 (1993) 577-597.

* NORTH[94] Robert, "Medical Discoveries of Biblical Times", in the Festschrift for Philip J. KING, *Scripture and Other Artifacts*, ed. COOGAN M., al. (Louisville 1994, Westminster-Knox) p. 311-332; 6 fig.

♥ NORTH[95] R., "Did Ancient Israelites Have a Heart ?", *Bible Review* 11,3 (1995) 33; 1 fig.; 11,5 (1995) 9-10, objection of Lawrence BOWEN, "Did the Israelites Know the Heart Pumped Blood ?" with response.

° NUTTON[87] Vivian, *John Caius and the Manuscripts of Galen*. Cambridge 1987, Univ. 117 p.

NUTTON[88] Vivian, *From Democedes to Harvey; Studies in Ancient Medicine*. London 1988, Variorum.

° NUTTON[91] Vivian, "John of Alexandria Again: Greek Medical Philosophy in Latin Translation", *Classical Quarterly* 85 (1991) 509-519.

° NUTTON[95] Vivian, "GALEN and the Traveller's Fare", in WILKINS John, ed., *Food in Antiquity* [meeting 1992; Exeter 1995, Univ.] 259-270.

OEPKE Albrecht, "*Iáomai*" [German ThWNT 3 (1938) 194-215], tr. BROMILEY G.W., in KITTEL Gerhard, *Theological Dictionary of the New Testament* 3 (Grand Rapids 1966, Eerdmans) 194-215 (just as German!).

* OPPENHEIM A.L., "On the Observation of the Pulse in Mesopotamian Medicine", *Orientalia* 31 (1962) 27-33.

* ORTNER D.J., "A Preliminary Report on the Human Remains from the Bab edh-Dhra Cemetery, 1977", in RAST W.E., SCHAUB R.T., *The Southeastern Dead Sea Plain Excavation*: Annual of the American Schools of Oriental Research 46 (1981) 119-132.

° ♦ PAHL[85] W.M., "Trepanation", in HELCK W. & OTTO E., ed., *Lexikon der Ägyptologie* 6 (Wiesbaden 1985) 756-757.

° ♦ PAHL[93] Wolfgang M., *Altägyptische Schädelchirurgie*. Stuttgart 1993, G. Fischer. xiv-410 p.; 356 fig. + 16 color.

PALMER Bernard, ed., *Medicine and the Bible* (9 art., Christian Medical Fellowship). Exeter 1986, Paternoster. 272 p.

PANGAS J.C., "La 'mano de un espectro', una enfermedad de la Antigua Mesopotamia", *Aula Orientalis* 7 (1989) 215-233.

† PANIKKAR Raimon, *Medicine and Religion:* Interculture 27,4. Montreal 1994, Intercultural Institute. 40 p.

♦ PAPAGIANNOPOULOS John G., "Eye Afflictions in the Old Testament and their Sociological Implications", *Theología* 60 (Athens 1989) 751-3 in Greek; Eng. 885.

* PARDEE Dennis, "Quelques remarques relatives à l'étude des textes hippiatriques en langue ougaritique", *Semitica* 45 (1996) 19-26.

‡ PARK Rosalind, "Kidneys in Ancient Egypt", *Discussions in Egyptology* 29 (1994) 125-129; 1 fig.

¶ PATRICH Joseph & ARUBAS Benny, "A Juglet Containing Balsam Oil (?) from a Cave near Qumran". *Israel Exploration Journal* 39 (1989) 43-55 (-59, chemical analysis).

* PENN R.G., *Medicine on Ancient Greek and Roman Coins.* London 1994, Seaby Batsford. vi-186 p.

° PENSO G., *Les médecins romains.* Paris 1984, Dacosta. 608 p.

† PERHO Irmeli, *The Prophet's Medicine; a Creation of the Muslim Traditionalist Scholars*: Studia Orientalia 74. Helsinki 1995, Univ. 158 p.

* PERIZONIUS W.R.K. & GOUDEMIT J., "Ancient DNA and Archaeo-virology: a question of samples", *Göttinger Miszellen* 110 (1989) 47-53.

* PETTINATO Giovanni, "Nascita, matrimonio, malattia e morte a Ebla", in HAUPTMANN H., *Wirtschaft und Gesellschaft von Ebla*, Tagung Heidelberg 4.-7. Nov. 1986 (Heidelberg 1988, Orientverlag) p.299-316.

° PHILLIPS E.D., *Aspects of Greek Medicine.* Sydney 1987 = 1973.

° PIGEAUD[87] Jackie, *Folie et cures de la folie chez les médecins de l'antiquité gréco-romaine. La manie*: Études Anciennes 112. Paris 1987, Belles Lettres. 266 p.

° PIGEAUD[93] Jackie, [Zu den medizinischen 'Sekten':] "L'introduction du Méthodisme à Rome", ANRW 2,37,1 (Berlin 1993, de Gruyter) 565-599.

PILCH J.J., review of JACKSON[88] in *Critical Review of Books on Religion* 3, ed. GAVENTA Beverly J. (Atlanta 1990, Scholars) 271-3.

♥ PINKUS Lucio, al., *Epilepsia, la malattia sacra*: Ricerche sull'esistenza umana. Rome 1992, Borla. 103 p.

° POHLENZ M., *Hippokrates und die Begründung der wissenschaftlichen Medizin.* Berlin 1938.

* POMPONIO Francesco, "Épidémie et *revenants* à Ebla", *Ugaritische Forschungen* 21 (1989) 297-305.

° POTTER[88A] Paul, *Short Handbook of Hippocratic Medicine.* Sillery QUE 1988, Sphinx. 59 p.

° POTTER[88B] Paul, tr., ed., *Hippocrates* vol. 5s: Loeb Library. Cambridge 1988, Harvard Univ. (vol. 1-4 c. 1938 are by JONES W.H.S.).

PRECOPE J., *Medicine, Magic and Mythology.* London 1954.

PREUSS Julius, *Biblical and Talmudic Medicine* [= *Biblisch-Talmudische Medizin* 1911], tr. ROSNER Fred. NY 1993 = 1978, Hebrew Publ. Co. xxx-652 p.

PRINCIPE Salvatore, *Le conoscenze anatomiche degli antichi Ebrei; il lessico anatomico e l'immagine dell'uomo nella Misnah*: Henoch quad. 7. Turin 1992, Zamorani. x-111 p.

PRIORESCHI P., *A History of Medicine, I. Primitive and Ancient Medicine.* Lewiston NY 1991, Mellen. xix-642 p.

* PRITCHARD James B., *Ancient Near Eastern Texts Relating to the Old Testament*[2]. Princeton 1995, Univ.: p. 175, Code of Hammurabi, tr. MEEK Theophilus J.

RAD Gerhard von, "Naaman (eine kritische Nacherzählung", in SIEBECK R. Festgabe, *Medicus Viator*, ed. CHRISTIAN P., RÖSSLER D. (Tübingen 1959, Mohr) p. 297-305.

* RAK Y., al., "Evidence of Violence on Human Bones in Israel, First and Third Centuries C.E.": *Palestine Exploration Quarterly* 108 (1976) 55-64.

RAMSEY P., *The Patient as Person.* New Haven 1970.

° RECHENAUER Georg, THUKYDIDES *und die hippokratische Medizin. Naturwissenschaftliche Methodik als Modell für Geschichtsdeutung*: Spudasmata 47. Hildesheim 1991, Olms. xii-396 p.

‡ REEVES Carol, *Egyptian Medicine*: Egyptology 15. Princes Risborough 1992, Shire. 72 p.; 63 fig.

REMUS[85] H.E., "Disease and Healing", in ACHTEMEIER P.J., ed., *Harper's Bible Dictionary* (San Francisco 1985) 222s.

† REMUS[97] Harold, *Jesus as Healer:* Understanding Jesus Today. NY 1997, Cambridge Univ. 149 p.

* RICHARDSON Sheila, "Ancient Medicine and Anatomical Votives in Italy", *Bulletin of the Institute of Archaeology* 30 (London 1993) 29-40.

♥ ° RICHARDSON W.F., "First find your part, then name it" [medical terminology for the heart in ARISTOTLE, GALEN, VESALIUS]: *Prudentia* 25,2 (1993) 29-46.

¶ RIDDLE[92] J.M., Quid pro quo ? Studies in the History of Drugs: Collected Studies 367. Aldershot 1992, Variorum, xi-341 p.; 2 fig.

♦ RIDDLE[94] John M., al., "Ever Since Eve ... Birth Control [plants] in the Ancient World", *Archaeology* 47,2 (1994) 29-35; 7 color. phot,

RINALDI G., "Introduzione allo studio della medicina nei Padri della

Chiesa", *Studi della storia della medicina* 111 (Pisa 1968) ..

¶ RIPPINGER Léon, "Les noms de médicaments en *dia-*", *Latomus* 52 (1993) 294-306.

† RITSCHL Dietrich, "Medizinische Ethik", *Evangelisches Kirchenlexikon³*. Göttingen 1992, Vandenhoeck & Ruprecht. Vol.3, p.349-356. (No article on Medizin or Krankheit.)

* ROBERTS Charlotte & MANCHESTER Keith, *The Archaeology of Disease²*. Ithaca 1995, Cornell Univ, x-243 p.

° ROESCH Paul, "Médecins publics dans les cités grecques à l'époque hellénistique", → GUILLERMAND, Antibes VII (1986-7) 57-67.

ROSNER⁷² F., "Yerakon in the Bible and Talmud: Jaundice or Anemia?", *American Journal of Clinical Nutrition* 25 (1972) 626-628.

ROSNER⁷⁷ Fred, *Medicine in the Bible and the Talmud: Selections from Classical Jewish Sources.* NY 1977, Ktav/Yeshiva. 247 p.; p.3-21, MUNTNER S., "Medicine in Ancient Israel".

ROSNER⁸³ F., "Earliest Description of Gout", *Arthritis and Rheumatism* 26 (1983) 236.

¶ ROSNER⁸⁵ Fred, "The Illness of King Hezekiah and the 'Book of Remedies' which he Hid" (in KOTTEK S. 1984), *Koroth* 9 (1985) 190-7.

ROSNER⁹² Fred, *Jewish Law and Medicine.* Northvale NJ 1992, Aronson. 202p

ROTHSCHUH K.E., ed., *Was ist Krankheit ? Erscheinung, Erklärung, Sinngebung* (Wege der Forschung 362, Darmstadt 1975) p. 414 [p. 397-420, "Der Krankheitsbegriff: Was ist Krankheit ? < *Hippokrates* 43 (1972) 3-17].

¶ ROUANET-LIESENFELT Anne-Marie, "Les plantes médicinales de Crète à l'époque romaine", *Cretan Studies* 3 (1992) 173-190.

ROUILLARD Hedwige, "El Rofé en Nombres 12,13", *Semitica* 37 (1987) 17-48.

‡ ROWLING J. Thompson, "The Rise and Decline of Surgery in Dynastic Egypt", *Antiquity* 63 (1989) 312-9.

★ RUPP Alfred, "Der Zwerg in der ägyptischen Gemeinschaft", *Chronique d'Égypte* 40 (1965) 260-304; 8 fig.

† RUSSELL E.A., "Divine Healing and Scripture", *Irish Biblical Studies* 4 (1982) 123-157.

° SABBAH G., *Études de médecine romaine*: Mémoire 8. St-Étienne 1988, Centre Palerne. 178 p.

SACHS A. memorial → LEICHTY E.

° SALAZAR C.F., *The Treatment of War Wounds in Greco-Roman Antiquity*: diss. Cambridge Univ. 1991.

diss. Cambridge Univ. 1991.

† SANFORD John A., *Healing Body and Soul; the Meaning of Illness in the New Testament and in Psychotherapy*. Leominster / Louisville 1992, Gracewing / Westminster-Knox. 136 p.

SANTANA HENRÍQUEZ Germán, "En torno a la composición [compound words] en la prosa médica griega antica [HIPÓCRATES, GALENO]", *Emerita* 59,1 (1991) 123-132.

‡ SAUNDERS J.B., *The Transitions from Ancient Egyptian to Greek Medicine*: Logan Clendening Lectures 10. Lawrence 1963, Univ. Kansas.

† SAUSER Ekkart, "Christus medicus -- Christus als Arzt und seine Nachfolger im frühen Christentum", *Trierer Theologische Zeitschrift* 101 (1992) 101-123.

° SCARBOROUGH[69] John, *Roman Medicine*. London 1969, Thames & Hudson.

SCARBOROUGH[84] John, ed., *Symposium on Byzantine Medicine*, 1983. Dumbarton Oaks 1984.

¶ SCARBOROUGH[91] John, "The Pharmacology of Sacred Plants, Herbs, and Roots", in → FARAONE C., *Magika Hiera* (NY 1991) 138-174.

° SCARBOROUGH[93] John (till Galen), NUTTON V. (assimilation ..), JACKSON R.P.J. (practitioners), "Roman Medicine" in *Aufstieg und Niedergang der Römischen Welt* 2,37,1 (Berlin 1993, de Gruyter) p.3-48 / p. 49-78 / p. 79-101 (*al.*)

¶ SCHADEWALDT H., "Die Apologie der Heilkunst bei den Kirchenvätern", *Veröffentlichungen der Internazionalen Gesellschaft für die Geschichte der Pharmakologie* 26 (1965) 115-130.

‡ SCHÄFER H., "Die Wiedereinrichtung einer Ärzteschule in Saïs", *Zeitschrift für ägyptische Sprache* 37 (1899) 72-74.

SCHARBERT[55] Josef, *Der Schmerz im Alten Testament*: Bonner Biblische Beiträge 8. Bonn 1955, Hanstein.

SCHARBERT[90] Josef, "Krankheit, Altes Testament", *Theologische Realenzyklopädie* 19 (Berlin 1990, de Gruyter) 680-683 [684-6 NT, MÜLLER Ulrich B.; 695-9 Religionsgeschichtlich, GERLITZ P.]

* SCHARF Joachim-H., "Anfänge von systematischer Anatomie und Teratologie im alten Babylonien", *Sitzungsberichte der sächsischen Akademie Leipzig,* math./nat.w. 120/3. Berlin 1988, Akademie. 68 p.

° SCHEIDEL Walter, "Libitina's Bitter Gains; Seasonal Mortality [September deaths double normal] and Endemic Disease in the Ancient City of Rome", *Ancient Society* 25 (Louvain 1994) 151-167 + 17 fig.

♥ SCHIPPERGES[89] H., *Die Welt des Herzens. Sinnbild, Organ, Mitte des Menschen*. Frankfurt 1989, Knecht.

SCHIPPERGES[90] Heinrich,*Die Kranken im Mittelalter*.Munich 1990, Beck.250p

♦ SCHRIJVERS   P.J., *Eine medizinische Erklärung der männlichen Homosexualität aus der Antike* (Caelius Aurelianus, De morbis chronicis IV 9). Amsterdam 1985, Grüner. 75 p.

° SCHUMACHER J., *Antike Medizin; die naturphilosophischen Grundlagen in der griechischen Antike²* (= ¹1940). Berlin 1963, de Gruyter. 327 p.

SEIDE J., *History of Medicine* (in Hebrew). Tel Aviv 1954.

* SENDRAIL M., "Les sources akkadiennes de la pensée et de la méthode hippocratique", *Annales de la Faculté de Lettres,* Toulouse févr 1952.

° SERBAT Guy, tr., CELSE, *De la médecine*: Coll. Budé. Paris 1995, Belles Lettres.

‡ SETHE Kurt, *Imhotep, der Asklepios der Ägypter.* Leipzig 1902.

† SEYBOLD[73] K. *Das Gebet des Kranken im AT*: Beiträge zur Wissenschaft des ANT 99. Stuttgart 1973.

SEYBOLD[76] K., "*Hālâ*", ThWAT 2 (1976) 960-971, tr. GREEN D., *Theological Dictionary of the Old Testament* 4 (1980) 399-409.

SEYBOLD[78] K., *Krankheit und Heilung: biblische Konfrontationen* (Taschenbuch 1008; Stuttgart 1978, Kohlhammer) p. 9; AT p. 11-79; NT with Ulrich B. MÜLLER, p. 80-176. -- English tr. by STOTT D.W., *Sickness and Healing*: Biblical Encounters. Nashville 1981, Abingdon.

‡ SEYFRIED K.-J., "Zwerg", *Lexikon der Ägyptologie* 6 (Wiesbaden 1986, Harrassowitz) 1432-5.

SHIMSHONY A., "Rift Valley Fever Caused the Fifth Plague and that of 1977": *Journal of the American Medical Association* 256 (1986) 1444 [as in *Veterinary Record* 104 (1979) 411].

SHORT A.R., *The Bible and Modern Medicine.* 1953.

SIGERIST Henry E., *A History of Medicine* (unfinished), I. Primitive and Archaic Medicine; II. Early Greek, Persian, and Indian Medicine. NY 1955 = 1951, Oxford; vol. I, p. xix, "could well have included a chapter on Jewish/OT medicine, strongly influenced by both Mesopotamia and Egypt, but I put this off to treat with the Middle Ages"; nothing further in vol. II.

♥ SIMUNDSON Daniel J., "Mental Health in the Bible". *Word & World* 9 (1989) 140-146.

° SKODA[88] Françoise, *Médecine ancienne et métaphore; le vocabulaire de l'anatomie et de la pathologie en grec ancienne.* Paris 1988. Peeters/Selaf. xxii-341 p.

♥ SKODA[94] Françoise, "Le marasme ['consomption'] dans les textes médicaux. Sens et histoire du mot", *Revue des Études Grecques* 107 (1994) 107-128.

SMITH C.R., *A Physician Examines the Bible.* 1950.

* SMITH Patricia, "The Trephined Skull from the Early Bronze Period at Arad", Festschrift for AMIRAN Ruth, *Eretz-Israel* 21 (1990) 89*-93*; 4 fig.

SMUTNY Robert J., *Latin Readings in the History of Medicine.* Lanham MD 1995, UPA. xii-453 p.

¶ SNYDER Geerto, *Instrumentum medici -- Der Arzt und sein Gerät im Spiegelbild der Zeiten.* Ingelheim 1972. Boehringer. 199 p.; 159 fig.

SODEN W. von, "*Tmryq* (Prov. 20,30) Kränkung", *Zeitschrift für Althebraistik* 2 (1989) 81-82.

SOKOLOFF Michael A., *Dictionary of the Jewish-Palestinian Aramaic of the Biblical Period.* Ramat-Gan 1990, Bar-Ilan Univ.

♥ SPERLING S. David, "Blood", *Anchor Bible Dictionary* 1 (1992) 761-3.

STÄHLIN Gustav, "*Asthenēs*" [German TWNT 1 (1933) 488-492], tr. BROMILEY G.W., in KITTEL Gerhard, ed., *Theological Dictionary of the New Testament* 1 (Grand Rapids 1964, Eerdmans) 490-3; → OEPKE.

STENDAHL Krister, "Gamla Testamentets föreställningar om Helandet. Rafa'-utsagorna i kontext och ideologi", *Svensk Exegetisk Årsbok* 50 (1950) 1-33.

¶ ‡ STETTLER A., "Der Instrumentenschrank von Kom Ombo", *Antike Welt* 13,3 (1982) 48-54.

STOEBE H.-J., "*Rp'* ", & STOLZ F., "*Hlh*", in JENNI Ernst & WESTERMANN Claus, ed., *Theologisches Handwörterbuch zum AT* (Munich 1976, Kaiser) 2,803-9 & 1 (1971) 567-570; English tr. BIDDLE Mark E., *Theological Lexicon of the OT* (Peabody MA 1992, Hendrickson) 3, p.1254-1299 & 1, p.425-7.

STÖHR Martin, "Denn ich bin der Herr, dein Arzt". Gedanken zur Pathologie der Geschichte", *Junge Kirche* 51 (Bremen 1990) 294-303.

♦ STOL[87] M., "Leprosy: New Light from Greek and Babylonian Sources", *Jaarbericht Ex Oriente Lux* 30 (1987-8) 22-31; skin-diseases also focused in his review of PALMER in *Bibliotheca Orientalis* 46 (1989) 128-130.

♦ * STOL[89] M., "Old Babylonian Ophthalmology", in FINET André Festschrift, *Reflet des Deux Fleuves,* ed. LEBEAU Marc & TALON Philippe (Akkadica supp.6; Leuven 1989, Peeters) 163-6.

♥ * STOL[91] Marten, *Epilepsy in Babylonia*: Cuneiform Monographs 2. Groningen/Broomall PA 1993, Styx. vii-155 p.; 2 pl.

* STOL[92] M., "Diagnosis and Therapy in Babylonian Medicine", *Jaarbericht Ex Oriente Lux* 32 (1991-2) 42-65.

† STOLZ Fritz, "Gott, Kaiser, Arzt. Konfigurationen religiöser Symbolsysteme", in Festschrift COLPE C., *Tradition und Translation,* ed. ELSAS Christoph (Berlin 1994, de Gruyter) p. 113-130.

* STOREN Horatio R., *Medicina in nummis.* Boston 1931 [Gnomon 63 (1991) 558].

STRUYS Thuis, *Ziekte en genezing in het Oude Testament.* Kampen 1968.

STUCKELBERGER Alfred, *Bild und Wort. Das illustrierte Fachbuch in der antiken Naturwissenschaft, Medizin und Technik*: Kulturgeschichte der Antiken Welt 62. Mainz 1994, von Zabern. 139 p.; 39 pl.

† SULLIVAN Lawrence E., ed., *Healing and Restoring: Health and Medicine in the World's Religious Traditions.* NY 1990, Macmillan. 468 p. Scarcely relevant to the biblical era.

♥ SULLIVAN S., *"kradíē"*, *Revue Belge de Philologie* 73 (1995) 17-38.

SUSSMAN Max, "Sickness and Disease", *Anchor Bible Dictionary* 6 (NY 1992, Doubleday) 6-15 gives a genuine survey of the data on Medicine in the Bible, with reference to CECIL [19]1988 and other secular medical texts; whereas H.C. KEE, "Medicine and Healing", 4, 659-666, offers only a theological treatment of "Yahweh as healer" and punisher by inflicting sicknesses; p.660 "Physicians Offer Useless Advice". Further 5,60-69, JONES R.N., "Paleopathology".

°SVENBRO Jesper,"Notes sur le calendrier hippocratique",*Ktema*18(1993)69-78

° SWAIN Simon, "Man and Medicine in THUCYDIDES", *Arethusa* 27 (1994) 303-327.

¶ TABANELLI[58] Mario, *Lo strumento chirurgico e la sua storia dalle epoche greca e romana al secolo decimosesto*: Romagna Medica 9. Forlì 1958, Valbonesi.

♥ ° TABANELLI[62] M., *Gli ex-voto poliviscerali etruschi e romani.* Florence 1962, Olschki.

‡ TAVARES A. Augusto, "Medicina e médicos no antigo Egipto e na Mesopotámia", *Brotéria* 126 (1988) 169-181.

° TEMKIN[71] Oswei, "Griechische Medizin als Wissenschaft und Handwerk" [= "Greek Medicine as Science and Craft", *Isis* 44 (1953) 213-225, tr. FLASHAR Dorothea], in FLASHAR Hellmut. ed., *Antike Medizin*: Wege der Forschung 221 (Darmstadt 1971, Wiss.B.) 1-28.

TEMKIN[89] Oswei, "Hippokrates", *Reallexikon für Antike und Christentum* XV/115 (1989) 466-481.

° TEMKIN[91] Oswei, HIPPOCRATES *in a World of Pagans and Christians.* Baltimore 1991, Johns Hopkins Univ. xiv-315 p.

† TESTA Emanuele, "Le malattie e il medico secondo la Bibbia" [Esodo 15,26 ... Mt 8,1-16; -- Sir 38.1-15], in Festschrift GALBIATI E., *Rivista Biblica Italiana* 45 (1995) 253-267; Eng.267.

THEISSEN Gerd, *The Miracle Stories of the Early Christian Tradition* [= *Urchristliche Wundergeschichten*: Studien zum NT 8 (Gütersloh 1974)], tr. F. MCDONAGH. Philadelphia 1983, Fortress.

° THIVEL Antoine, "Theorie und Empirie in der römischen Medizin und bei GALEN", in KÜHNERT Barbara, ed., *Prinzipat und Kultur im 1. und 2. Jahrhundert*: Wissenschaftliche Tagung Univ. Jena\Tbilissi 27.-30.X.1992 (Bonn 1995, Habelt; 332 p.) p.90-99.

* THOMPSON R. Campbell, *Assyrian Medical Texts from the Originals in the British Museum* (facsimiles only). Oxford 1923, Univ.

* TIGAY J.H., "Examination of the Accused Bride at Qumran", *JANES* 22 (1993) 129-134.

‡ TILL W.G., *Die Arzneikunde der Kopten*. Berlin 1951, Akademie. 154 p.

TOURNIER Paul, *Bible et Médecine* (Neuchâtel 1951, Delachaux et Niestlé); tr. SIEBECK Richard, *Bibel und Medizin* (Zurich 1953, Rascher), a doctor's medico-humanitarian reflections.

¶ ° TOUWAIDE Alain, "L'histoire des sciences pharmaceutiques en Grèce et à Byzance", *Byzantion* 63 (1993) 451-4.

° TSEKOURAKIS D., "PLATO's Phaedrus and the Holistic Viewpoint in HIPPOCRATES' Therapeutics", *Bulletin of the Institute of Classical Studies* 38 (London 1991-3) 162-173.

TUFNELL Olga, *Lachish III, The Iron Age* (Oxford 1953) p. 62.

VAN BEEK Gus & Ora, "The Function of the Bone Spatula", *Biblical Archaeologist* 53 (1990) 205-9.

VAN DER EIJK P.J., *Ancient Medicine in its Socio-Cultural Context*: Clio Medica. Amsterdam/Atlanta 1995, Rodopi. 637 p.

VATTIONI Francesco, *Le iscrizioni di Hatra*: *AION* 28 supp. (Naples 1981).

VEGETTI Mario, "Tra passioni e malattia. Pathos nel pensiero medico antico", *Elenchos* 16 (1995) 217-230.

VELTRI G., "Zur Überlieferung medizinisch-magischer Traditionen. Das *métra*-Motiv in den Papyri magicae und der Kairoer Geniza", *Henoch* 18 (1996) 157-175.

♦ VERBOV J.L., "Skin Disease in the Old Testament": *The Practitioner* 216 (1976) 229-236.

VON → RAD; SODEN

° VON STADEN Heinrich, HEROPHILUS: *the Art of Medicine in early Alexandria*. Cambridge/New Haven 1989, Cambridge Univ./Yale Univ. 666 p.

WEBER T., "Gadara of the Decapolis: Preliminary Report on the 1990 Season at Umm Qeis", *Annual of the Department of Antiquities of Jordan* 35 (1991) 323-331.

WELLS Louise, *The Greek Language of Healing from Homer to New Testament Times*: *BZNW* 83. Berlin 1998, de Gruyter.

‡ WESTENDORF Wolfhart, *Erwachen der Heilkunst. Die Medizin im Alten Ägypten.* Zurich 1992, Artemis & W. 297 p.

WESTERMANN Claus, "Gesundheit, Leben und Tod aus der Sicht des Alten Testaments", in *Ärztlicher Dienst weltweit,* ed. ERK Wolfgang, SCHEEL Martin (Stuttgart 1974) p. 153-166.

♥ WHARTON J.A., "Tooth", "Sinew", *Interpreter's Dictionary of the Bible* 4 (1962) 670; 379.

‡ WILDUNG⁷⁷ᴬ Dietrich, *Imhotep und Amenhotep. Gottwerdung im alten Ägypten*: Münchener Ägyptologische Studien 36. Berlin 1977, Deutscher Kunstverlag. Redimensions SETHE 1902.

‡ WILDUNG⁷⁷ᴮ Dietrich, "Imhotep", *Lexikon der Ägyptologie* 3 (1977) 145-8.

* WILHELM Gernot, *Medizinische Omina aus Hatttuša in akkadischer Sprache* (mit Übersetzung): Studien zu den Boğazköy-Texten 36. Wiesbaden 1994, Harrassowitz. 106 p.; ix pl.

† WILKINSON John, *The Bible and Healing; a Medical and Theological Commentary.* Edinburgh / Grand Rapids 1998, Handsel / Eerdmans. P. 32-52. OT epidemic & systemic disease; 63-260 NT; 261-294 in the modern Church.

WILKINSON Lise, *Animals and Disease; an introduction to the history of comparative medicine.* Cambridge 1992, Univ. x-272 p.

WINTER Richard, "Homosexuality", in PALMER 1986, p.145-163.

WISEMAN Donald J., "Medicine in the Old Testament World", in → PALMER, *Medicine and the Bible,* 1986, p. 13-42.

WÖHRLE⁹⁰ Georg, *Studien zur Theorie der antiken Gesundheitslehre*: Hermes Einz. 36. Stuttgart 1990, Steiner. 295 p.

° WÖHRLE⁹² Georg, "CATO und die griechischen Ärzte", *Eranos* 90 (1992) 112-5.

* WOLSKA Wanda, "Zwei Fälle von Trepanation aus der altbabylonischen Zeit Syriens", *Mitteilungen der Deutschen Orient-Gesellschaft* 126 (1994) 37-50; 7 fig.

WOLTER M., "Arznei, Arzt", in *Neues Bibel-Lexikon* 1 (Zurich 1991) 177-9.

♦ WRIGHT David P. & JONES Richard N, "Leprosy", *AnchorBD* 4 (1992) 277-282.

WUNDERBAR R.J., *Biblisch-talmudische Medizin.* 1950/60.

♥ YOUNG Allan, "Psychiatry and Self in Bible and Talmud; the Example of Posttraumatic Stress and Enemy Herem", in → KOTTEK S., ed., *Third Symposium 1987, Koroth* 9 (1989) 194-210. -- Further, on p. 151-164 see the essay of RUBIN Nissan, "Body and Soul in Talmudic and Mishnaic Sources".

♦ ZAGHLOUL El-Hussein, "An Eye-disease Mentioned in a Private Letter from Tuna el-Gebel (Pap. Mallawi Inv. no. 484)": *Mitteilungen des Deutschen Archäologischen Instituts Kairo* 42 (1992) 255-260; 1 fig.; pl.48.

ZIAS[82] J.,"Three Trephinated Skulls from Jericho", *BASOR* 246 (1982) 55-58.

♦ ZIAS[85] Joseph E., "Paleopathological Evidence of Leprosy in Palestine during the Talmudic Period .. Leprosy in the Byzantine Monasteries of the Judean Desert [Martillous 614 C.E.]", *Koroth* 9/1 (1984/5) 242-8.

♦ ZIAS[89] Joseph, "Lust or Leprosy ? Confusion or Correlation?", *BASOR* 275 (1989) 27-31.

* ZIAS[91] J., "Death and Disease in Ancient Israel", *Biblical Archaeologist* 54 (1991) 146-159.

† ZIEGLER Ruprecht, "Aigeai, der Asklepioskult, das Kaiserhaus der Decier und das Christentum", *Tyche* 9 (1994) 187-212.

* ZIMMERMANN R. & KELLEY M.A., *An Atlas of Human Paleopathology*. NY 1982.

ŽIVANOVIĆ Srboljub, *Ancient Diseases: the Elements of Palaeopathology*. London 1982, Methuen. Mostly on bones.

2

a) **Brain and Nerve in the Biblical Outlook**
Biblica 74 (1993) p. 577-597

b) **Medical Discoveries of Biblical Times**
Philip J, KING Festschrift
Scripture and Other Artifacts
Louisville 1994, p. 311-332; 6 fig.

both summarized and adapted as (c)

Did Ancient Israelites Have a Heart ?

Bible Review 11,3 (June 1995) 33; 1 fig.

To the ancient Israelites the *lēb*, often translated heart, was the seat of the emotions. The heart could be "gladdened" (Proverbs 27:11) or glum-- "Why is your face sad, since you are not sick ? This can only be sadness of the heart" (Nehemiah 2:2); "trembling" (1 Samuel 4:13) or courageous -- a brave man has "the heart of a lion" (2 Samuel 17:10); full of love--"Love the Lord your God with all your heart" (Deuteronomy 6:5) or full of hate -- "[Michal] saw King David leaping and dancing before the Lord, and she despised him in her heart" (2 Samuel 6:16).

But the Israelites also associated the heart with knowledge, meditation and morality. The Bible speaks of "the thoughts of the heart" (1 Chronicles 29:18) and "great searchings of the heart" (Judges 5:16) and includes instructions to "commune with your own heart" (Psalm 4:5). The heart can plan wicked deeds -- "a heart that hatches evil plots" (Proverbs 6:18) -- and can become hard -- "The Lord hardened Pharaoh's heart" (Exodus 10:27). The heart can turn away to follow other gods (1 Kings 11:2) or can remain "true" (Nehemiah 9:8).

These various meanings have led some to interpret *lēb* as "the mind". Proverbs 6:18, for example, is variously translated as "a mind that hatches evil plots" (Jewish Publication Society Version) and "a mind given to forging wicked schemes" (Revised English Bible) as well as "a heart that devises wicked plans" (New Revised Standard Version). But this distinction between mind and heart is a relatively modern one. Ancient Israelites had no word for brain and did not associate thinking with the head[1]. Instead, thought and will were entwined with what we call emotions. The biblical *lēb* corresponded largely to the functioning of the nervous system, which the ancients identified as the internal organs of the torso[2]. The seat of intelligence and emotion lay in what we refer to as the stomach. Although the term *lēb* (and its variant form *lēbāb*) occurs more than 850 times in the Bible, it never refers specifically to an organ pumping blood. Ancient Israelites were apparently unaware that the blood circulated throughout the body.

A second-century B.C.E. Etruscan statue [photo p.16, Fig.1; from *King Festschrift* p.314] now in the Museo Arqueológico of Madrid, illustrates what ancients really *meant* by the *lēb*[3] Both the Etruscan statue and the biblical word share a common heritage: medical knowledge from Egypt transmitted by the Greeks. Medicine flourished in Egypt during the early biblical period, and after Alexander the Great conquered Egypt and founded Alexandria in 331 B.C.E., this city became the world-center of medicine. From here, medical knowledge spread to Rome, where for many years all doctors were Greek. The Etruscans, who at this time were well attested from Rome to Florence, would certainly have interacted with the Romans in matters of such importance as medical care. At the same time, the prominence of the now-Greek medicine of Egypt reached Israel, where it is perceptible in the apocryphal [Catholic deuterocanonical], Hellenistic book of Sirach (38:1-3), which praises physicians:

> "Honor physicians for their services,
> for the Lord created them;
> for their gift of healing comes from the Most High,
> and they are rewarded by the king.
> The skill of physicians makes them distinguished,
> and in the presence of the great they are admired."

---

1. See my "Brain and Nerve in the Biblical Outlook", *Biblica* 74 (1993) pp. 577-597.

2. See Angel GIL MODREGO, *Estudios de lēb/ab en el Antiguo Testamento. Análisis sintagmático y paradigmático*; dissertatio. Universidad Complutense, Madrid 1992.

3. See Antje Krug, *Heilkunst und Heilkult. Medizin in der Antike*, 2nd ed. (Munich, C.H. Beck, 1993.

An arched panel of "skin" has been cut out below the lungs and heart of this [above-mentioned Madrid] sculpted male torso, creating a "window" through which we can observe the internal organs of cognition. Although the components seem a jumbled mass to the untrained eye, experts have distinguished various organs and variously identified them by modern medical terms. The large, teardrop-shaped organ at center, for example, is thought to be the liver. Apparently this torso was offered with a prayer that the relevant organ would be healed, or with thanks for a cure.

Under the title "Did the Israelites Know the Heart Pumped Blood ?" in *Bible Review* 11,5 (1995) 9-10 appeared this Reader's Reply by Lawrence BOWEN:

I am a regular reader of both BR and *Biblical Archaeology Review*, which I find interesting, informative and generally factual. However, I noted an incorrect statement in the article entitled "Did Ancient Israelites Have a Heart?" (June 1995). In paragraph three, Robert North writes, "Although the term *lēb* (and its variant form *lēbab)* occurs more than 850 times in the Bible, it never refers specifically to an organ pumping blood. Ancient Israelites were apparently unaware that the blood circulated throughout the body."

True, in the great majority of its occurrences in the Scriptures, the word "heart" is used figuratively. However, the Bible does refer to the actual organ pumping blood. In Exodus 28:30 we read: "And in the breastpiece of judgment you shall put the Urim and the Thummim, and they shall be upon Aaron's heart [Hebrew, *lev*]" (RSV). The breastpiece was put over the area of the chest where the organ pumping blood is located (i.e., over the heart). Speaking of Joram's (or Jehoram's) death, 2 Kings 9:24 also refers specifically to the organ pumping blood: "And Jehu ... shot Yoram between the shoulders, so that the arrow pierced his heart [Hebrew, *mil-libboh*]" (RSV).

Hebrew scholars recognize that the Bible specifically refers to an organ pumping blood. *Lexicon in Veteris Testamenti libros.* by Koehler and Baumgartner, notes regarding the use of *lev (levav)*: "*pumping organ, the heart*: ... 2K 9,24". Also, the *Theological Wordbook of the Old Testament*, by Harris, Archer and Waltke, states: "Concrete meanings of *lēb* referred to the internal organ and to the analogous physical locations. However, in its abstract meanings, 'heart' became the richest biblical term for the totality of man's inner or immaterial nature". Typically, Hebrew vocabulary is composed of concrete words from which abstract and figurative meanings have been derived.

Does North really have any basis for his statement, "Ancient Israelites were apparently unaware that the blood circulated throughout the body"?

On the same page 10 of *BR* 11,5 is subjoined the author's invited response:

I am grateful for reader Bowen's attention. "In the Bible the heart is not an organ of the blood circulation" (J. Preuss & F. Rosner, Biblical and Talmudic Medicine *[1933] p.194) and similar statements (like mine) can be disproved only by citing concrete contrary examples. This cannot be done.*

As for "a shot through the heart" being fatal (2 Kings 9:24), it is true that our modern outlook would normally assume that the (blood-pumping) heart was meant, but equally fatal would be a shot through the "internal organs," which I claim lēb *to mean.*

I confess I do not find in Exodus 28:30 Bowen's implication that the breastpiece is to be put "where the organ pumping blood is located". Like some other biblical occurrences, this use is compatible with the assumption that lēb *is properly "heart" but also compatible with the claim that "internal organs of cognition and control" is meant.*

3

How Loud was Jesus' Voice ? (*Mk 4,1*)

awaited in *The Expository Times* 111 (2000)
with kind permission (excluding electronic diffusion) of the publisher, T&T Clark, Edinburgh, per Dr. Geoffrey Green

Apparently no commentator notes that by getting into a boat, Jesus would have been *farther* from even the nearest fringes of the crowd, and hence less audible to all. The text does not in fact say that his motive was to be better heard; hardly a single commentator infers this. It may be that the aim of Jesus, or that of the evangelist in creating this setting as a literary flourish, was rather a pleasant little scene such as we have admired in paintings[1]. The crowd shown in these is sometimes not *'very* large', but this term can be quite relative. Anyway the sea-cove and boat are the focus.

Few commentators find anything at all noteworthy in verse 1. 'The effect of the boat is to picture the difference between teacher and hearers'[2]. A similar judgment may underlie Gnilka's casual reference to the boat as a 'lake-pulpit' (*Seekanzel*) considered a Markan addition (the pre-Markan exordium having been only 'And Jesus spoke'), but Räisänen cites some who claim that Mark took over the boat from his source[3]. Tuckett while finding the framework-verses 1 and 2 both 'due to Mark alone; they are full of

---

1. Chiefly inexpensive colour-illustrated New Testaments. Jan BRUEGEL's masterpiece shown to illustrate Mk 4,1 for J. MURPHY-O'CONNOR's article 'Why did Jesus Return to Galilee ?' in *Bible Review* 12,1 (1996) 20 (& 42), is rather dark for early daytime, and shows a fairly large milling crowd, many of them busied about other things as the caption notes, and surprisingly little focus on Jesus in the boat.

2. K. KERTELGE, *Markusevangelium*, NEchter 2 (Würzburg 1994) 46. His 1987 Stuttgart commentary mentions Mk 4,1 on p.52 but skips at once to 4,3: so also P. PERKINS, NIntB 1995; D. ENGLISH 1992; J. HEIL, CBQ 1992; A. COLLINS 1992; W. SCHMITHALS 1979; E. LEMCIO 1978; J. CROSSAN, JBL 1973; M. DIDIER in Fest. A. CHARUE 1969; J.P. BROWN, JBL 1961; F. GEALY, ExpT 1936. -- No specific item is cited for Mk 4,1 or 4,2 in W.E. MILLS, *Bibliographies for Biblical Research 2, Mark* (Lewiston NY 1993).

3. J. GNILKA, *Das Evangelium nach Markus* (Ev.-Kath.Komm. 2/1, 1978) p. 156; Heikki RÄISÄNEN, *Die Parabeltheorie im Markusevangelium [Mk 4]*, Helsinki 1973, p. 64. -- Jesus teaches from a boat also in Luke 5,3 and Matthew 13,2.

Markianisms' gives no clue to what these were[4]. For Boismard the boat and crowd are not in Proto-Mark but due to a Lucan redactor[5]. Others further point the link of this boat backward toward 3,9. More obviously for many it points forward to 4,36, where Jesus is (still) in a boat[6].

The lake itself, especially the frequent crossing of the lake, is noted by several exegetes as a sign of ecumenism, an opening out toward the Gentiles[7]. In this sense the approach to our pericope is 'the lake as the place of passage toward pagan peoples'; in the midst of 'a great Jewish multitude, Jesus interrupts his teaching, climbs into a boat and starts over'[8].

'It has become common practice to study the parables of Jesus in isolation from the contexts in which they were transmitted in the Gospels', begins Vorster in an essay arousing our hopes[9]. Then under the subhead 'Mark 4:1-34 and the Markan Narrative', in emphasizing 'time' and 'space', he says that 'signs' which he calls 'topological' like mountain, sea, boat have 'special' meaning since they are used to create specific scenarios: 'the *sea* is where the crowd receives specific teaching' (nothing added about 'boat'). So it is clear that 'space' here has nothing to do with geography (or with

---

4. C.M. TUCKETT, 'Mark's Concerns in the Parables Chapter (Mk 4,1-34)', *Biblica* 69 (1988) 1-26; p.8. More helpfully Greg FAY, 'Introduction to Incomprehension: the Literary Structure of Mark 4:1-34', *Catholic Biblical Quarterly* 51 (1989) 65-81, finds a 'Marcan redactional frame' (p.70) in the chiastic Teaching--Crowd--Boat--Crowd--Teaching.

5. E. BOISMARD, *L'Évangile de Marc, sa préhistoire* 1994, p.93.

6. R.McL. WILSON, 'Mark,' in *Peake's Commentary on the Bible*[2], ed. M. BLACK (London 1962, Nelson) 803. -- 'A similar picture' is suggested by the boat in Mk 5,21 to H.M. HUMPHREYS, *He is Risen: a New Reading of Mark's Gospel* (1992) 41.

7. Werner H. KELBER, *The Oral and the Written Gospel* (Philadelphia 1973 [2]1997), frequently. -- In *The Kingdom in Mark: a New Place and a New Time* (1974) 27 on Mark 4,1 he says the emphasis is not on sitting in the boat but on sitting on the sea.

8. Juan MATEOS & Fernando CAMACHO, *Marcos, texto y comentario* (Madrid 1994, Almendro) 106.

9. Willem S. VORSTER, 'Meaning and Reference; the Parables of Jesus in Mark 4,' in [his ed. with] R.C. LATEGAN, *Text and Reality; Aspects of Reference in Biblical Texts* (Atlanta 1985, Scholars) 27-65; cited p. 34 & 43. See also P. HARTIN, 'Disseminating the Word; a Deconstructive Reading of Mark 4:1-9" in his (with J. PETZER) *Text and Interpretation* p.187-200; J. LAMBRECHT, 'Redaction and Theology in Mark 4", in M. SABBE, ed., *Marc*, Bibliotheca EphTheolLov 34 (1974, [2]1988) 269-308.

narrative)[10].   Vorster's 'topology' is of purely symbolic *tópoi* or *loci communes*. Later he says it is necessary not only to examine (with Lambrecht 1969, p.106) how the speech is organized internally, but also 'to see chapter 4 as part of the Markan narrative world (as we have done above)'. He has indeed done this above, but chiefly in insisting how the parables themselves are also narrative, by which ultimately is meant 'charged with symbolism'. Nothing is finally said in the essay about a real boat or a real sea-cove[11].

Boobyer, giving far more prominence to verse 1 than is usual and seeing the same boat in verse 36 (whence Jesus seems to have spent the whole day in the boat), deplores the 'incongruous shifts of place'[12]. Despite the 'multitude' of verses 1 and 36, in verse 10 Jesus is virtually alone with the Twelve (*hoi perì autòn sỳn toîs dódeka*). Boobyer therefore also concludes that the *tópoi* by which Mark was motivated were topics, 'topical considerations', rather than geographical details of location.

But there could be a geographical aspect to our concern for Jesus' speaking in such a way as to be heard by 'the multitude', or 'the crowd', or even 'the group'. There are certainly many coves along the northwest coast of the Sea of Galilee. And there are places where a hilltop near the water's edge slopes down not too steeply. Where and if the cove and hill coincide, especially if the slope is rather rounded, we would have a kind of natural amphitheatre. This is the impression the paintings sometimes give. Such a situation would presumably have made for improved audibility. But it

---

10. Similarly D. CHRISTIANE, 'Le jeu entre l'espace et le temps en Marc 4,1-34', in P. BONNARD Festschrift *La mémoire et le temps* (Genève 1959, 127-140); on p.135, verse 1 goes with the preceding but verse 2(-34) marks a distancing from the main narrative. -- N. PETERSEN, 'The composition of Mk 4,1-8,26', *Harvard Theological Review* 73 (1980, 185-217) 193 finds a key in the topographical content; but p.197 on Mk 4,1 says only that the boat is the same as in 4,36. But for W.KELBER,'Jesus and Tradition: Words in Time, Words in Space', *Semeia* 65 (1994) 139-167 'in space' means 'in print'.

11. So Paul BEAUCHAMP, 'Paraboles de Jésus, vie de Jésus. L'encadrement évangélique et scripturaire des paraboles (Mc 4,1-34)', in J. DELORME ed., *Les paraboles évangéliques* (ACFEB 1987; LDiv 135, 1989; 151-170) on p.152 apparently refers to the arrangement of teachings by content, citing 'No Gospel, even Mt 5, has a more didactic *mise en scène*', from V. FUSCO, *Parola e regno; la sezione delle parabole (Mc 4,1-34) nella prospettiva marciana* (1980), where p.80 on verses 1 and 2 notes only the verbs used for Jesus. More literally perhaps W. EGGER, *Frohbotschaft .. Mk-Ev* (Frankfurt 1976) 111 'Mark thus creates a magnificent setting (Szenerie)'.

12. G.M. BOOBYER, 'Redaction of Mark 4:1-34', *New Testament Studies* 8 (1961) 59-70.

would still be likely that both the far and the near fringes of the group would find it harder to hear Jesus.

Even granting that this may have not been the primary concern in choosing the décor of the present episode, most readers' reaction to Mk 4,1 would doubtless be the importance of making his teaching as audible as possible to the listeners -- and that the 'very many' of them must bear at least some relation to more concrete indications elsewhere. Nowhere else, doubtless, as many as the Five Thousand of all four evangelists; but we could have to reckon with a couple of hundred[13].

Though we are informed about the *persona* or mask ingeniously constructed to project the voice in Greek-era theatres, and there may have been similar helps to Roman oratory, still it has never been easy for an open-air speaker to make himself *adequately* audible to two hundred people, even clustered closely together in a relatively quiet area. In the past century we never had experience of any such thing; there were always megaphones and eventually electronic loud-speakers. Some emergencies occasionally forced an unusually loud-voiced policeman to shout to a larger crowd to disperse or avoid danger.

But it has surprised me that no reader of Mark 4 seems to have asked himself just how large the crowd would have been, and how loud would have to be the voice of anyone who is conveying to them information which is new and profound though in simple familiar words. And in fact even specialists in the parables are not much concerned about that. It has become an acquired fact among exegetes that Matthew's Sermon on the Mount (like other sections of his) was never spoken publicly in that form, but contains in some order of similarity many teachings of Jesus given in entirely different context by Mark or others. The *teaching* is generally held to be indisputably

---

13. The '(large) crowds' of Mark 4,1 are vaguely stressed by R.H. GUNDRY, *Mark* (Eerdmans 1992) 190; B.W. HENAUT, *Oral Tradition and the Gospel: the Problem of Mark 4* (JSNT supp. 82, 1993) 150; C.S. MANN, *Mark* (Anchor Bible 27, 1986) 261; J. ERNST, *Das Evangelium nach Markus* (1981) 126; Robin GUELICH, *Mark 1-8* (Word Comm. 34A, 1989) 190; M. HOOKER in *Black's Commentary* (1991) 122; and W. GRUNDMANN, *Ev.Mk.*[3] (1965) 88, crowd larger than usual. -- B. VAN IERSEL, *Leggere Marco* (1993 < 1986) 112 ventures that Jesus got into the boat in order not to be trampled by the crowd. -- Elizabeth S. MALBON, 'Disciples/Crowds/Whoever: Markan Characters and Readers", NT 28 (1986) 104-130, is more concerned with whether the listeners were opponents (T. WEEDEN) or sympathizers (R. TANNEHILL, likelier). -- Only R.A. COLE, *Tyndale Mark* ([2]1989) 88 says that Jesus did not rejoice over big crowds as other teachers do, but here he was forced to resort to the boat as an unusual mode of teaching.

that of Jesus; the *occasion* or *setting* may quite often be the literary creation of an evangelist who did not even waste any particular thought on the matter. His interest, his *convictions* lay elsewhere.

If Matthew was unconcerned to indicate the (presumably known to him) various settings from which successive teachings came, Mark too had no interest in estimating roughly *how many* people his 'crowd' represented, and he may well never have attempted to inquire. Even less was the concern of either for how loud a voice on Jesus' part would have been required to reach however large a crowd it was. It was the *teaching* which was important, and indeed also the reception accorded to it, even if by a group of only twenty.

The 'setting' furnished by Mk 4,1 (though similar also in Mt 13,2) may well be an imaginative literary flourish, which is not exactly the same as 'fictional'. But even frankly invented details in a purely fictional historical novel can convey valuable factual information, even about the author's own or periods other than those being written about. It has often been pointed out that we should not seek from the evangelists (or anyone else) the answers to questions which they simply did not ask. Obiter dicta like 'there was much grass in the place' (Jn 6,10) are not intended to convey botanical or climatic information.

True enough; but with the burgeoning of scientific and other information it becomes increasingly imperative to seek from the Bible, for example, help on quite recent moral or medical problems with which it never explicitly dealt. And human curiosity in general legitimately seeks answers to its inquiries wherever it can find them. If no one has hitherto been impelled to wonder 'how loud was Jesus' voice' (and if that is not an indiscreet or totally useless un-problem), then there is no likelier place to seek an answer than in the New Testament. Doubtless most people rightly draw from it the impression that Jesus normally used a pleasant or even soft voice. There is one clear indication of his 'loud voice', *phōnē megálē*, with which Jesus died (Mt 27,50). And one may suspect that in driving money changers from the Temple (Mk 11,15) Jesus 'raised his voice'.

But a rather louder, or even very loud, voice would have been required with a crowd as small as 200, or even a group of 20. These seem satisfactory parameters, in default of any proof or concrete indication whatever for practically all the parables and other oral teachings of Jesus. But we can no longer escape facing up to the 5000 of all four evangelists (including Mk 6,43; distinguished from the 4000 of an apparently different event by Mk 8,9 and emphatically in 8,20-21). This would seem to be an undoubted parameter for the size of the crowds by whom Jesus was heard.

But two important points are raised by the observation that in Mark 6,33 (confusedly[14]) Jesus was trying to escape the crowd, but they knew where he was going and got there before him[15]. We must notice in this intriguing detail two separate factors relevant to our problem. First, many of the 'crowd of listeners' would have got tired along the way and for this or other reasons dropped out, so that the number of original listeners would have been even larger than 5000. And secondly, the multiplication of the loaves would not have been performed in direct relation to the number of those who had just been listening (though more so than in the 'communal meal' consensus noted below).

But to return to our concern for the 5000: Even the exegetes who profess no more interest than the evangelists themselves in such numbers or concrete settings, seemingly hesitate to admit that we have here a typical case of biblical scribal copying, adding a couple of zeroes to make a meagre figure give more glory to God. *Some* exaggeration or casual reckoning may well be admitted, but hardly any exegete cares or dares to estimate any 'lowest' figure[16].

And of course the focus of attention is the feeding, the miracle. The day's portion of actual teaching was finished; the 5000 itself is not a number

---

14. Jouette M. BASSLER, 'The Parable of the Loaves', *Journal of Religion* 66 (1986) (152-) 172 also notes a 'gap' in Mark's text, 'puzzling' the implied reader.

15. Ivor BUSE, 'The Gospel Feeding of the Multitudes', *ExpT* 74 (1962s) 167(-170). -- In *ExpT* 97 (1985s) 112-5, S. BARTON, 'The Miraculous Feeding in Mark' is concerned with symbolisms (OT, Passion, Mission).

16. Adolf POHL, *Das Evangelium des Markus*, Wuppertal 1986, 269, on Mk 6,44 notes that in the Bible big numbers are 'valued' but even whole cities like Bethsaida had at most 3000 population; Ralph W.KLEIN, 'How Many in a Thousand?' in *The Chronicler as Historian* (ed. K. HOGLUND; JSOT supp. 238, 1997) 271-282, notes other possible meanings for Hebrew *aleph* in the huge numbers of Babylonian armies in 2 Chr 13,3.7; Berndt SCHALLER, '4000 Essener -- 6000 Pharisäer. Zum Hintergrund und Wert antiker Zahlenangaben' in Fest. H. STEGEMANN, *Antikes Judentum und Frühchristentum* (ed. B. KOLLMANN, 1999 de Gruyter) 172-182 [there on p. 253-265 G.A. BROOKE, '4Q252 and the 153 Fish of John 21:11' notes that in the Qumran fragment (not so simply in Gen 8,14) Noah's Ark landed on the 153d day. -- No concern for what actual countable number the figure 5000 may have represented is shown by either R. LATOURELLE, *The Miracles of Jesus and the Theology of Miracles* (1988) 72-78, or by the study he cites as 'the best and the one that most faces up to the problem of historicity', I. DE LA POTTERIE, 'Le sens primitif de la multiplication des pains', in J. DUPONT, ed., *Jésus aux origines de la Christologie*: BiblETLov 40 (1975 ²1989, 303-330), p. 321 (L'événement historique): 'une foule' (a crowd).

which relates to how well Jesus' voice could be heard. But in all four gospels it is more or less the same group. And the miracle of 'the 5000' is so frequently singled out that it can justly be regarded as a veritable cornerstone of many people's faith. Are we to say casually that this concrete number meant no more to the evangelists than the 'very large crowd' meant to Mark ?

John Meier's very recent, thorough, and moderate treatment of the 5000 in 17 pages has nothing to say of this number except (as most admit[17]) that the 4000 is a variant tradition of the same event. Only at the end he sets forth his view that the historical event behind this story was one among many occasions of table fellowship celebrated by Jesus, but 'memorable because of the unusual number of participants' and at the bottom of the same page 'a memorable communal meal with a large crowd'[18]. An almost identical proposal was made by Kollmann, emphasizing that such meals had eschatological-paradisiacal overtones[19]. Both mention as minor the influence of 2 Kgs 4,42-44 (Elisha's 20 loaves, no fish, 100 men) in the formulation of the NT narrative. No concrete number of participants is even hinted by these exegetes, and in any case would be wholly irrelevant to our inquiry, since the fellowship-meal as a (very probably, says Meier) historical event is shown as standing in no relation at all to any long session of

---

17. Concerning the '4000', the only debatable point remaining, according to K.P. DONFRIED, 'The Feeding Narrative and the Marcan Community (Mark 6,30-45 and 8,1-10)' in the 1980 BORNKAMM Fest. *Kirche* 95-104, is whether Mark found the two doublets in his source or (Donfried's view) had his own reasons for creating the duplication. Still a defender of the (also) 4000 is Austin FARRER, 'Loaves and Thousands', in *Journal of Theological Studies* NS 4 (1953) 1-14, but only because of a symbolism with which he is concerned. Raymond BROWN's 1966 *Anchor Bible John* on p. 233 seems to have no comment on the 5000 of John 6,10; his p. 237 seems concerned only in view of the 4000.

18. John MEIER, *A Marginal Jew; Rethinking the Historical Jesus* (New York 1994, Doubleday) vol. 2, p.967.

19. Bernd KOLLMANN, *Ursprung und Geschichte der frühchristlichen Mahlfeier* (Diss. 1989): Göttinger Theologische Arbeiten 43. Göttingen 1990, Vandenhoeck & Ruprecht; p. 195-206, Die Traditionen von der wunderbaren Speisung; summarized in his *Jesus und die Christen als Wundertäter. Studien zu Magie, Medizin und Schamanismus in Antike und Christentum*; FRLANT 170 (Göttingen 1996, Vandenhoeck & Ruprecht), p.274. A similar view is attributed to earlier exegetes (and apparently dismissed) as 'naturalistic' by LATOURELLE n.16 above, p.72.

teaching and auditory experience[20].

We end up unable to exclude the possibility that Jesus is in general portrayed as making himself heard by some twenty, or at any rate hardly more than two hundred; and the fringes of such gatherings commonly enough scarcely hear what is being proclaimed. As a matter of simple human interest, from sympathy or advantage Jesus must have been aware of how difficult it was to make himself heard by a normally large crowd, even if rarely as many as 200. His ability to use on occasion a very loud voice warrants comparison with known political and other leaders. It also warrants conclusions with regard to his own personality: *noverim me, noverim Te.*

---

20. H. VAN DER LOOS, *The Miracles of Jesus*: NT Supp.9 (Leiden 1965, Brill) (619-) 637: a 'messianic' (S. BERKELBACH VAN DER SPRENKEL) or communal meal, historical except for 'all were sated'; not a show-off feat (*Schauwunder*), though we remain uninformed where the food came from.

4

Could Hebrew have been a Cultic Esperanto ?

adapted from Kohlhammer-Verlag *Zeitschrift für Althebraistik* 12,2 (1999)
(updated Catholic Biblical Association research-report, San Diego 1994)

Prominent above in our first chapter, on Medicine, was the fact that there is no word for "brain" in the Hebrew Bible, nor indeed for "heart" in its proper sense of the specific bodily organ, nor for "nerve" or "lung". There are also lacking words for "comb" and "spoon" actually found in Palestine excavation; and many other words needed for ordinary daily life-communication. This situation was responsible for the approach of Ullendorff to be noticed presently, and for our own here.

But our title and theme are due to Knauf's provocative 1990 "Was 'Biblical Hebrew' a language ?"[1]. Actually the idea of an "invented" language can only mean "produced by combining elements of neighboring languages actually in use" as Knauf suggests, and as was the case with Esperanto which we will notice in conclusion. Much of the documentation here was involved in my 1993 *Biblica* research on "brain" in the Bible[2]. Now will be added chiefly some dialogue with Rendsburg's *Diglossia, and* with some insights of Garbini.

Then chiefly thanks to some unusual outlooks of Philip Davies in 1992 we will be pointed toward the problem of when and how such an "invented" language as he also holds, could have originated. Then we will feel impelled to make an insertion not contained in our ZAH article, querying whether the audacity of putting an existing partial or oral Bible into an "invented" language has (in Kirkpatrick) some instructive parallel to the audacity of (Kelber's) Mark changing Jesus' message from orality to textuality.

---

1. E. A. KNAUF, "War "Biblisch-Hebräisch" eine Sprache ?", ZAH 3 (1990) 11-23.

2. R. NORTH, "Brain and Nerve in the Bible", *Biblica* 74 (1993) 577-587.

1. Knauf's many mini-languages

We may begin with our rendition of this statement of Knauf (p.11). "It is undeniable that the Hebrew parts of the Old Testament are in a code which has all the earmarks of a natural language: a limitedly-recognizable phoneme system, a grammar, a vocabulary, 'dialects' like hymnic and pro-saic, and even a history, from archaic Judges 5, through standard-classical, down to 'sub-classic' Qoheleth, Sirach and Qumran. But an entirely different question is whether that language was ever spoken by anyone ... Indeed even as a *written* language in no time or place did Biblical Hebrew ever serve as a means of communication (letters, permits, receipts)".

Facile refutation of these bold statements springs immediately to mind. What of the Lachish Letters ? the tax-receipt "for the king" ostraca? the Siloam inscription ? the Gezer calendar ? and the Deir'Alla Balaam documents ? Knauf is well aware of these, and takes them up one by one, with observations which he claims tend to prove his own thesis.

In general what he aims to show is that these inscriptions were indeed part and proof of genuinely *used* language; but he means by this rather *many* separate languages, *none* of which can be reasonably called "biblical Hebrew".

Knauf focuses chiefly the northerly dialects, or what he calls rather "the Israelite languages" in plural[3]. His clearest case is the word for "year", which is *št* [*šat(t)*], not *šana(t)* as in what he calls Judaean (which in this case happens to coincide with biblical Hebrew). This *šat* is one of the only eight real nouns in the Samaria ostraca; and along with more obscure phonemic and grammatical details is said to prove that "Israelite" at least was a separate language. Knauf invokes here the fact that Phoenician and Ugaritic also use *šat* for year. He thereby seems to make of this fact a criterion of northerly pertinence as distinct from the "Judaean language".

---

3. Note further KNAUF's "Place Name Provinces in Semitic-Speaking Ancient Near East", *Proceedings of the Leeds Philosophical and Literary Society* A/8/ii (1956) 83-110; and fn. 65 below. In A. SÁENZ-BADILLOS, *A History of the Hebrew Language*, tr. J. ELWOLDE (Cambridge 1993) p.62-64, "The Language of the Inscriptions" is quite updated, including 'Ajrud, Izbet Sarta, the silver Nm 6.24, and the ivory pomegranate; on p. 42 Mesha is suggested to have used an Israelite scribe; and p. 54 accounts for the obsolescence of greater Akkadian influence demanded by H.P. BAUER (1910; *Historische Grammatik* with P. LEANDER, 1922).

Thus it is a bit surprising that the rest of his article scarcely follows up any relevance of Phoenician or even Ugaritic[4].

The brief Gezer Calendar, dated around 900 when Gezer was under North-Israel rule as in 1 Kgs 9,15, shows both similarities and differences vis-à-vis the Deir'Alla (called here Sukkoth) inscriptions. This fact constitutes the chief basis for maintaining that there was not one but there were *several* (North-)"Israelite" languages, none of which was really "standard"[5].

Knauf's p. 16 further makes a remarkable statement which we may render "While the profane [Sukkoth] inscriptions of the same stratum already show pure Aramaic, the language of the Bileam inscriptions is *not yet Aramaic, but also no longer Canaanite*"[6]. These last words, which we have italicized, may be taken to mean not of course that the or an Aramaic language was just then first coming into existence, but rather that a local group's use of Aramaic borrowings was just then becoming so strong that

---

4.   Knauf p.13 n.8 disapproves J. H. TIGAY, *You Shall Have No Other Gods; Israelite Religion in the Light of Hebrew Inscriptions*: Harvard SemSt 31, Atlanta 1986, for failing to distinguish north and south in concluding chiefly from theophoric names that polytheism was not as prevalent as the biblical strictures would lead us to think. -- Coastal Phoenician lacks the rich Biblical Hebrew Aramaic "substratum", says I. YOUNG, *Diversity in Pre-Exilic Hebrew*: FAT 5, Tübingen 1992, (63-) 70, adding that Phoenician/Aramaic represent "the battle of two prestige-languages for the role of *lingua franca* in Syria-Palestine" [p.203-5 his review of Knauf]; further "The 'Northerners' of the Israelite Narrative in Kings" [1Kgs 17 - 2Kgs 10], ZAH 8 (1995) 63-70. -- The "extreme view" apparently attributed in a note 4 to GARBINI, that Phoenician itself was the language used in North-Israel, is concluded to be untenable in a chapter of the 1992 doctorate of Françoise BRIQUEL-CHATONNET, "Hébreu du Nord et Phénicien: étude comparée de deux dialectes cananéens": *Orientalia Lovaniensia Periodica* 23 (1992) 89-126. P. DHORME, "La langue de Canaan", *RB* 22 (1913) 369-393 was just a systematization of then-known forms. -- Punic (as well as South-Arabian) is included by L.C. SCOTT, *Archaic Features of Canaanite Personal Names in the Hebrew Bible*: Harvard SemMg 47, Atlanta 1990.

5.   Note J. MACDONALD, "Some Distinctive Characteristics of Israelite Spoken Hebrew", BiOr 32 (1975) 162-175, with whom Y.T. RADDAY and H. SHORE, *Genesis, an Authorship-Study in Computer-Assisted Statistical Linguistics* (Rome Biblical Institute 1985) agree that the language of direct speech differs notably from that of narrative.

6. "A stage before definitive separation of Aramaic from Canaanite" in the view of H.-P. MÜLLER, "Die Sprache der Texte von Deir'Alla im Kontext der nordwestsemitischen Sprachen mit einigen Erwägungen zum Zusammenhang der schwachen Verbklassen", ZAH 4 (1991) (1-)31. -- On "East-Jordan Canaanite", see K.P. JACKSON, *The Ammonite Language of the Iron Age*: Harvard SemMg 27, Chico CA 1983 (77-80 on Abinadab seal in Knauf 23); W. AUFRECHT, *A Corpus of Ammonite Inscriptions*: Ancient Near Eastern Texts 4, Lewiston 1989.

there was question of henceforth calling their language "Aramaic" instead of whatever it had been been called before[7].

His p. 20 will insist that when biblical Hebrew came into being after the fall of Judah, Aramaic was not only the official language there but also in part the language of common people's daily use. Moreover already in footnote 4 of his second page he had stated, "Just as the authors of [OT] dissertations today can presume their readers know the main European languages and some Latin, Greek, Hebrew, Aramaic, and Arabic, so the author of Job expected of his public a good knowledge of Aramaic and a smattering of Phoenician and Arabic"[8]. Though there was no occasion for mentioning Ugaritic here, it is emphasized that Aramaic was more familiar to the biblical people than Phoenician was[9].

These references to Aramaic are mentioned in passing because of what will concern us farther on. But for Knauf they are not as important as the existence of many mini-languages, including Judaean and at least two

---

7. Attention should be called here to the Dan Aramaic inscription then not yet discussed: É. PUECH, "La stèle araméenne de Dan", *Revue Biblique* 101 (1994) 215-241; H.-P. MÜLLER, "Die aramäische Inschrift von Tel Dan", ZAH 8 (1995) 121-139 [and T. MURAOKA there, 11 (1998) 74-81]; P.-E. DION, "Balaam l'Araméen d'après de nouveaux documents du VIIIe siècle", *Église et Théologie* 22 (1991) 85-87.

8. Our Job is a translation from an original Aramaic, according to N.H. TUR-SINAI, *The Book of Job: a New Commentary* (Jerusalem 1957) xxx; approved by André LEMAIRE, "Aramaic Literature and Hebrew Literature: Contacts and Influences in the First Millennium B.C.E.", *Ninth Congress "C"* (Jerusalem 1988 ..) 9-24; p. 23; denied by KAUFMANN there p.55; and by Gary RENDSBURG, "Linguistic Variation and the 'Foreign Factor' in the Hebrew Bible", *Israel Oriental Studies* 15 (1995) 179, though A. IBN EZRA had also favored an Aramaic Job original; advertence by James BARR, *Comparative Philology and the Text of the Old Testament* (Eisenbrauns 1987) 226, amid four senses of "Aramaism". -- Rendsburg's *Israel Oriental Studies* 15,179 also rejects the view that the Job original had been Arabic: F.H. FOSTER, "Is the Book of Job a translation from an Arabic Original ?", *American Journal of Semitic Languages* 49 (1932s) 31-45; A. GUILLAUME, "The Arabic Background of the Book of Job", in the S.H. HOOKE Festschrift, *Promise and Fulfilment*, ed. F.F. BRUCE (London 1963) p.106-127; and *Studies in the Book of Job*, London 1968.

9. Little can be added from N.M. WALDMAN, *The Recent Study of Hebrew; a Survey of the Literature and Selected Bibliographies*, Winona Lake 1989; p. 9-15 cognates, in Biblical Hebrew p. 1-78; Aramaic Influence and Language Change [2 Kgs 18,26 ..] p.79-86. -- The "common but altogether untenable" view that Old-Hebrew dialects arose from a post-Exodus Takeover (Landnahme) attributed by Knauf p.13 n.7 to p.110 of the Neukirchen 1985 edition of Winfried THIEL's 1976 dissertation *Die soziale Entwicklung Israels in vorstaatlicher Zeit* was not verified in the 1980 edition available to me.

Israelite, amid what is called "Canaanite" (and by some Moabite, Edomite, Ammonite). His proof that so many mini-languages were in use in the production of the inscriptions which are commonly attributed to Biblical Hebrew, suffices for his forceful conclusion (p.21) "Biblical Hebrew was not a language that was ever spoken by anyone. ... There was no updating of the spelling of the compositions which had been handed down, other than their definitive literary formulation in the fifth century. ... Not only is Biblical Hebrew no [used] language, but there was also no 'Old-Hebrew' in existence from the 8th to the 6th centuries; there were just some five languages, distinct though nearer to each other than to Phoenician and the other Canaanite languages".

2. Ullendorff's Proto-Mishnaic Vocabulary Pool

Knauf's p.11 is satisfied that Ullendorff no less than himself answers with an emphatic No the question "Is Biblical Hebrew a language ?", though he must immediately go on to reject what Ullendorff's answer really means: Biblical Hebrew was a "linguistic fragment" or *part* of a real language, namely the presumed "Old Hebrew" which meanwhile continued in use until it was transformed into "Middle" or Mishnaic Hebrew. Ullendorff reaches his conclusions by an approach very different from Knauf's, inquiring into the total lack in Biblical Hebrew of so many words without which a real *used* language could not exist. One such word, incidentally, was "brain", which accounted for my interest in the present problem (ftn.[2] above).

Ullendorff says, "I am simply interested to know whether the words, forms, and constructions that *happen* to occur in this corpus of relatively modest size, which we call the Hebrew Bible, would be adequate to serve as a basis for the ordinary day-to-day requirements of a normal speech community"[10]. There is no word for "comb" or "spoon", though the use of these is firmly attested by archeology.

In our Hebrew Bible there are some 300,000 words in all, but only some 7500 *different* words (p.253 = p.5), as compared with 40,000 of a *small* and 500,000 words of a *large* English dictionary. Moreover of the 7500-some words, there is only one single occurrence of at least 1500, or perhaps

---

10. E. ULLENDORFF, "Is Biblical Hebrew a Language ?", BSOAS 34 (1971), p.241 (-255) = (his) *Studies in Semitic Languages and Civilizations*, Wiesbaden 1977, p. 3 (-17).

as many as one-third (p,262 = p.14): 2440 in Rabin's estimate[11]. It seems obvious that only a quirk of chance saved *these* words from perishing in the oblivion which must have been the fate of the other words useful or necessary if Biblical Hebrew had been a real used language.

"To consider that which is preserved in the Masoretic text as sufficient even for the limited needs of daily life in ancient Palestine" is a fallacy pilloried by G.R. Driver[12]. Albright calculates, "the known biblical Hebrew vocabulary cannot represent over a fifth of the local stock of North-west Semitic words in use between 1400 and 400 B.C"[13]. Ullendorff's foot-note purports to give from a letter of Albright some justification for this "gloomy, pessimistic" calculation. More relevant would it have been to note that the Albright statement glides casually from "Biblical Hebrew" to "Northwest Semitic"; and in fact appears *not* in the adjacent article on the Biblical Languages (by Ryder), but in a section of the "Archaeology" article entitled "Light from Ugarit on the Bible" -- almost as if Albright considered it to be obvious that the vocabulary-pool out of which the measly 7500 words of Biblical Hebrew have been saved from extinction *included* also the not-so-different "Ugaritic dialect of Canaanite"[14].

This view seems shared by the very outset of Ullendorff's paper (p. 241 = p.3). "The major part of the OT is written in a Canaanite tongue clearly distinguished from [Daniel/Ezra] Aramaic. While we have no

---

11. C. RABIN, *Millîm bod'dot*, in *Ensiqlopediyâ miqrā'ît*, Jerusalem 1962, vol. 4, p.1066-70. Ullendorff attributes his own figure of 1500 hapax to a "Jewish Encyclopedia vi,226-9".

12. G.R. DRIVER, "Hebrew Notes", JBL 68 (1949) 58. His "Colloquialisms in the OT", *Mélanges Marcel Cohen*, Hague 1990, is more relevant to Rendsburg below.

13. W.F. ALBRIGHT, "The Archaeology of the Ancient Near East", in *Peake's Commentary on the Bible*[2], ed. M. BLACK (London 1962) p.62. On p. 68 there, E.T. RYDER estimates only some 5000 separate words in the Bible (instead of over 7500; "too low" says Ullendorff p. 243 = p.5 n.12).

14. Stephen A. KAUFMANN, "The Classification of the North West Semitic Dialects of the Biblical Period and Some Implications Thereof", *Ninth World Congress of Jewish Studies* (1985 "C": panel Hebrew and Aramaic). ed. M. BAR-ASHER, Jerusalem 1988, p. 41-55, in a paper aimed to show that the Deir'Alla inscriptions are slightly more Aramaic than Canaanite, begins on p. 41 with Cyrus GORDON's latest ever-changing view: Ugaritic and Biblical Hebrew were the same language (in 1965 with M. DAHOOD he had held that Ugaritic is a Canaanite dialect). But Ugaritic is not even to be classed with Canaanite, held J.BLAU, "On Problems of Polyphony and Archaism in Ugaritic Spelling", JAOS 58 (1968), p.523-6, and *A Grammar of Biblical Hebrew*, Wiesbaden 1976, p.1.

knowledge of the precise nature of the language spoken by the Hebrew immigrants into Canaan, it is likely that from a linguistic point of view the OT owes more to the vanquished Canaanites than to the conquering Hebrews".

Leaving aside the historical presupposition of "immigrants" (from Egypt? or even ultimately from Ur or Harran) "vanquishing" Canaanites, which would hardly go unchallenged today, the above citation poses neatly the precise question with which we are concerned. What indeed *was* that language spoken by the so-called "Hebrew immigrants" (Egyptian ? if after 400 or even 100 years there; or if not, the Amarna-wise crumbling Akkadian of their "origins" ? or more plausibly, the language of their long wandering through Aram, which had somehow meanwhile replaced Amarna-Akkadian as *the* international language) ?

In spite of his saying that we do not know, Ullendorff will end up by holding that we know quite well (p. 250 = p.20): it was a proto-Hebrew language [he seems to require already a "Canaanite"[15] picked up on the fringes of Egypt before the "vanquishing"] out of which Biblical Hebrew drew -- a relatively small part -- but which went on being used until it was transformed gradually into the basically identical Middle Hebrew, a spoken Mishnaic Hebrew[16].

By way of proof, assuming as "obvious" that the Mishnaic Hebrew so well described by Segal was the "continuation" of Biblical Hebrew,

---

15. It may be doubted that exegetes commonly make Hebrew the language of Adam and Eve (Knauf ZAH 3,13), but "the language of the Patriarchs was [already] the language of Canaan", according to Mireille HADAS-LEBEL, *Storia della lingua ebraica* [*L'hébreu, trois mille ans d'histoire* 1992], tr. Vanna LUCATTINI VOGELMANN, Firenze 1994, p.13.

16. See also J. FELLMAN, "The Linguistic Status of Mishnaic Hebrew", *Journal of Northwest Semitic Languages* 5 (1977) 21s; A. SAMELY, "Is Targumic Aramaic Rabbinic Hebrew ? a Reflection on Midrashic and Targumic Rewording of Scripture", *Journal of Jewish Studies* 45 (1994) 92-100; D. GOODBLATT, "Palestinian Talmud: Language", in *The Study of Ancient Judaism*, ed. J. NEUSNER, Hoboken 1982, vol. 2, p. 201-8 (= p. 63-70). -- G.M. SCHRAMM, "Hebrew Language Scholarship" (under Biblical Languages: Hebrew) in *Anchor Bible Dictionary* 4,211-4, is pretty much limited to Masoretic. -- H.-P. MÜLLER, "Zur Theorie der historisch vergleichenden Grammatik dargestellt am sprachgeschichtlichen Kontext des Althebräischen", in *Semitic Studies* in Honor of Wolf LESLAU, ed. A.S.KAYE, 2 (Wiesbaden 1991, p.1100-1118), p. 1104 ftn. 15 sees Ullendorff's p. 17 (Mishna from a colloquialization of OT diction) as relevant to gradual use of the participle to supply lack of distinction between present and future in the standard-biblical "fientisch" longform-preformative.

Ullendorff notes only some few of the 300 roots it "retrieves" while losing 250[17]. The surprising absence of *šā'â*, "hour" from the Bible had already been studied by James Barr[18]. To this are added chiefly "comb", "spoon", and "kitchen" [19].

Ultimately Ullendorff seems to be saying: Needful words not found in the Bible must have come from *somewhere; -- Atqui*: many of them turn up in the Mishnah; -- *Ergo*: Mishnah must represent the total and *real* language of which Biblical Hebrew gives us only a fragment.

3. Rendsburg: Hebrew as Mutant, like Egyptian and Arabic

In turning now to Rendsburg's *Diglossia*, we may note at once that he claims to reach conclusions fully in agreement with this lengthy citation from Ullendorff: "The language of the Mishnah, principally derived from these oral sources, was in fact the product of the colloquial used during the Biblical period; the amalgam of its standard and sub-standard versions ... Perhaps BH, in its Masoretic garb, is simply the literary counterpart to the Mishnaic colloquial"[20]. To this Rendsburg frankly adds that this view, and also similar insights of Chomsky and Bendavid, have really anticipated the conclusions which he himself will have reached[21]. He points out how he

---

17. M.H. SEGAL, *Mishnaic Grammar*, English 1927 reprinted 1958. "but the 1936 Hebrew edition goes far beyond it"; p.99-134.

18. J. BARR, *Biblical Words for Time*, London 1969; *Semantics of Biblical Language*, Oxford 1962.

19. So E. Y. KUTSCHER, *A History of the Hebrew Language* (Jerusalem/Leiden 1982) 135: "Non-biblical Hebrew Vocabulary: ... 3. New Hebrew elements. Here belong those elements which most probably existed in the original stock of Hebrew, but do not appear in BH [mostly agriculture; no list] but *t*[e]*hol* 'spleen' is a good example (Arabic cognate *tuḥal*)". I am grateful for a letter of John Pairman BROWN (Nov.5,1992) on the "thousands of words" in Mishnaic Hebrew not in the Hebrew Bible, including "Old Semitic" *pyl*, "elephant, ivory" in Kilaim 8,6 for Ezek 27,25 and possibly a *mks* "publican" of origin different from the "tax" of Nm 31,28; but the others which he indicates are admittedly post-biblical.

20. G.A. RENDSBURG, *Diglossia in Ancient Hebrew* (American Oriental Series 72, New Haven 1990) p. 15-16 (from Ullendorff p.249 = p.11).

21. W. CHOMSKY, *Hebrew, the Eternal Language* (Philadelphia 1964), p.161; A. BENDAVID, *Leshon ha-miqra' 'o leshon hakamim ?* Tel Aviv 1951, [2]1967-71 (*û-lshon*).

hopes to have gone farther.

The principal base of Rendsburg's Diglossia is Kurt Sethe's 1925 demonstration that we possess literary Egyptian in six successive stages, of which each is the colloquial "used" form of the preceding one: Old Egyptian becomes Middle Egyptian, New Egyptian becomes demotic, and especially demotic becomes Coptic[22]. This simplified model was used also by Pulgram to show a similar development of Latin[23]. Independently but in basic agreement, diglossia has been detected also in Arabic by Corriente and Blau[24]. Rendsburg maintains (p. 31) "Biblical Hebrew remained relatively stable [while] popular Hebrew underwent the development found in all languages ... finally becoming attested as Mishnaic Hebrew".

Though this conclusion does seem to support or coincide with Ullendorff, we may here interpose a caution. Ullendorff supposes a pre-biblical existing proto-Mishnaic language with an extensive vocabulary-pool from which biblical Hebrew then drew the relatively few words it needed. This procedure seems to turn upside-down the Sethe-Rendsburg model, in which biblical Hebrew would be the pre-existing standard, and Mishnaic its colloquial corruption which only later *becomes* standard. This is doubtless the more common view even now. We are familiar with the apparently similar phenomenon of a classical Latin being progressively colloquialized as it continues in use for the preservation of religious traditions.

The bulk of Rendsburg's *Diglossia* is devoted to enumerating long lists of cases in which our Hebrew Bible is "ungrammatical" or does not conform to its more commonly attested norms[25]. These cases for him point

---

22. K. SETHE, "Das Verhältnis zwischen Demotisch und Koptisch und seine Lehren für die Geschichte der ägyptischen Sprache", *ZDMG* 79, 1925, 290-318; his diagram in English in RENDSBURG, Diglossia p.29. -- H.-W. FISCHER-ELFERT, "Randnotiz zur spätägyptischen Diglossia (P BM 10298)", *Göttinger Miszellen* 127 (1992) 44-47.

23. E. PULGRAM, "Spoken and Written Latin", *Language* 28 (1950) 458-486.

24. J. BLAU, "The Beginnings of Arabic Diglossia: a Study of the Origins of Neoarabic", *Afroasiatic Linguistics* 4/4 (1977) 1-28; F. CORRIENTE, "Marginalia on Arabic Diglossia and Evidence Thereof in the Kitab al-Agani", *Journal of Semitic Studies* 20 (1975) 38-61; S. ALTOMA, *The Problem of Diglossia in Arabic; a Comparative Study of Classical and Iraqi Arabic*, Harvard diss. 1969; B.H. HARY, *Multiglossia in Judaeo-Arabic .. Cairene Purim Scroll*, ÉtJudMédv 14, Leiden 1992.

25. Rendsburg has published many specialized word-studies in support of his thesis, including "The Northern Origin of 'The Last Words of David' ", *Biblica* 69 (1988) 113-121; "More on the Hebrew *šibbōlet*", JSS 33 (1988) 255-8; "The Ammonite Phoneme /T̠/", *BASOR* 269

up *within* our Bible itself, sometimes but by no means only in reported oral statements, portions of the "second language" or real *used* language of the biblical people. It must be admitted that much of what we call corruptions or mistakes in the use of a standard language, are in fact elements of the nascent local variations which we call "dialects". But it is far from clear that a simple tabulation of the ungrammaticalities occurring within the use of a standard language, suffices to prove and constitute a "second language"[26].

Moreover Rendsburg is careful to justify the fact that he seeks these evidences solely within the Masoretic text, admitting its inadequacies. And as for the archeologically attested inscriptional materials of the relevant period, which loom so large for Knauf and indeed for most Semitists, Rendsburg courageously maintains (p.32) "By and large the language [of the small corpus of Iron Age inscriptions from Israel] is identical to BH, and few colloquialisms seem to have penetrated them"[27].

———

Finally we may call attention to an echo of Rendsburg's position in the arresting titles of the two key chapters in A. Sperber's *Historical Grammar*. Under the title "Two Hebrew dialects combined form biblical Hebrew", he devotes a hundred pages to pre-Masoretic pronunciation, largely preserved from Hebrew in Jerome's commentaries but from Greek in his onomastica. Under a subhead "Two dialects of biblical Hebrew" he asserts that Israel and Judah are the respective homelands of these dialectal differences. His other key chapter bears the title "The composite character of the Bible". Sperber's emphatic declarations are supported by very little prose, but a dense mass of cited cases, which constitute a veritable mine for

---

(1988) 73-79;   "Morphological Evidence for Regional Dialects in Ancient Hebrew", in *Linguistics and Biblical Hebrew*, ed. W.R. BODINE, Winona Lake 1992, p.65-88; *Linguistic Evidence for the Northern Origin of Selected Psalms*, SBL monograph 43, Atlanta 1990 (p. 29, Phoenician scribes wrote the account of the Temple-building and dedication); "Israelian Hebrew Features in Genesis 49", *Maarav* 8, 1992, p. 161-170.

26. See now D.C. FREDERICKS, "A North Israelite Dialect in the Hebrew Bible ? Questions of Methodology", *Hebrew Studies* 37 (1997) 7-20.

27. His p.23 n.70 insists that his understanding of "colloquialisms" differs greatly from that of G. ABRAMSON, "Colloquialisms in the Old Testament", *Semitics* 2, 1971-2, p. 1-16 meaning rather idioms. Unsupportive of Rendsburg is S. ÓLAFSSON, "On Diglossia in Ancient Hebrew and its Graphic Representation", in the A. CZAPKIEWICZ memorial *Folia Orientalia* 28 (Warsaw 1991) p.193-205; 3 fig.

research-scrutiny, but are hard to use for an evaluation of whether they tend more to favor the Knauf position or its alternatives[28].

4. Naville's ill-starred parallel with Coptic

In view of the importance which Coptic has for the Sethe-Rendsburg model, it seems imperative to dispose of a view understandably passed over in complete silence by modern experts. And in fact despite the prestige of the Schweich Lectures and of himself as excavator of Maskhuta and Yehudiyya, Naville's pronouncements on the origins of biblical Hebrew are embarrassingly mingled with outdated fantasies, immediately and adequately refuted by Gressmann[29]. What then are we forced to say here of the man who for better or worse pioneered the view that biblical Hebrew was not a "used" language but an artificial literary creation ?

Naville's earlier volume and its subsequent French form start out squarely with the assertion that the Pentateuch was written in an Amarna-style cuneiform, in conformity with Moses' background[30]. In supporting this view, he admits on p. 21 that if Abram as an Aramean had brought from Mesopotamia any more cursive language than his undoubted cuneiform, it would have been Aramaic and not any Hebrew or *yehudit*. Also, throughout their Egyptian stay the Israelites always considered themselves Arameans, so that the use of this language in the eventual Elephantine diaspora may not be considered an abandonment of their linguistic tradition.

The 1915 Schweich Lectures start out with a chapter on deficiencies of the Higher Criticism, which as noted from A. van Hoonacker in the preface shows no approval for Naville's view[31]. Cuneiform is discussed in the second lecture, and Aramaic in the third. Thus in none of these books does he get around to explaining his view of what Biblical Hebrew really was, and how it arose. That task was left for his 1920 French volume on the evolution of Egyptian and its relation to the Semitic languages[32]. His essential claim is that the biblical books, including now the

---

28. A. SPERBER. *A Historical Grammar of Biblical Hebrew, a Presentation of Problems with Suggestions to their Solution*, Leiden 1968.

29. H. GRESSMANN, "L'archéologie de l'Ancien Testament", *Revue de Théologie et de Philosophie* 48 (NS 4/18), 1916, 26-53; p. 36 on Naville's tracing of the early Arameans, starting from Mesopotamia.

30. É. NAVILLE, *Archaeology of the Old Testament: Was the Old Testament Written in Hebrew ?*, Library of Historical Theology, London 1913, p.11 = *L'Archéologie de l'AT: l'AT a-t-il été écrit en Hébreu ?*, tr. A. SEGOND, Paris/Neuchâtel sans date.

31. NAVILLE, *The Text of the Old Testament*, Schweich Lectures 1915, London 1916.

32. NAVILLE, *L'évolution de la langue égyptienne et des langues sémitiques*, Paris 1920; p. 152-178. L'hébreu; his p. 154 proceeds chiefly from the fact that Coptic was a new writing-system based on a principle absolutely different from that previously in use; this change to

Prophets written mostly in Aramaic, were transcribed after 176 B.C. into an entirely new alphabet invented for that purpose; and that just as in the case of Coptic so sweeping a change could not remain merely a matter of external form, but involved a revision of the language of composition itself. On the analogy with Coptic, Naville claimed that square-script Hebrew was invented to utilize and unite the various Aramaic-related dialectal differences actually in use[33].

5. Rab-Shaqeh Speaking Yehudit and Aramaic

We will return now to a point which we have seen varyingly emphasized by all the above scholars, the prominence and indeed dominance of Aramaic among the various dialects claimed to be identifiable in the background of the biblical Hebrew record[34].

This situation is most vigorously and picturesquely exemplified in the episode of 2 Kings 18,26. Sennacherib's official, called the Rab-Shaqeh, came and stood before the walls of Jerusalem, and called for the king to come and hear him. The king, Hezekiah, sent instead the minister Eliakim and two assistants[35]. To them, ostensibly, is addressed the lengthy and eloquent speech of verses 19-25.

Only with verse 26 we learn two items of great importance. The Rab-Shaqeh's words were really intended not for the king or his three

---

writing *yehudit* in the new (Biblical Hebrew) alphabet was made by "the rabbis" near the Christian era (p.158) though Ezra had "united" the whole Bible in Aramaic (p.191).

33. NAVILLE, *La Haute Critique dans le Pentateuque*, Paris/Neuchâtel 1921, further answered the "courteous" P. HUMBERT, "M.É. Naville et la critique du Pentateuque", in *RThPh* NS 9 N° 38, 1921, p.59-88, citing E. DOUMERGUE, *Moïse et la Genèse d'après .. Naville*, Paris 1920. -- See recently D. VAN BERCHEM, *L'égyptologue genevois Édouard Naville*, Genève 1989,cited by J.LECLANT in the *Comptes Rendus de l'Académie des Inscriptions* (1991) 126-7.

34. Chaim RABIN, "The Emergence of Classical Hebrew", in *The World History of the Jewish People I/V (The Age of the Monarchies II. Culture and Society*, ed. A. MALAMAT) 71-78, begins by calling this origin "surrounded by mystery", but cites with approval the role of Aramaic in S. MOSCATI, "Il semitico di nord-ovest", in the Festschrift for G. LEVI DELLA VIDA, *Studi orientalistici*, Roma 1956, vol.2, p.202-221. Note W. VON SODEN, "Gab es bereits im vorexilischen Hebräisch Aramaismen in der Bildung und der Verwendung der Verbalformen ?", *ZAH* 4 (1991) 32-45 (No!); also his *Sprache, Denken und Begriffsbildung im AT*, Mainzer Akadamie geist./soz. Abh. N° 6 für 1973, p. 34-40.

35. P. BORDREUIL, F. ISRAEL, "[(Isa 22,20) 2 Rois 18,18; 19,2] À propos de la carrière d'Elyaqim: du page au majordomo (?)", *Semitica* 4ls (1991s) 81-87; 2 fig.

officials but for the beleaguered population of Jerusalem who were listening. And the harangue has been, thus far at least, in what is called *yᵉhûdît*, "the language of Judah". Clearly dismayed by the force of his arguments, the trio ask him to continue in Aramaic instead.

This episode raises issues enormously momentous for our present discussion: issues which are passed over with surprising brevity and assurance by almost all the commentators. Like Begg in the New Jerome Commentary, they mostly say that *yᵉhûdît* was just a word for (biblical) Hebrew as in Neh 13,24, and that Aramaic was known only by the highly educated[36]. Hobbs adds that only with the Persian period Aramaic had become the language of the general population[37]. Specialized studies by Ben-Zvi and others point up the greater complexity of the situation[38].

The more recent researches which we have been citing above tend to regard the *yᵉhûdît* of 2 Kgs 18,26 as a term for the language actually spoken in daily use, *differing* from biblical Hebrew and varyingly akin to neighboring language-uses like Ammonite and Aramaic itself. The case of Job is especially noticed (ftn.[8] above). Garbini's brief advertence in the English volume of his ever-forceful and original attacks on biblical cruces, insists that *yᵉhudit* "was certainly not used in the monarchical period to denote the language of the Israelites of the two kingdoms", and considers anachronistic in 701 B.C. an international ("imperial") Aramaic[39].

But as for the diffusion of *some* kind(s) of Aramaic around Jerusalem, already in 1957 we had occasion to point out that a diagram of the distinguished expert Haiim Rosén, aimed primarily to show the divergences of other West-Semitic dialects from Moabite, really proves

---

36. C.T. BEGG, "2 Kings", *New Jerome Biblical Commentary*, ed. R.E. BROWN, *al.*, Englewood Cliffs NJ 1990, p.182.

37. T.R. HOBBS, *2 Kings*, Word Comm. 23, Waco 1985, p.258.

38. E. BEN-ZVI, "Who Wrote the Speech of Rabshakeh and When ?", *JBL* 109 (1990) 79-92 [much later than the three current views: an Assyrian / an Aramean or Judahite called Assyrian / a real Judean]. -- See also A.R. MILLARD, "Please speak Aramaic", *Buried History* 25 (1989) p.67-73 [and his "The Knowledge of Writing in Iron Age Palestine", *Tyndale Bulletin* 46 (1995) 207-217].

39. G. GARBINI, *History and Ideology in Ancient Israel* (London/Philadelphia 1988) 46.

biblical Hebrew more different from Moabite than from biblical Aramaic[40]. Several experts today maintain that the various speech-usages attested in the biblical homeland all form a "linguistic continuum" with Aramaic[41].

We must here take into account the historical connections previously always assumed to exist between the Aramaic-speaking "Arameans" and the biblical people from beginning to end of what the Bible tells us about them. It has been generally agreed from Deut 26,5 that their "father" was called an Aramean at one of the earliest stages at which they are encountered. Even if Abraham, and with him the racial group of which he formed a chief part already (allegedly) in Mesopotamia, is called Aramean, it is far from clear that these "earlier Arameans" are identical with or even related to the racial entity which much later became prominent there[42]. It is these "later Arameans" whose Aramaic language from roughly the Iron Age became the extremely important medium of communication throughout the whole Middle East as far as Elephantine.

And even if Abraham is called by the same name Aramean which later became common as an *ethnic* designation in the same area, it is not an attested fact that the Aramaic *language* was spoken by any "Abrahamic clan". Still it is likely that such a migratory group would carry with them some language or dialect *of their own*, and to that extent (ambiguously) "Aramaic". The attested fact of proto-Hebrews as some kind of Arameans could retain its validity even in the recently-burgeoning supposition that the biblical people never had any roots *inside* Mesopotamia at all, and that their "remembrance" of them is mythical[43].

---

40. H.B. ROSÉN, *Ha-'Ivrit še-lānû*, Our Hebrew Language in the Light of Linguistics, Tel Aviv 1955, diagram p. 22; my review in *Orientalia* 25 (1957) 388-391.

41. Notably W.R. GARR, *Dialect Geography of Syria-Palestine 1000-586 B.C.E.*, Philadelphia 1985, p. 205, Canaanite Hebrew was rather near to Aramaic; rejected by KNAUF, *ZAH* 3 (1990) p. 13, n.8.

42. R.A. BOWMAN, "Arameans, Aramaic, and the Bible", *JNES* 7 (1948) 65-90; J.C. GREENFIELD, "Aramaic Studies and the Bible", 1980 Vienna Congress, *VTS* 32 (Leiden 1981) 111-130; H. TADMOR, "On the Role of Aramaic in the Assyrian Empire", in the Festschrift for Prince Takahito MIKASA, ed. M. MORI, *al.* (Wiesbaden 1991, p. 419-423); p. 422 accepts "the ability of an Assyrian envoy to deliver an eloquent speech in the 'Judean tongue'".

43. R. NORTH, "Symposium on the Mythic in Israel's Origins (Roma Accademia dei Lincei, Feb.10-11,1986)", *Biblica* 67 (1986) 440-448. In acceptance of an offprint of this report of a meeting in which he had played so large a part, along with an inquiry as to his views on our present topic, Professor Giovanni GARBINI under date of January 30,1994, kindly informed me

Also being redimensioned nowadays is the far more emphatic biblical "remembrance" of a liberation from Egypt, after a sojourn there of some hundred(s of) years, by Abraham himself briefly and then by all his descendants. Some take the "400 years" as a mystical number or a typical number-exaggeration, or as meaning really "4 generations". But even this minimum is a decisive period of time in which the use of their own language by a minority group would be likely to have given way to the use of (or notable contamination by) the official local language.

Acts 7,22 says, possibly as a literary flourish, that Moses was given an education in Egyptian scholarship. Some exegetes have noted that an Egyptian court-training would have included also Mesopotamian laws and language[44]. The Amarna letters show that cuneiform was indeed then a chancery language for Egypt's dealing even with nearby Canaan. And despite Naville there remains food for thought in the question, "What language *did* the (? wandering) biblical people use ?", and in the fact that biblical Hebrew shows virtually no trace of Egyptian influence in grammar or vocabulary.

These few historical facts (or largely *possibilities* opened out by the biblical text) tend perhaps to support the "linguistic continuum" view. Aramaic itself, or some Canaanite dialect-variant of it, was already the likeliest "used" language of the biblical people at the time of their installation in Canaan. This was the beginning of their history anyway, according to a currently popular view; but the same judgment holds in any plausible interpretation of their "recorded" history. The question thus becomes, not so much when or where, but rather *how* and *why* "Biblical Hebrew" was invented to be the vehicle of their traditions.

6. *Philip Davies' solely socio-political origins of the Hebrew Bible*

Precisely to this question a head-on answer has now been offered, not on any linguistic grounds at all, by a highly original and thought-provoking

---

he feels that "brilliant" approaches (Knauf, Ullendorff) tend to obscure the real problem of the origins of biblical Hebrew, namely "the artificiality of the Masoretic interpretation and the corruption of our biblical text", comparing the vowels of Origen's *Secunda* which force a complete rewriting of the JOÜON and GESENIUS-KAUTZSCH grammars.

44. H. CAZELLES, *Études sur le Code de l'Alliance*, Paris 1946, has thoroughly studied these problems.

little volume which risks being rejected out-of-hand as destructive of the whole basis of both the Jewish and the Christian religions[45]. It in fact holds that the *whole* of our Hebrew Bible *and* its language, with purely *civil* aim having nothing to do with religion except slightly as part of a unitive general culture, were created out of nothing (though incorporating scraps of tradition) by scribes paid by the Persian government to support its takeover of administration in Judah[46].

These (heuristic) scribes were organized in four main "colleges", named for (1) Moses, the legal documents; (2) David, the liturgical poetry; (3) Solomon, wisdom; (4) dizzyingly named for W.F. Albright, because it had (not "would have had" p.121) "a highly optimistic view of what was historical". Actually the role assigned to the scribes is not so different from that filled by Albright in his century: "preserving, annotating, amplifying" and eruditely making acceptable to a conservative populace the older traditions.

"The production of a large-scale and complete history from the creation to the beginning of the [Persian-era: p.117] society of Yehud was not the primary task" (p. 132), but rather classifying, copying, and filling the gaps of scraps of various existing fragmentary scrolls. However, these salaried scribes (far different from Albright) had to *invent* the overall tradition. "There *was* no pre-existent history to be written about, no 'tradition', and so various accounts had at first to be invented ... Such an absence follows from what I have said [in chapters 1-5] about the non-existence of 'ancient Israel'" (p.132; note further p. 119 on the "non-Exodus" and Egypt)[47].

---

45. Philip R. DAVIES, *In Search of "Ancient Israel"*: JSOT supplement 143, Sheffield 1992: Ch.6, "Who Wrote the Biblical Literature. and Where ?"; ch.7, "How Was the Biblical Literature Written, and Why ?"; p. 120 "an exercise in imagination whose purpose is purely heuristic .. not to be taken as a hypothesis", [though p. 16 had called it a "working hypothesis"]; anyway it is really set forth (p. 130-3) as not merely a hypothesis but a fact.

46. See however D.W. JAMIESON-DRAKE, *Scribes and Schools in Monarchic Israel, a socio-archeological approach*: JSOT supp.109, Sheffield 1991.

47. "*Histories* of *an* ancient Israel *can* be written, [but not] *the* history of *the* ancient Israel", says Davies now in "Whose history ? Whose Israel ? Whose Bible ? Biblical Histories, Ancient and Modern", in *Can a 'History of Israel' be Written ?* (1996 Dublin meeting of 20 European scholars; *JSOT* supp. 245, ed. L.L. GRABBE, 1997) p.104 (-122). -- It is surprising that Tamara ESKENAZI, "Current Perpectives on Ezra-Nehemiah and the Persian Period", *Currents in Research: Biblical Studies* 1 (Sheffield 1993) 59 (-86) in praising Davies for

We have perhaps been unfair in thus leaping to the "colleges" and their function without first following the sociological presentation of why such scribes *must* have existed in the allegedly Ezra's day[48]. We begin with the arresting statement of p.107, "Even in modern societies with 90% literacy, fewer than 1% write books". No source is indicated for this plausible-enough statistic, nor is it implied whether or not another percent or more write for periodicals. And as for the likely "reading public" of the 95% *non*-literate societies, readers must have been mostly among those who *wrote* the books: surely much less than the above 1%, though p.108 seems to admit as many as 5% of Judah as scribal. "Writing is an economically supported activity .. [arising] from ideological, economic, and political preconditions (p.106). ... The origin of biblical literature [is] certainly within the temple and court", cooperating even if possibly as two separate power-centers suggested in the Ezra books[49]. In any case, despite their non-religious aim, the Temple would have been the depository of scribal products (p.111)[50].

Finally (though already p.102), "Biblical Hebrew", despite exegetes' claims of early and late and Knauf's north and south, was an "artificial scribal language" (p. 104), created by scribes partly (pure) Aramaic-speaking,

---

recognizing the Ezra-era as the earliest in which "we can use the Bible (critically) as a source for [Israel] history", does not mention that for him the whole of that "history" had to be "invented" from a few scraps by the "scribes in the pay of the Persian government".

48. The "lien social" plays no relevant role in C. FONTINOY, "La langue, lien social; ombres et incertitudes concernant les origines de l'hébreu biblique", in the Festschrift for É. LIPIŃSKI, *Immigration and Emigration within the Ancient Near East*, ed. K. VAN LERBERGHE & A. SCHOORS, Orientalia Lovaniensia Analecta 65, Louvain 1995, p.65-77; perhaps more in S.B. NOEGEL, "Dialect and Politics in Isaiah 24-27", *Aula Orientalis* 12 (1994) p. 177-192.

49. Intriguing though not mentioned here is the Temple of Haggai explained as a bank in operation: David J.A. CLINES at the Rome 1991 SBL meeting, "Haggai's Temple: Constructed, Deconstructed and Reconstructed", in *Second Temple Studies 2*, ed. T. ESKENAZI: JSOT supp. 175, Sheffield 1994, p. 60-87. So also J. BLENKINSOPP, "Temple and Society in Achaemenid Judah", in *Second Temple Studies 1*, ed. P. DAVIES: *JSOT* supp. 117, Sheffield 1991, p. 22-53: by the time of Neh 12,13; 2 Mcb 3,5-18; Josephus War 6,282 & Ant 14,110-3. "the Temple served as a kind of bank in which private funds could be deposited" & p.163 (-174), R. HORSLEY, the Temple was a politico-economic institute.

50. "The Significance of the Temple Archive" is a subtitle on p.40 of Roger T. BECKWITH, "Formation of the Hebrew Bible", in J. MULDER, ed., *Mikra: CRINT* 2/1, Assen/Philadelphia 1988, p. 39-86; but despite Beckwith's titles, his whole article is really only about the Canon, with no hint of scribal activity or the origins of Biblical Hebrew (nor is there anything here relevant on p. 21-23, "The Scribes" by M. BAR-ILAN).

partly ("colloquial/oral") "Hebrew"-speaking. This *Bildungssprache* is a post-Iron-Age-Judah scholarly construct, scarcely differing from that claimed by Knauf. *Why* this creation of the scribes was necessary for embodying their socio-political *content* is not made clear and is ultimately not the focus of Davies' interest. His later chapters will go on to explain how the purely civil-political ("Bible") books produced by the (heuristic!) scribal colleges later became sacred (Scripture) and canonical. If he has given us a challenging model for the How and Why of the *content* of the books, we must still seek a model for the How and Why of the origin of "Biblical Hebrew".

[§7 which follows is an insertion not in our ZAH text.]

7. The Kelber-Ong Transit from Orality to Text

It is impossible to envision any author(s) standing before the production of a largely oral work in an entirely new literary medium without considering how similar was the position of Mark in Kelber's orality-research from A. Lord to Ong[51]. In his first two chapters Mark is the hero of an orality no longer ineptly judged by our ingrained standards of literacy. This orality constantly involves social interaction and easy rememberability without memorization. These two qualities in Mark 10 are found to imply that a notable number of Jesus' listeners were rootless vagrants who here found approval for having left father and home[52]. Orality also involves freedom; the spoken words as transmitted are freely adapted in accord with the various transmitters' convictions, pre-Mark included.

---

51. Werner R. KELBER, *The Oral and the Written Gospel; the Hermeneutics of Speaking and Writing in the Synoptic Tradition, Mark, Paul, and Q.* Philadelphia 1983, Fortress [²1997, Bloomington, Indiana Univ., with new introduction by Kelber p. xix-xxxi]. 430-item bibliography, of which 250 on orality; only BEN-AMOS relevant to OT, or also GUNKEL as real discoverer of orality, p. xiii. The preface of both Kelber editions is by Walter ONG, to whom deep indebtedness is often acknowledged in the text; see KELBER, "Walter Ong's Three Incarnations of the Word: Orality -- Literacy -- Technology", *Philosophy and Theology* 23 (Milwaukee 1979) 70-74.

52. KELBER ²24, from G. THEISSEN, "Wanderradikalismus; Literatursoziologische Aspekte der Überlieferung von Worten Jesu im Urchristentum", *Zeitschrift für Theologie und Kirche* 70 (1973) 245-271 [= "Itinerant Radicalism .. ", tr. Antoinette C. WIRE, *Radical Religion* 2 (1975) 84-93].

But with Kelber's chapter 3 we see Mark standing before the temptation to transcodify everything good about orality into the new and unfamiliar medium of textuality. It is chiefly Mark who makes clear "that preservation of oral tradition is not a primary function of writing" (p. 207, *sic*). And his motive in writing is precisely that the oral transmission of his rivals has been *too* free. So he must begin by plotting a narrative to discredit the clearly enough evidenced "incomprehension" of "the" (some) disciples and prophets (p.97). Thus even the mother of Jesus (maybe, p.104) and his brothers, as oral transmitters, have to be discredited with the help of preserved oral statements, in part (*hoi par'autoû* 3,21) for having tried to get Jesus arrested as insane, in part for having been ignored and disowned by Jesus himself (3,34). Like Kelber, we have singled out these statements for their shock value, and we found the whole of the exposition reasonable and fascinating, sometimes almost convincing.

We must here call attention to a delightful trait of Kelber's exposition, the anthropomorphisms which it attributes to the elements of speech whether oral or written. In fact words are portrayed like the tiny men and girls of Disney cartoons, shouldering their new duties and marching cheerfully in straight forward linearity (p. 106). "To allocate each letter, word, and verbal unit to a single position, 'where it stands in a definite, permanent, and unambiguous relationship to the others' is equivalent to the construction of a world"[53].

"Conscripted into the service of textuality, the once-spoken words have to alter their semantic behavior and live up to new hermeneutic responsibilities" (p.109). "Didactic stories .. relinquish their role as autonomous carriers of information [and] conform to a project not only larger than but different from their own" (p.111). "Writing and print .. liberate" from audience controls[54]. The written text, ironically, "conveys a sense of 'realism' that in its total impact exceeds that of reality ... Written language .. can live and create out of its interior potential" (p.116). The goal of these mesmerizing observations is the very serious one of proving that just by being written down a large part of the *message itself* is reordered.

In a third stage, this Mark whom we followed first as a confirmed and successful oralist, then as defecting because other oralists were not doing

---

53. KELBER[2] p.107, citing Jack GOODY, *The Domestication of the Savage Mind* (Cambridge 1977, Univ.) p.68.

54. KELBER[2] p. 114, citing ONG, *The Presence of the Word* (1981 = 1967), p.88.

the job adequately, now appears finally (ch. 5; [2]p. 184) as the sole and literary author of the (first) whole and tightly organized Passion narrative -- and with *no* oral antecedents (because a Jesus of death would have conflicted too strongly with the oralist presentation of a *present* Jesus of life).

––––

     Much of Kelber's analysis could be made just as apt for the Old Testament. Nielsen's key-chapter begins hopefully "The written Old Testament is the creation of the postexilic Jewish community; of what existed earlier only a part was in fixed written form" [lists and such needed by government][55]. But this book is rather thin and outdated.

     A more promising study of the oral life-span of Old Testament materials has been made by Kirkpatrick, admitting as source-material a limited amount of the listener note-taking which Kelber also admits, but not attacking the overliteracy of most so-called "oralist" studies[56]. She fully supports Kelber's key point that we can seek no such thing as an original (oral) form, because every repetition was an original creative performance. She also with Kelber puts Gunkel at the fountainhead of current oralist research[57], but deplores how quickly he fell into the snare of Olrik's thirteen

––––––––––––––––––

55. E. NIELSEN, *Oral Tradition: a Modern Problem in Old Testament Introduction* (SBT 11, London 1954, SCM) p.39 (from NYBERG's *Hosea* p.6); p.43. Susan NIDITCH, *Folklore and the Hebrew Bible* (Minneapolis 1993, Fortress), also brief (case-studies) but updated; and now her *Oral World and Written Word: Ancient Israelite Literature* (Louisville 1996, Westminster-Knox) 107, against the view that after writing appeared it *replaced* oral transmission, insists on the continuing interplay between orality and literacy; writing is respected, but as part of a different and sacral world; she concludes "source-criticism theories become suspect, as do other theories about the composition of the Hebrew Bible that are grounded in modern-style notions about Israelites' use of reading and writing".

56. Patricia G. KIRKPATRICK, *The Old Testament and Folklore Study: JSOT.S* 62. Sheffield 1988. She is explicitly the only exception in the surprising 1997 statement of Harold M. WAHL, *Die Jakobserzählung: BZAW* 258 (Berlin 1997, de Gruyter) 61: "Virtually all exegetes today ignore oral tradition and use only literary methods".

57. Herman GUNKEL, *The Legends of Genesis; the Biblical Saga and History* [1901, [6]1964; tr. W.H. CARRUTH], was reprinted with a preface by W. F. ALBRIGHT. NY 1964, Schocken. Gunkel's *Genesis* [[8]1963] was published in English only in 1997 (Mercer; tr. Mark E. *Biddle*). -- See too C. CONROY, "Hebrew Epic [F.M. CROSS 'prose variants' ...]: Historical Notes and Critical Reflections", *Biblica* 61 (1988) 1-30.

too rigid "laws" for detecting pre-text orality[58].

She surveys fairly the work of Heda Jason and D. Ben-Amos on the importance of genre-classification, but adds warnings from Dorothy Irvin's *Mytharion*[59]. She goes beyond Kelber toward Davies in endorsing fully P. Irwin's "Tradition does not merely transmit the past; it creates it"[60]; and creates it in such a way as to embody sociological conditions of its later date, and also to support the existing regime. Though querying a figure as precise as Dorson's 150 years for the duration of historical reliability of oral transmission, she in fact categorically adopts that figure as a maximum[61].

All in all, Kirkpatrick furnishes for the Old Testament a thorough and sober survey of pre-text orality studies. To that extent she is doubtless more convincing than Kelber. But heuristically we remain sadly in need of a Kelber's stimulating and imaginatively anthropomorphic portrayal of the batch of OT material clamoring for unity in confronting some person whom we can call Ezra just as we call some person Mark. In some ways it appears

---

58. Axel OLRIK, "Epic Laws of Folk Narrative" [= Epische Gesetze der Volksdichtung 1908, in *Zeitschrift für Deutsches Altertum* 51 (1909) 1-12], tr. Jeanne P. STEAGER, in Alan DUNDES, ed., *The Study of Folklore* (Englewood Cliffs 1965) 129-141 (Kirkpatrick p.56).

59. Dorothy IRVIN, *Mytharion: the Comparison of Tales from the Old Testament and the Ancient Near East* (Ägypten und Altes Testament 32; Neukirchen 1978; 91-104, The Theological Meaning of Angels in the Genesis Narrative) p. 113; classification preferred to Heda JASON, *Ethnopoetry* (Bonn 1977); "Content Analysis of Oral Literature", in (with Dimitri SEGAL) *Patterns in Oral Literature* (World Anthropology; Hague/Chicago 1977) and to D. BEN-AMOS ed., *Folklore Genres* (Austin 1976) and five cited articles.

60. P. IRWIN [not D. Irvin above, cited oftener], *Liptako Speaks: History from Oral Tradition in Africa* (Princeton 1981) p.163: but Kirkpatrick (p.109) really bases herself on less-categorical proclamations from other African researches by J. VANSINA, *Oral Tradition as History* (London ²1985, p.94; ³1988); p. 172 and three earlier cited works; and J.C. MILLER, *Kings and Kinsmen* (Oxford 1976) p.23. She mentions on p.101 the dismay that oral stories are valued more for their historicity than just because they are interesting: R.C. CULLEY, *Oral Tradition and Historicity*, in J. WEVERS & D. REDFORD, *Studies in the Ancient Palestinian World* (Toronto 1972) 106-116; she gives three other works of his, but cites unusably as op.cit. his warning that the improvisation of transmitters was less free than has become accepted.

61. KIRKPATRICK p.103,109,114; R.M. DORSON, "Oral Tradition and Written History: the Case for the United States", *Journal of the Folklore Institute* 1 (1964) p. (220-)230 [five other writings cited]; also on using modern cases to determine the reliability of oral transmission, L. DUPRÉE, "The Retreat of the British Army from Kabul to Jalalabad in 1842 (History and Folklore)", *Journal of the Folklore Institute* 4 (1967) 59-74.

less audacious to hypothesize the adaptation of these materials to a brand-new language, "invented" from Aramaic, than their transfer from the oralist (doubtless partly based on note-taking or fragmentary scrolls) to the organized written medium of a Kelber-Ong world.

8. *The Esperanto model*

[§7 in *ZAH*

It does not seem unreasonable to seek in modern experience a parallel for the alleged ancient creation of an artificial language. The best known is Esperanto, with two million users (2000 within the USA: wherefore the prestigious Modern Language Association offered in Chicago a seminar in Esperanto, but no one showed up)[62].

The language was invented in 1877 by the Polish oculist and linguist Ludovic L. Zamenhof. He combined Indo-European elements chiefly of western Europe, "hoping" (*esperanto*) that it would become an easily-learned second language for international use.

It did in fact have relatively quick and wide acceptance chiefly in Europe; and its universal organization founded at Rotterdam in 1908 has received recognition from UNESCO. It is used at least once each week for a Vatican newscast; and its *Biblia Revuo* published at Ravenna since 1964 has only recently been renamed. How many Esperanto users have found it to be of genuine practicality rather than just a fad or "hope" is of course hard to decide[63].

In any case, the word and concept of Esperanto as an artificial language made up by combining elements of the actually used languages in its nearby background, is now widely understood and utilized. As thus defined, it is evidently applicable to the situation which has been claimed for the late origins of biblical Hebrew. But almost equally instructive may prove to be the *differences* in concept between the two, and the question of *why* such an artificial language should be invented.

All the recent researches which we have been investigating, though often using a sensational title or approach, ultimately claim chiefly that

---

62. Martin MARTY, "M.E.M.O.[-randum]", *Christian Century* 108 (1991) p. 471.

63. S. LEVIN, "Can an Artificial Language be More than a Hobby ?", in *Aspects of Internationalism, Language and Culture*, ed. I. RICHMOND (8 papers on Esperanto from the 1985-1990 conferences of the Center for World Languages), NY 1993, p. 1-8.

biblical Hebrew was a literary or even poetic *language*, something beyond the easily-recognized fact that *no* literary writing is identical with oral use in common daily life by the relevant people[64]. And this claim really is aceptable to *all* who have seriously studied biblical Hebrew and have some acquaintance with the inscriptional materials of the cognate then-contemporary languages and especially of Aramaic.

Doubtless most of those who have dedicated their lives to the study of the Bible tend to think of its language as *the* real vital existing reality, in comparison with which all those cognates are mere shadows or spinoffs. But a moment's reflection would force these scholars to agree that in the known historical background it was rather Aramaic which held the position of the most important and real widely used and influential language. Moreover the Canaanite inscriptional materials in part show closer relations with Aramaic than with biblical Hebrew.

It nevertheless would have been a rather colossal achievement, far surpassing Zamenhof's, to have invented out of the whole cloth a brand-new language for a very restricted literature destined to have the importance of biblical Hebrew in world history. Those who maintain, or are at least not unfavorable to, such a hypothesis, seem to have given but little attention to the concrete physical circumstances in which such a change would have been made.

Davies is an audacious exception, though focusing the content rather than the language-origination itself. A fuller exception, though a totally uninfluential one, was Naville. He maintained that it was about the time of Christ when some important Jewish authorities turned to putting their religious traditions into the new language of their own creation. "Creation" of course here can only mean as in the case of Esperanto, recombining elements of familiar existing languages. Naville was quite explicit in claiming that the emergence of the Coptic language was an example of similar procedure, though the "whodunit?" remains obscure. He further claimed that in the case of Coptic this was done for greater convenience and accessibility, since the new language would have been more easily used than its Egyptian predecessor subject to so much corruption and divergence. This

---

64. In tacit opposition to DAVIES' purely secular-political not religious origin, GARBINI's letter (fn. 43 above) still holds the (virtually universal) majority opinion that our biblical Hebrew involves a limited number of texts, "all of religious origin" and of postexilic redaction, hence does not represent the literarization of the "whole" of the language commonly spoken at Jerusalem before the exile.

would be true also of the Sethe model which we noted as used by Rendsburg.

But it seems likelier that the motive for introducing the new and invented Biblical Hebrew language would have been just the opposite. The aim was not wider accessibility, but the preservation of sacred traditions in an arcane and ritual language, which the common people would recognize as only vaguely familiar. To this extent Biblical Hebrew was something like medieval Latin, understood and even used with great facility by the clergy (scribal schools!), but chiefly for the perpetuation and discussion of religious traditions. It is thus in fact that most scholars both Jewish and Christian doubtless regard the origins of Mishnaic Hebrew, rather than as the ampler preexisting language from which Biblical Hebrew was drawn according to Ullendorff.

As for the date of this great changeover, the Ezra-period seems to be agreed by all who do not offer any other specific proposal. For the implantation of a new language, the need of civil authority postulated by Davies seems agreed by Knauf[65]. Exegetes in general relate this period, as culmination of immediately-preceding scribal activities in Babylon, to the actual formulation and ordering of our Pentateuch (-Kings).

Jerome wrote "I have no objections whether you wish to call Moses the author of the Pentateuch or Esdras the reviser (*instaurator*) of the same work"[66]. Thus also Robert Bellarmine: "Until the time of Esdras, the Scriptures were not edited in the form of books available in easy and convenient form, but were dispersed among various annals and papers [4 Kgs 22 ...]. But it was Esdras who after the Captivity collected and edited them in a single corpus, adding to Deuteronomy the last chapter concerning the life

---

65 KNAUF, *ZAH* 3,12: "a standard language presumes specific social and political conditions, notably an administration that can establish and impose it", invoking his "Haben Aramäer den Griechen das Alphabet vermittelt ?", *Welt des Orients* 18 (1987) 45-48 [now see B. SASS, *Studia alphabetica*, OBO 102, Fribourg/Wiesbaden 1991]; further Knauf's *Midian*, Wiesbaden 1988, 137.

66 Adversus Helvidium, ch.7: Migne PL 23 (Hieronymus 2), 190; (JEROME) *Dogmatic and Polemical Works*, ed. J.N. HRITZU, Fathers of the Church 53, Washington 1965, p.19 with no note; the edition of M. Ignazia DANIELI, *La perenne verginità di Maria* (Collana di Testi Patristici 70, Roma 1988), p.40 adds a note on the proliferation of Jewish tradition regarding Ezra's "funzione restauratrice"; and her p.43 notes that she there uses a 7*bis* (and an 8*bis* but with no 8, though Migne has 8 as well as 7 twice) "to avoid confusion with the usual citation of Migne". Her 7*bis* is 9 in H. HURTER's ²1894 p.264, her 8*bis* is his 10, her 9 is his 11 and so on to her final number 22, his 24 (though he has a 45 by misprint for 15 p.274).

of Moses, and various other transitional remarks"[67].

It remains significant and in need of explanation that amid the lavish praise of Nehemiah and others in Sirach 49,11 (180/130 B.C.) Ezra is totally unmentioned. This leads Garbini and others to maintain that Ezra never existed and is a mythic fabrication of scribes to impose authority upon their tampering with received texts: In 159 B.C., "with this name, which no one ever bore, there really came into being that 'Judaism which, through Pharisaism, has come down to our own days'", Dead Sea Scrolls included[68].

Admitting that much of his argumentation is plausible, we have maintained that it would still hold good in the likelihood that Ezra really existed in more or less the functions his books attribute to him, but was "mythologized" by later scribes[69]. Our final essay N° 6 below will be entirely focused on this problem, intensely relevant to *when* and *how* our Bible *could* have been put into an alleged and always purely hypothetical "invented" language.

---

67 R. BELLARMINE, *Controversiae*: the 1721 Milan edition (1, p.166) cited in A. VAN HOONACKER, *De compositione litteraria et de origine mosaica Hexateuchi disquisitio historico-critica*, posthumously published by J. COPPENS, Verhandelingen der Vlaamse Academie Letteren 11/11, Brussels 1949, p. 78; the text does say "life" (*vita*) of Moses rather than "death" as some exegetes think more relevant.

68 GARBINI, *History and Ideology* (fn. 39 above) p. 169; the citation is from the outset of the article p. 153, P. SACCHI, *Storia del mondo giudaico*, Turin 1976, 51. But Garbini's p. 155 admits the parallel of Ezra with the Moses of J.A. SOGGIN, *A History of Israel, from the Beginnings to the Bar Kochba Revolt*, London/Philadelphia ¹1984, p. 133-7: a "historically elusive" figure "put to use" only in the exilic period. (In relation to Soggin's p.276 is mentioned his privately expressed agreement with Garbini).

69 R. NORTH, "Ezra (person)", in *AnchorBD*, NY 1992, vol.2, p.727: treated in detail along with GARBINI in ch. 6 below.

5

Civil Authority in Ezra

Festschrift E. VOLTERRA

Milan 1972, Giuffré (with permission); vol 6, p. ‖377‖-‖404‖ unchanged

[In view of recent developments involving especially Garbini and Davies (→ p.169 & 155) it would be naive to offer these statements of a half-century ago as simple historical facts without defense; but it is still important today to recover, against the current view, what the biblical text really said -- and says. The bibliography will be updated in the next article.]

Within the field of juridical history in which Professor Edoardo Volterra has attained eminence, three interesting questions arise during the Persian Biblical period. The first is whether the biblically affirmed official mission of Nehemiah from the Achaemenid government was a permanent and replaceable magistracy. The second is whether Ezra held the status of government representative at all. And the third is whether the aid given by the Persian chancery to Ezra and Nehemiah for their reform-activities ought to be called a kind of Concordat, or treaty between civil and religious authority.

It may be foreseen that this topic would not have been chosen unless there were some hope of gaining adherence for convictions different from those which now prevail. And in fact our stimulus to this study came from the dissatisfaction we felt for some premises on which the current consensus is based.

That we should query the term Concordat will surprise no one, though the issues involved may generate some new viewpoints of juridical importance. To regard Ezra's mission as a purely spiritual one is also fully in accord with the tenor of the biblical text, though it affronts the almost universal agreement which has greeted an ingenious proposal to make of him the "Persian Cabinet Undersecretary for Jewish Affairs". But finally to deny to Nehemiah any civil governorship at all undoubtedly holds out less hope of success, since it is contrary to a current consensus based on certain explicit expressions of the text.

Ninety verses out of the 686 in the books of Ezra, or some thirteen percent, seem to ‖378‖ refer to the wielding of civil authority. Of these, fifteen refer to the Zerubbabel Temple-building period. Sixteen others deal with the alleged allotment of funds from the Persian treasury for sectarian religious activities. Twenty-two verses relate to Ezra's authority, and thirty to Nehemiah's, beside some seven on the status of Nehemiah's antagonists.

1. *Sequence of the Records: Ezra*. Before making an analytical dissection of these 90 verses according to their separate themes or contexts which interest us, it will be instructive to begin with a synthesis. Here is a simple connected narrative of what is said about the two leaders regarding the use of authority by and toward them.

Ezra first appears (7.1) qualified only as a remote descendant of the high-priest Aaron. He was a scribe "quick" in the Torah of Moses, and the King "granted him all his request" according to the hand of YHWH his God upon him (7.6).

An official document of Artaxerxes is given "to Ezra, the priest, the writer, writer of the words of the commands of YHWH and his statutes for Israel" (7.11). The document bears as its salutation, "Artaxerxes to Ezra, the priest, writer of the law of the God of Heaven".

The direct object of the decree is that Jews who wish to return to Judah with Ezra may do so, and may take along Temple-vessels and whatever money they can get by free-will offerings. To this, addressing Ezra in second person, is subjoined a parenthetical and really ungrammatical motive clause: "because emissary to inquire according to the law of your God which is in your hand"(7.14). "And you, Ezra, according to the wisdom which is in your hand, appoint magistrates and judges ... who know the laws of your God; do you also teach those that do not know it" (7.25). "And for whosoever will not do the law of your God, speedy execution of judgment: death, banishment, fine, or prison" (7.26).

Here is Ezra's reaction to the receiving of this decree: "Blessed be God who has put into the King's heart to beautify the house of God" (7.27). This, like the reference to Temple-vessels in 7.19, seems to fit Zerubbabel's Temple-building activities more proximately than anything in subsequent chapters about Ezra's own commission and activities.

When the caravan arrives in Jerusalem, the immediate administrative procedures needed are described in 7.33 but not linked to the person of Ezra. The gold "was deposited" without indication of by whom. The "children of the captivity" performed sacrifices. "And ‖379‖ 'they' gave the decrees to the King's satraps and governors (*pahawôt*) of Eber-Nahar" (7.36).

At a later point, initiative in the mixed-marriage problem is taken by the "princes", *śārîm*, who come to Ezra (9.2). However, the *śārîm* themselves, or their colleagues, along with certain other "rulers" (*s^egānîm*) were the worst offenders. Ezra thereupon functions like a preacher or activist on the order of Savonarola. It is chiefly the priests whom he forces to pledge reform of their marital status (10.5). Ezra shuts himself up in a room to fast and pray, while "they" make a proclamation "according to the counsel of the *śārîm* and the elders" (10.8). Because of the rain and the complexity of the matter, the people propose to Ezra that a committee of *śārîm*, elders, and judges should make the needed determinations. The book ends abruptly with no decrees or recommendations from this committee, but only a list of those who had foreign wives.

With equal abruptness, in Nehemiah 8.1, all the people gather in the street and ask Ezra the writer to bring the Torah. Ezra the priest brings it and reads (8.2). It is on a wooden platform that Ezra the writer is standing. (8.4).

A reprimand, oratorical rather than juridical, and not for connubial or other offenses but for their failure to be joyful and festive, is addressed to all the people by "Nehemiah the *tiršātā'*, and Ezra the priest the writer, and the Levites that taught the people", but with no mention of governor, princes, rulers, elders, judges, or nobles.

Next day the "patriarchs", *rāšê hā-ābôt*, and the priests and Levites had a meeting with Ezra the writer (Neh 8.13). A crowd is marshaled in 9.5 by Levites, not by government officials. The pledge, presumably fruit of Ezra's preaching, is signed in first place by Nehemiah the *tiršātā'* (10.1), but as part of a list of 23 names of which verse 8 says "these were the priests". Whether the narrative of Ezra's activities comes to an end with or before this chapter, or includes also Neh 11 or even 12, is a matter on which the evidence is vague and varyingly interpreted.

2. Contexts of Nehemiah's authority. -- Nehemiah is the king's "cupbearer" (1.11), a function which in attested usage may be the equivalent either of "favorite, playboy", or of "Lord Privy Chamberlain" (akin to the "eunuch" by which the term is rendered in Greek), or possibly any one of a wide range of variations in between. He asks Artaxerxes, "Send me to Jerusalem to build it" (2.5), ‖380‖ and Artaxerxes' only hesitancy concerns how long he will be away (2.6).

Nehemiah then asks that letters be given for the *pahawôt* of Eber-Nahar (2.7), and timber allotted from the royal domain (2.8). Arriving in

Eber-Nahar, he went to "the *pahawôt*" and gave them the letters (2.9). No reaction of theirs is recorded. The arrival of Nehemiah made Sanballat angry, but it is not said that he was one of the "governors" (2.10).

The rulers called *sᵉgānîm* are left unaware that Nehemiah takes a night-ride around the walls, because he had said nothing about his plans to the priests or "nobles". or *sᵉgānîm* (2.16). The word here and often in Nehemiah rendered "nobles" is *horîm*, "the free", but in 3.5 is *addîrîm*, "the majestic". Ezer the son of Jeshua was *śar* of Mizpah (3.19).

To Nehemiah has thus far been attributed neither authority nor official position at all. He is a charismatic building-contractor, in favor with the Emperor, yet relying chiefly on his personal energy and magnetism to get the job done on time despite weather, shortages, wars, or strikes. To cope with these obstacles he appeals to the *hōrîm* and the *sᵉgānîm* (4.8H = 4.14G). He arranges that if danger threatens, all the workers should form a phalanx around him; it may be selfish, but is not strategic, thus to let the enemy know where their major target is (4.14H = 4.20G). Nehemiah "disputed" with the *horîm* and the *sᵉgānîm* (5,7) over moneylending procedures which he himself had shared (5,10).

Suddenly he says, "From the time that Someone commanded me to be *pehām* (ungrammatical if it means 'their governor') in Judah ... that is, twelve years, I and my brethren -- governor's bread I have not eaten" (*sic*, 5.14). But the former *pahôt* took food-requisitions beside money taxes (5.15). Though immense meals were prepared for Nehemiah's freeloaders, yet he never applied for "governor's bread" (5.18). In his two recorded contacts with Ezra, Nehemiah is not called *pehâ* but *tiršātā'* (Neh 8.9; 10.1).

Nehemiah says in 7.1, "When the wall was built, and I had set up the doors, then guards were appointed (by 'somebody')", and "I gave charge over Jerusalem to my brother Hanani, and to Hananiah, commandant of the fortress" (later called Antonia: Neh 7.2).

In Jerusalem dwelt *śārîm* of the people (Neh 11.1) and *śārîm* of the state (11.3), of whom Nehemiah was not one. Adaiah's brethren [Neh 11.5; and Pedaiah's, Neh 11.7] were patriarchs; but were nevertheless, along with some others, ‖381‖ supervised by Zabdiel (Neh 11,14). Nehemiah brought some *śārîm* of Judah up on the wall to watch the religious procession he had organized (12.31). At that time there were some appointed (by "somebody") for collecting tithes and such (12.44).

An unnamed "they", not Nehemiah nor Ezra, read in the Torah about not fraternizing with Ammon and Moab (Neh 13.1). Nehemiah was not in Jerusalem while the priest Eliashib was giving a room in the Temple to

Tobiah; because Nehemiah had gone to Artaxerxes and after a short visit taken leave of him (without indication of receiving from him any title or mission either new or reaffirmed, 13.6). Nehemiah got into a quarrel with the $s^e g\bar{a}n\hat{i}m$ (13.11), but himself set treasurers over the treasuries (of Temple tithes, 13.15). He again quarreled with the $hor\hat{i}m$ of Judah (13,17), then without awaiting their action he got his own servants to picket or blockade the city-gates against unlawful sabbath-entry (13.19). His final claim to God's mercy is that he straightened out the priests' and Levites' schedules.

3.   *Did Artaxerxes Sign a Concordat ?* -- Among Rome's numerous contributions to juridicism both secular and religious is an essay from Saint Anselm's on the Aventine Hill, in which Fruhstorfer maintains that in Ezra 7-8 we have "a Concordat drawn up between the secular Persian regime and the biblical people of God"[1]. We have only admiration for the imaginativeness and common-sense which tries to bring the biblical narrative to life by re-expressing it in the terms familiar to. our local and twentieth-century milieu. But as said above, we will permit ourselves some rather pedantic queries in the hope of shedding light on incidental useful issues.

Webster's English dictionary defines concordat as "an agreement between a pope and a sovereign or government for the regulation of ecclesiastical matters". Of course neither Ezra nor "the biblical people of God" is claimed to be a pope, but they would seem to be the equivalent, "supreme religious authority".

Before assenting to this, we must reflect that the word concordat first came into existence in connection with the Pope, and has never been used since then except for a document involving the Pope. The name is used only since Constance 1418, though the reality is found already in the Worms investiture truce of 1122. Mörsdorf even ‖382‖ proclaims that Mercati wrongly includes in his compilation of concordats a concession of Urban II to Roger of Sicily in 1098, for the reason that though papal it is unilateral.[2]

Hence, not only is Webster's term sufficiently generalized for the term being defined; it is even too general. The Pope has historically com-

---

1   Karl FRUHSTORFER [msgr.; not Früh-], *Ein alttestamentliches Konkordat (Esr. 7-8)*, in *Studia anselmiana* 28, 1951, 178-186.

2   K. MÖRSDORF, s.v. *Konkordat*, in *Lexikon für Theologie und Kirche*[2], VI. Freiburg, 1961, 454.

bined two functions of authority, religious and political. In a concordat it is his position as political sovereign which is involved. At least it is maintained by scholastic theorists that temporal sovereignty is needed for the Pope precisely in order that he may negotiate with secular sovereigns for the safeguarding of religion.

But another and perhaps more enduringly valid aspect of the Concordat may be discerned in the fact that by it a civil ruler concedes certain civil advantages favoring the practice of one particular religion, in return for which he expects to get certain political and not merely spiritual benefits for himself.

As Fruhstorfer points out, in Ezra's case the advantages were not all on the side of religion. Artaxerxes stood to gain considerable political advantages by this concession[3]. Cyrus himself, and Darius, have left monuments as far away as Egypt, attesting their deliberate and efficient policy of not merely tolerating but positively furthering local sectarian religious practices. The most conspicuous example is the Elephantine Jewish passover regulated by Darius[4]. Also in Egypt the Persian government fostered a codification of local Egyptian cult laws. Other examples are recorded in Mesopotamia and Phoenicia[5].

‖383‖ This seems to be a reasonable or even a thoroughly self-interested policy for a conqueror to follow. Religious laws and practices generally encourage the population toward peacefulness and submission to authority. When the lawfulness of the authority itself is questionable, or contrary to the traditions of conservatism also favored by religion, then

---

3 K. EDDY, *The King is Dead: Studies in the Near Eastern Resistance to Hellenism,* Lincoln 1961, 48.

4 E.A. COWLEY, *Aramaic Papyri of the Fifth Century B.C.,* Oxford, 1923. n° 30; J.B. PRITCHARD, *Ancient Near Eastern Texts Relating to the Old Testament[2],* Princeton, 1955, 491.

5 Compilation of evidence by R. DE VAUX, *Les décrets de Cyrus et de Darius sur la reconstruction du Temple,* in *Revue Biblique* 46, 1937, 29-57 [Eng. "The Decrees of Cyrus and Darius on the Rebuilding of the Temple", in *The Bible and the Ancient Near East,* tr. Damian McHUGH (1971 Doubleday) 63-96]: *RB* p.31, Rassam cylinder (ANET[2] 294) shows Cyrus favoring Mesopotamian sanctuaries; confirmed at Warka. J. JORDAN, *Erster vorläufiger Bericht über die deutschen Ausgrabungen in Uruk-Warka,* Berlin, 1930, 10-20; cf. Nabonidus Chronicle (ANET[2] 316, 309; DE VAUX p. 34); Cyrus cylinder, line 5 (ANET[2] 316), confirmed at Ur: L. WOOLLEY, *Ur of the Chaldees,* London, 1929, 205; the Demotic Chronicle shows Cambyses guaranteeing revenues of Egyptian temples (DE VAUX p.41); the Magnesia inscription shows Darius angry because a Persian viceroy has taxed the Apollo temple.

religions do sometimes become a front for sullen resistance or active rebellion. But more often, especially if the hierarchs are positively honored and favored by the regime, they end up finding that there is some good and some bad in all human systems and the best thing is to cooperate not only with the good but also with the disagreeable.

To evaluate whether in this light the commission of Ezra may be called a Concordat, we must consider some similar cases. If the parish priest secures from the village mayor authorization for a Fatima procession interrupting traffic on a main street, is this a Concordat? Or even if Cardinal Frings secures from the Bundestag a dispensation of seminarians from military service, is this a Concordat? Obviously not. Even if the supreme religious authority of the land, backed up by the Popes' strong recommendation, secures a concession from his own lawful and supreme political authority, this is not a Concordat. The essential element which is lacking is that the political sovereign in making his concession be really putting it in the form of a contract, with a partner whom he thereby acknowledges to be in at least some sense not subject to his own jurisdiction, but possessed of an equal and parallel jurisdiction of his own.

Finally we must notice a dilemma. If the mandate of Ezra partook in any way of the nature of a Concordat, then there can be no question of regarding him as a Persian government representative in Judah, whether as Persian Cabinet Undersecretary for Jewish Affairs or not. A cabinet-member, or any civil-service functionary of a bureaucracy, is even more subject to the regime and under its jurisdiction than the rest of the citizens. The other citizens had no choice in the matter; they might actively disapprove either the existing regime or the whole political structure of the region where economic or family factors force them to live. A religious leader in this situation would not be compromising his principles by accepting or even demanding concessions from the regime. But to accept a post of honor and salary within the structure is an acknowledgment of submission rather incompatible with the spirit of a Concordat.

‖384‖ Recent commentaries fail to make clear that in Ezra we cannot simultaneously discover the equivalent of a Concordat and of an Undersecretary. There may have been either or neither, but not both.

4. *Three Traits of Public Office for Ezra.* -- The Persian government maintained on its staff certain officials charged with regulating and mediating the purely religious or indeed purely sectarian interests of local groups. The Persian government also officially charged and empowered Ezra to see to the promulgation and enforcement of Jewish religious law within the

community of Judah. But these two functions are not automatically the same[6]. It remains to clarify whether the regime was installing Ezra as one of its own employees, or simply declaring and enforcing his freedom and legitimacy in performing purely religious functions among his countrymen.

Careful re-reading of the relevant passages will show that the claim of government position for Ezra is based on only three statements. He can appoint judges disposing of extreme sanctions. He can demand immediate action by the king's treasury. And he is called an ambassador.

Ezra 7,25f reads, "And you, Ezra, according to the wisdom of your God which is in your hand, appoint magistrates and judges to judge for all the people of Eber-Nahar, for all those acknowledging the laws of your God; and whoever has not acknowledged them, you (plural only here) will instruct. And whoever will not do the law of your God, and the law of the king, immediately let judgment be done upon him either for death, or for uprooting, or for a fine of possessions, or for imprisonment".

Undoubtedly anyone with a document signed by the King entrusting him with these powers would seem to be an official government representative. He was even able to appoint other official government representatives who could inflict such punishments as death or the confiscation of wealthy citizens' entire property without even referring the matter to Susa or to any higher tribunal for review. Or can we be so sure that certain normal legal practices are not taken for granted as underlying these provisions ? At least the right of appeal to the King or some intermediate representative does not seem to be abrogated.

‖385‖ Upon closer look, Ezra himself does not have power to execute or even pass these sentences. As for the execution, no machinery for this is hinted. In some preceding verses, Ezra had been told to turn to royal treasuries for the implementation of his decisions. If the judges' sentences were indeed to be carried out by the Persian army of occupation and police-force, no examples of such procedures are indicated anywhere in the Ezra books. As Eduard Meyer admits, "Ezra was provided with religious and political authority ... but with no troops or means of enforcing it"[7].

And even if the judges "appointed" by Ezra were truly Persian government officials, it might perhaps not follow from this that Ezra was.

---

6 H.H. ROWLEY, *Nehemiah's Mission and its Background*, in *Bulletin Rylands*, 37,1955, 534 [= his *Men of God* (1963) 211-245], is one of the few studies to query with detachment whether Ezra was an officeholder.

7 E. MEYER, *Die Entstehung des Judentums*, Halle, 1896, 240 f.

Sometimes a respected local leader is empowered to present nominees, who thereupon actually receive their jurisdiction from the regime and not from the counselor who named them.

Two kinds of judges are named, the *šôpēt* and the *dayyān*. A sort of religious implication has come to attach to *dayyān*, as in mishnaic and Arabic *dîn*. *Šôpēt* recurs in Ezra 10,14; preeminently in the Bible it means one who "executes God's judgments" as a charismatic warrior. not really a ruler or official but nearer to that than to a legal diagnostician.

To Ezra's judges is accorded jurisdiction over "the whole Eber-Nahar province"[8]. Here certainly at least we are confronted with language which is not to be taken literally, king's signature or no king's signature. There is no reason to suppose that Ezra or his appointees had any say at all over the Samaria regime or any parts of North Syria. They are strictly limited to Judah, or rather to the people of "Jewish religion", that is to say Mosaic religion as practiced in the southern region, those who acknowledge "the laws of his God"[9]. His further mandate to "those who do not acknowledge them" is rightly taken by Rudolph to mean not proselytizing but bringing backsliders into conformity[10]. The character of the mandate of both Ezra and his judges is qualified by the phrase "according to the wisdom of your God which is in your hand", an indication that it is a religious authority approved as such by Artaxerxes.

‖386‖ A second indication of Ezra's government position may be seen in the lengthy passage about his financial support (Ezra 7,15-24). He is told by Artaxerxes that he is empowered "(15) to bring the silver and the gold which the King and his counselors have freely contributed to the God of Israel who is in Jerusalem, his abode, (16) and all the silver and gold which you will find in all the state of Babylon, what with the generosity of the people and the clergy donating to the temple of their God who is in Jerusalem; (17) so that you may promptly buy with the money bullocks, rams, lambs, with corresponding offerings and libations, and may offer them on the altar of the Temple of your God who is in Jerusalem. (18) And whatever it suits you and your brethren to do with the rest of the silver and

---

8 We write Eber-Nahar as a neutral combining of Assyrian Ebirnari, Aramaic Abar-Naharā', and Hebrew Ēber ha-Nāhār, a term which does not mean necessarily either Samaria or Syria.

9 H. SCHNEIDER, *Die Bücher Esra und Nehemia*, Bonn, 1959, 135.

10 W. RUDOLPH, *Esra und Nehemia mit 3.Esra*, in *Handbuch zum Alten Testament*, 20, Tübingen, 1949, 74.

gold, you shall do in accordance with the views of your God. (19) And the vessels which have been given you for the cultus of the temple of your God, deposit before the God of Jerusalem. (20) And the rest of the requirements of the Temple of your God which it will befall you to give, you shall give from the King's treasury. (21) From me myself, King Artaxerxes. is established a decree to all treasurers in Eber-Nahar; whatever Ezra the priest, writer of the law of the God of heaven, shall ask you, will be promptly done (22) up to: silver, 100 talents; wheat, 100 bushels; wine, 100 quarts; oil, 100 quarts; salt, no limit ... (24) Declaring to you that all priests and Levites and cantors and doorkeepers and oblates and ministers of that Temple of God: tribute, tax, or revenue it is not authorized to impose upon them".

The most noteworthy thing about this passage is that it seems to relate more to installing a Temple-cultus than to promulgating a Law. And in fact Ezra's reaction in verse 27 stresses only this aspect of the decree: "Blessed be YHWH, the God of our fathers, who put such an idea into the heart of the King, to adorn the temple of YHWH which is in Jerusalem." Verse 19, though not using the term "confiscated (vessels)", nevertheless unmistakably echoes the terms of Ezra 1.7 ff in which Cyrus authorized and promoted the original rebuilding of the Temple. This does not exclude that since both bureaucracy and religion are strong for doing only what has solid precedent no matter how irrelevant it may be to the present need, again now Ezra may have received vessels and free-will offerings for Temple-cultus as a token of approval for his religious mission of quite different type.

As for the further financial support offered by the Persian crown, this is made to consist in free-will offerings. The King and his ||387|| counselors were, as is usual in such cases even today, "Patrons", donors, benefactors. Moreover the exemption of clergy from taxes in 7.24 is an important sign of good will, but not truly a form of government support or political position. The original grant of Cyrus had been altogether limited to his donations (Ezra 1.4-7; 3.7; 5.14; 6.5), and this holds predominantly for Artaxerxes also. But this cannot be said of Ezra 7.10ff or 6.4-9. In verse 7.20 the Aramaic word "give" occurs twice, but in the Jerusalem Bible its sense is changed from "procure" to "receive", to fit the qualification "from the King's treasury". Verse 22, while seeming to limit this authorization by indicating exact maximum amounts, actually reinforces it.

We notice that the wording of Ezra 6.9 is echoed in 7.17-22. The part about bullocks, lambs, and rams is taken up as what Ezra is to purchase from the free-will offerings he had collected. But the part about wheat, salt, wine, and oil is made the matter of a concession by the royal treasury[11]. It is claimed that this concession is rendered perfectly plausible by the known historical fact that Cyrus himself and other monarchs paid for setting up religious installations. But this is simply not applicable to the Temple-rebuilding under Cyrus and Darius described in Ezra 1-6. The Jews' building-activities are shown in Ezra 1.4 to have been dependent on what free-will offerings they could collect, either from their countrymen or from Persian lords. Moreover, the stagnation and vicissitudes of the project show clearly that it was not dependent on a budget furnished annually from public funds, much less an unlimited expense-account on which they could draw[12].

Haggai 1.8f (recalled in Ezra 6.13) shows that the work on the Temple had bogged down because the people were not keeping up their pledges in the building fund; and Haggai 2.7 warns that the Temple benefits will be shared by the Gentiles, upon whose contribution reliance will have to be placed. In this light, the words of Ezra 6.4 and 7.21 are to be taken merely as an expansive formula of royal good will: as when a top statesman or executive says, after casually meeting one ‖388‖ of the "little people" on whom his position depends, "If there's anything at all I can do for you, just call on me"[13].

In Ezra 6.5, the Cyrus decree as rediscovered orders the restoral of confiscated vessels, but no further contribution. In 6.8, the *niksim*, "treasures, property" from which "expenses" are to be "given" to the returning Jews, may also mean "confiscated property" as fits the context. Then in the next

---

11 Rudolph estimates the talent, *kor*, and *bat*, at $2000, 360 litres, and 36 litres respectively. We have rendered *kor* and *bat* simply as "bushel" and "quart" because they are plainly put as an offhand round number in terms of the most familiar measure. But according to our research in Nelson's *New Catholic Commentary on Holy Scripture* [1969, p.107] the talent is only $718; the *kor* is 220 litres or 6.4 U.S, bushels; and the *bat*, one-tenth *kor*, is 22 litres or 23.25 U.S. liquid quarts.

12 G. HÖLSCHER, *Die Bücher Esra und Nehemia*, in E.KAUTZSCH, A.BERTHOLET, *Die Heilige Schrift des Alten Testaments* II, Tübingen 1923, 314.

13 Ultimately this explanation is not so different from Rudolph's (p.37) based on Galling: Cyrus merely said the Jews could draw on tax-funds paid in by the Syrian population; but these were probably not coming in yet in very organized fashion, and ultimately their disbursement would depend much on the good will of local Samaritan treasuries: K, GALLING, *Königliche und nichtkönigliche Stifter beim Tempel von Jerusalem*, in *Zeitschrift des Deutschen Palästina-Vereins* 68, 1951, 134-143 [*Studien zur Geschichte Israels im persischen Zeitalter*, Tübingen, 1964]. Further E.J. BICKERMAN, *The Edict of Cyrus in Ezra I*, in *Journal of Biblical Literature* 65, 1946, 249-275.

verse, the command of Cyrus that various staples be furnished to the returnees for their sacrificial system is quite naturally to be understood as extra
ration coupons.   In a war-ravaged or occupied country, it is normal or
necessary that the government see to the apportionment of bare necessities
by head and not in accord with ability to pay for them.   Since such rationing
would imply genuine hunger and want, only a royal ukase could make such
goods available for outright destruction (or priests' supplementary nutriment)
in a sacrificial system.   The red-tape of rationing is a part of the functions of
"the king's treasury", especially since the goods themselves were probably
impounded in the same storehouses as the king's "taxes in kind".   A similar
explanation accounts for the "timber in the king's forest" in Neh 2.8.   In this
perspective, Ezra 7.22 simply explicitates and limits the amount of rationed
goods which could be drawn for the Temple worship, perhaps as a mere reaf-
firming of what had been granted for Zerubbabel's needs.

In the third place we come to the word šālîh (Ezra 7.14) which itself
means "ambassador" or "emissary", but is applicable also to such functions
as apostle, viceroy, inquisitor, lieutenant, trouble-shooter, or in general
whatever role could be called "representative" of a person in authority.   There
is no variant reading or textual note to account for the omission of any pronoun or other indication that Ezra ("you") rather than some third party is the
šālîh.   The Septuagint reading in fact says "he was sent" with no variant,
which must ‖389‖ correspond to a Hebrew meaning "someone".   In the
variant of Esdras-a' 8.12, šālîh drops out altogether.   Its impersonal use
without pronoun is justified by a parallel passage from Elephantine; "but
from the conclusion of this and the preceding verse it is clear that Ezra is
addressed; hence the pronoun 'you' is not indispensable, according to Hebrew
usage (cfr. 2 Chr 18.3; but in 2 Chr 19.6 there is haplography and hû' should
be restored).   Nevertheless it is clearer to accept Ehrlich's emendation of
šālîh to šᵉlihattā"[14].

Ezra's "mission" is unmistakably further qualified by the modern-
sounding term "fact-finding", lᵉbaqqārā.   This in turn is further qualified as
"according to the law of your God which is in your hand".   In the judgment
of numerous experts, the "law" in Ezra's hand, though here called dat and
not tôrâ, is the definitive edition of the Pentateuch which he himself had

---

14   W. RUDOLPH (→ n.10) Esra und Nehemia 1949, 68; E.A. COWLEY (→ n.4), n° 21,3.

finally succeeded in bringing to a conclusion[15]. What he requested from the royal authorities was no more than an exit-visa to go to Jerusalem to promulgate his Torah; but they, in accord with policy laid down by Cyrus, were only too happy to oblige, and to provide a royal edict fostering the move. But even for those who insist that "the wisdom" or "the law" in Ezra's hand means merely in a general way the sacred revelation already known to the Jews in Judea, it still remains true that the edict of Artaxerxes does not so much give as acknowledge the authority of Ezra, within the strictly religious realm[16].

5. *Ezra the Writer, the Priest.* -- In the much greater majority of passages, Ezra's authority and work are presented as bearing no relation to a Persian chancery-post at all. His titulature especially is insistently priest and *sôpēr*, Aramaic *sapar*. And the meaning of "writer" is given to *sôpēr* by Schaeder, though rejected by Rudolph in crediting him with having "proved to the hilt" that it is a Persian chancery-title.

‖390‖ Really Schaeder does not give any examples or proof of the existence of such a government-post, either in Persia or anywhere else. The *sôpēr* of 2 Sam 8.17 is a priestly assistant, not "next in line after the *mazkîr*", itself a Hebrew word meaning more properly "secretary". (In 2 Sam 20.23 the order and names are different.) The example of Neh 11.24 about "Pethahiah at the king's hand for every affair of the people", if valid, would put far ahead of Nehemiah and the other protagonists an obscure character whose influence is never once invoked in the various power-struggles[17]. The *rêš galûtâ* in later Judaism, from the Parthian-Sassanid and not Achaemenid period, is called by Browne not really parallel[18]. He does indeed hold a position similar to Ezra's. but it is rather that of a *consul* or representative of

---

15 J. MEINHOLD, *Esra der Schriftgelehrte?*, in *Festschrift K. Marti*, Giessen 1925, 199, brought to a new plane of convincingness by H. CAZELLES, *La mission d'Esdras*, in *Vetus Testamentum* 4, 1954, 113-140.

16 We may admit with C.C. TORREY, *Ezra Studies*, Chicago, 1910, 253, and F. AHLEMANN, *Zur Esra-Quelle*, in *ZAW* 39, 1943, 85, that Neh 8 f fits after Ezra 8,35 rather than after Ezra 10,44.

17 This corroboration from Nehemiah is "overlooked" in Schaeder's otherwise "brilliant demonstration", according to R. de Vaux (→ n.5), *Les décrets de Cyrus* in *RB* 46, 1937, 52 n.5.

18 L. BROWNE, in M. BLACK, *Peake's Commentary on the Bible*, London 1962, 375.

a minority-group, empowered to negotiate on terms of Concordat-style quasi-equality with a regime in matters over which that regime's competence is not fully acknowledged. The other examples given by Schaeder are by himself called "remote"[19].

In short, Schaeder rests his case on the term *soper-sapar*. And yet in doing so he admits that the greatest problem is how this term came to mean also "exegete" or "Scripture-scholar", a sense which he concedes it to have so prominently in the Ezra-narrative. His handling of the problem ends up linking it with Persian *dipir* and thus precisely making it an administrative term. What he really sets about to prove, and proves with relative satisfaction, is that the Hebrew word *sāpar* besides its normal meaning "to count", can mean also "to write", akin to the Akkadian *šapāru* "send a message", the Aramaic *sāprā* "chancery-official", and the Canaanite gloss *sofer yode* in Egyptian Anastasi Papyrus I under Ramesses II (the adjunct *yode* has nothing to do with *yᵉhûdâ* but is a loose ‖391‖ equivalent of "quick", *mahîr*, applied to Ezra himself in 7,6, and transcribed some sixteen times in other parts of the Anastasi text)[20].

Though Schaeder does suggest the rendition "Secretary (or Minister) of the Law of the God of Heaven", it would seem that we owe to Galling the current popularity of the "Undersecretary of State for Jewish Affairs" claimed to have been a recognized Jewish institution.

———

Ezra is every inch a priest and a scholar. For one whose life-achievement was the completing of a definitive edition of the Torah and its promulgation among Jews and Samaritans alike, to serve as a cog in an administrative machine would have been repugnant to both his temperament and his training. What is more important, he is at no point shown *exercising* any government-type authority. He is a preacher, a Billy Graham, a Padre Lombardi, enjoying the benevolence and even active help of civil authority

---

19 H.H. SCHAEDER, *Esra der Schreiber*, Tübingen, 1930, 48, citing W. WRESZINSKI, *Die Höhepriester des Amon*, 1904. where in §79 one Egyptian high-priest is called "writer of the divine book of Amon". -- On the *rêš galûtā'*, "Exilarch". A. CHRISTENSEN, *L'empire des Sasanides. Le peuple, l'état, la cour*, Copenhagen, 1907. 19 & 38.

20 RUDOLPH (Esra 1949 → n.10), p. 68, in rejecting the sense of "write" for Hebrew *sāpar* indicates that the most plausible specimens would be Ps 56,9, "You (numbered or wrote) my wanderings ... was it not in a book ?" and Ps 87,6, "YHWH will (count or write) in writing down the people, 'This man was born there'".

because religion of its very nature fosters submission and cooperativeness for the common good[21].

6. *Was Nehemiah "Tiršātā'" or "Pehâ" ?* -- A jurisdiction even more concrete and autocratic than Ezra's is claimed for Nehemiah. To him is given the name "Governor", rendering *pehâ* in Neh 5.14 and *tiršātā'* in Neh 8.9; 10.1. The interpretation of these terms must be dictated in general by the same norm as for Ezra: is Nehemiah presented as acting like one possessing civil authority ? But the two cases differ in that the title applied at least fleetingly to Nehemiah does in fact of itself, unlike *sōpēr*, imply civil authority. The following varied questions will call for an answer:

> (§1) Was any Jewish returnee a governor ?
> (§2) Is Nehemiah really called *pehâ* ?
> (§3) What is *tiršātā'* ?
> (§4) Is Nehemiah shown as governor only part of the time?
> (§5) What concrete functions does Nehemiah exercise ?
> (§6) Is "cupbearer" favorite or chamberlain ?
> (§7) Was Sanballat governor ?
> (§8) What was Nehemiah's relation to local officials ?

‖392‖ (6, §1) *Was any member of the postexilic Judah community a governor ?* What seems obvious to one expert on this point is contested or flatly denied by another. For Père de Vaux, Sheshbassar of Judah is governor in the same sense as Tattenai of Samaria[22]. Sheshbassar is in fact called *pehâ* in the claim of the Judeans reported to Darius by *pehâ* Tattenai (Ezra 6.15), but there it is perplexing why neither Sheshbassar nor Zerubbabel is shown actually treating with Tattenai as responsible for the work and the community. In Ezra 1.8, Sheshbassar is not called *pehâ*, only "prince", *nāśí'* not *śar*, and "for" not "of" Judah.

But in Ezra 2.2 the leader of the returning exiles is called Zerubbabel. It is quite commonly held that the compiler here envisions a

---

21 "The juridical structure has tended from the very beginning to separate itself from that of religion, even while it is just as today determined in its very essence by moral norms whose connection with religion can not of course be denied": J. KLÍMA, *La base religieuse et éthique de l'ordre social dans l'Orient ancien*, in *Archiv Orientální* 16, 1949, 334.

22 R. DE VAUX, *Les décrets de Cyrus* (→ n.5), *RB* 46, 1937, 29.

different person, perhaps a different office or a document misplaced from a later period. Rudolph holds that the compiler unquestionably identifies Zerubbabel with Sheshbassar, but simply made a mistake[23]. It is indeed strange that the compiler would so crassly fail to clarify the identification for his readers. Once this hurdle is leaped, there is no further reason to suppose that the compiler is not making Zerubbabel a variant name for Sheshbassar. This would hold especially if the proper spelling is Shenazar as in 1 Chron 3.18 (Senabassar in Esdras-*a*' 3.15) where he instead of Zerubbabel is the son of Shealtiel, and Zerubbabel is son of Shenazar's older brother Pedaiah.

At any rate, only Zerubbabel is seen exercising any kind of non-priestly leadership in the community, but not much, and without title. In the Ezra books he is neither *pehâ* nor *nāśí'*, though Haggai four times calls him *pehâ* of Judah. Zerubbabel doubtless owes his primacy to his inheritance of the Davidic dynasty (as a link in the genealogy of Jesus, Mt 1.12; Lk 3.27), but in Ezra he so constantly appears as a mere figurehead that his primacy may be one of prestige rather than jurisdiction. Rost thinks that Cyrus made "the prince of Judah" a Persian puppet-governor in order to gain popular favor away from some nationalist ferment perhaps caused by Haggai, but that afterwards no Son of David was ‖393‖ ever governor in Judah again, since the top authority passed to the high-priest[24]. Grosheide holds that if Sheshbassar (or) Zerubbabel was *pehâ*, he must have been governor of the whole Province of Syria (properly Eber-Nahar), or at least of Samaria sub-province[25]. This observation in a sense reinforces what we have said in footnote 8 about "jurisdiction over all Eber-Nahar" being too loosely used in the Ezra-books to be taken seriously; but *pehâ*, though the title of Samaritan governor Tattenai, is in fact used without protest for Sheshbassar in Tattenai's own letter.

Nehemiah, in calling himself *pehām* (5,14f) adds that his conduct distinguishes him from former *pāhôt*. These former governors are not of

---

23 We may dismiss as unconvincing the effort to prove that Zerubbabel is not from *zeru-babili* "born in Babylon" but from *zerûb ba-'ebel* "oppressed in grief", and is thus a variant of the name of Nehemiah, "God has consoled": P. RIESSLER, *Nehemias, die Zeit seines Auftretens und seine Person,* in *Biblische Zeitschrift* 1, 1903, 232-245, and *Wann wirkte Nehemias ?,* in *Theologische Quartalschrift* 90, Tübingen 1910, 1-6.

24 L. ROST, *Erwägungen zum Kyroserlass,* in W. RUDOLPH Festschrift *Verbannung und Heimkehr,* Tübingen, 1961, 302.

25 H.H. GROSHEIDE, *Juda als Ouderdeel van het Persische Rijk,* in *Gereformeerd Theologisch Tijdschrift* 54, 1954, 70.

Judah but of Samaria according to Rudolph, who denies that Sheshbassar and Zerubbabel were governors; but there is really no true sense in which Nehemiah was successor to a governor of Samaria[26]. In summary, though apparently no expert claims that there was no Judah governor, opinions are so divided on each aspect of the question that we cannot base any further assurance on any one of them.

(6, §2) *Is Nehemiah really called pehâ ?*   The only passage in which Nehemia is called a *pehâ*, only one single time (5.14), uses that word ungrammatically. He says indeed, here and again in 5.18, that he did not claim "the bread of the *pehâ*"[27]. But the only declaration assumed to mean that Nehemiah himself was governor involves serious exegetical difficulties,

First of all, even strong defenders of the governorship like Rudolph admit that the reading *pehām* is impossible. It is taken by the Septuagint to mean "their governor", which would require emendation to *pehātām*. But in the absence of any antecedent for the plural pronoun, Rudolph like Gesenius-Brown accepts rather the emendation *pehâ'*.

‖394‖ Secondly, he again admits that the omission of any subject with the verb "he commanded me" is inadmissible, and debates combining the two words *siwwâ ôtî* into one "I was commanded". But there would be no serious obstacle to supplying either the impersonal "one" as passive-equivalent, or "the King" as subject, ... if we were sure in advance what the authenticity and sense of the declaration is.

"From the twentieth to the thirty-second year of Artaxerxes" in Neh 5.14 is a clear and satisfying indication for those who maintain that Nehemiah was governor from the moment of his first arrival in Jerusalem. But this is altogether implausible in the light of how he is presented in Neh 2.1. Hence Hölscher deletes the phrase as a marginal gloss, supposing that its insertion caused the grammar-mixup of the word "commanded".

Instead of emending three times into a patchwork involving fourteen words, is it not more respectful both of the text and of critical principles to

---

26 W. RUDOLPH, *Esra und Nehemia* 1949 (→ n.10) p. 131 & 123, citing A. ALT, *Die Rolle Samarias bei der Entstehung des Judentums,* in O. PROCKSCH *Festschrift,* Leipzig, 1934, 24 (= *Kleine Schriften II,* Munich, 1953, 333).

27 On the current view that Nehemiah's [ch. 1-6] memoir was a votive offering set up at a shrine, following Egyptian usage compiled by E. OTTO, *Die biographischen Inschriften der ägyptischen Spätzeit,* Leiden, 1954, see G. VON RAD, *Die Nehemia-Denkschrift,* in ZAW 76, 1964, 176-187.

see what can be done about the one word *pehâ* ? This word is simultaneously the most incompatible with the remote context, and the most easily
explained as an intrusion in the proximate context. Referring to "living like
a governor" as a comment on quality of food occurs three times here, and
might well have given to a scribe the idea that Nehemiah is thereby referring
to himself as appointed governor.

    If we emend *pehām* to *bāhem*, for example, the sense would become
altogether natural: "Even from the day when it was commanded me to be
'among them' in the land of Judah. for the twelve years from the 20th to the
32d of King Artaxerxes, I and my brothers ate no governor's bread".
Whether one finds tolerable the concrete conjecture *bāhem*, unsupported by
ancient witnesses [except by their own emendation of the existing Hebrew],
is altogether secondary to the observation that something is wrong with
pehām both grammatically and exegetically.

    (6, §3) *What is tiršātā'* ? We will rely here on E. Meyer, whose
support is even more valid since he firmly holds that Nehemiah was the
pehâ. He also holds that Sheshbassar was, and Zerubbabel was, but that the
post had been left unfilled during the period in which Ezra and Nehemiah
had arrived in Jerusalem. Since he maintains a *second* governorship for
Nehemiah in 433 or later, he presumably dates the first term from 445 as in
Neh 2.1; "TRŠT', doubtless a Persian participle to be pronounced *taršatâ*, is
no name of an office like Pasha or the *Khšatrapavam* not yet used by the
Jews, but a title like Excellency. ||395|| It rightly stands in official
documents, but has no place in the narrating of history and none at all in an
autobiography"[28]. Hence it is to be expunged in Neh 8.9, but admitted in
10.2; where however apart what may be said about *pehâ* it no more indicates
an officeholder than the Cockney taxi-driver addressing his client as
"guv'nor". •

    This explanation of *tiršātā'* is adopted in the *International Critical
Commentary*[29]. When the word occurs in the census list of Ezra 2.63 =
Neh 7.65, it is in a purely religious context for the man who made the
decision that those who claimed to be priests but could not document their

---

28 E. MEYER, *Entstehung* 1896 (→ n.7) 194; also 75, 97, 131; and 4: "Judaism was made
possible only by an energetic intervention of the Persian king, in the fact that the authority of
the Empire stood behind Nehemiah and Ezra."

29 L.W. BATTEN, *Ezra and Nehemiah*, Edinburgh, 1913, 97.

claim were not to eat sacred bread until some priest could get an oracular pronouncement[30].

It must be further noted that the only application of *tiršātā'* to Nehemiah at all occurs in the vastly more embroiled question of whether his ministry was ever contemporary and shared with Ezra. Even then, in Neh 10.1 it has the further anomaly of being part of a list of priests. And the sudden appearance of these two major figures in cooperation is enigmatic and contrary to everything else recorded in the two books. Chiefly for this reason we might be emboldened to regret the "concordist chronology" popularized by such experts as Wellhausen, Albright, Rudolph, Pavlovský, and Bright, to elude the dilemma posed by van Hoonacker: Is Ezra's ministry thirteen years before Nehemiah's or thirty-one years after ? [31]   They claim that by the "negligible" alteration of "seventh" to "thirty-seventh" year of Artaxerxes [I] in Ezra 7.7 they salvage the "momentous attested fact" that Ezra and Nehemiah were contemporary. But a ‖396‖ more realistic attention to the true syndromes of emphasis in the text would show that the excision of the brief passages claiming contemporaneity would much better fit the total perspective.

(6, §4) *Is Nehemiah shown as governor only part of the time ?* Categorically we may answer from the text of Neh 5.14: Whatever is said about Nehemiah's *pehâ*-ship *at all*, shows it lasting from the first year of his arrival in Jerusalem.

The impossibility of reconciling this long term with the presentation in Neh 2.9 and elsewhere is one of the proofs of textual corruption, emphasized even by defenders of the governorship, in the only text which speaks of Nehemiah as *pehâ* at all.

---

30   K. GALLING, *Serubbabel* in *Fest.W.*RUDOLPH 1961 (→ n.13) 92; see further E. ROBERTSON, *Urim and Thummim*, in *Vetus Testamentum* 14, 1964, 73.

31 W. RUDOLPH, *Esra und Nehemiah* 1949 (→ n.10) 71; W.F. ALBRIGHT, *A Brief History of Judah from the Days of Josiah to Alexander the Great*, in *Biblical Archaeologist* 9, 1946, 13, renouncing *JBL* 46, 1921, 21; V. PAVLOVSKÝ, *Die Chronologie der Tätigkeit Esdras. Versuch einer neuen Lösung*, in *Biblica* 38, 1957, 257, 448; J. BRIGHT, *The Date of Ezra's Mission to Jerusalem*, in *Y.* KAUFMANN *Jubilee Volume*, Jerusalem, 1960, 70-87; 85. The view of A. VAN HOONACKER is set forth most recently in *Revue Biblique* 33, 1924, 33-64; and defended most imposingly by H.H. ROWLEY, *The Chronological Order of Ezra and Nehemiah*, in *J.* GOLDZIHER *Memorial*, Budapest, 1948, 117-149 (= *The Servant of the Lord and Other Essays*, London 1952, 129-159).

(6, §5) *What positively is Nehemiah shown doing ?* We have tried to give objective though not uncommitted attention to all the evidences relating to the *terms* by which Nehemiah's mission is described. Our conclusion had to be largely based on the risky "argument from silence", namely that our hero is nowhere shown *acting* as the alleged titles would indicate. Now it is time to take up more constructively what *is* in fact the authority of Nehemiah and his relation to other authoritative members of the community.

What actual functions does Nehemiah exercise ? For a long time he is seen only as a genial building-contractor. This is his mandate from Artaxerxes (Neh 2.5); this is his role even in the moments of greatest crisis (Neh 4.8H; 5.7). It is he who sets up the doors, while another appoints the doorkeepers (Neh 7.1). What powers he had, he left to his brother and the fort-commandant (Neh 7.2).

In getting the bricks moving again after the worker-demonstrations of 5.1, Nehemiah appeals to various leaders, and among other things induces the priests to support his moratorium-proposals (Neh 5.12). From this rather obscure and trivial hint, Pirenne sweepingly generalized that in reconstruction-Judah, "all powers, without any exception, belonged to the clergy"[32]. He at least does not give much for Nehemiah's governorship. But a more warranted application of his observation would be in the fact that where Nehemiah appears with most authority is in doing a priest's job, ‖397‖ in regulating certain details of mixed marriages, sabbath, cult-treasury, and tithes (Neh 12.44-13.13).

After his return from Babylon, however, Nehemiah's activities are harder to determine because there is no consensus about how much of chapters 10-12 is to be adjudged to him instead of Ezra[33]. All that surely relates to him is expressed primarily by the term "I put up a fight", *wā-ārîbâ* (Neh 5.17; 13.17). To get the Temple functioning properly he quarreled with the *seḡānîm*, Neh 13.11 (besides throwing out Tobiah from a sacristy-room on his own authority, 13.8f); to secure sabbath-observance he quarreled with the *hōrîm* (Neh 13.17). His "authority" in these matters is seen to be not

---

32 J. PIRENNE, *Institutions du peuple hébreu, V. La captivité et la restauration de Jérusalem sous l'empire perse*, RIDA III⁰ S., 1, 1954, 208.

33 A. JEPSEN, *Nehemia 10*, in ZAW 66, 1954, 87-106, links chapter 10 with 14; so also DE FRAINE and SCHAEDER. But it is left where it is by A. IBÁÑEZ ARANA, *Sobre la colocación original de Neh. 10*, in *Estudios Bíblicos* 10, 1951, 370-402. And even Neh 9 is referred to Nehemiah's own reforms by M. REHM, *Nehemiah 10*, in *Biblische Zeitschrift* NF 1, 1957, 39, following SELLIN.

only indirect, but also relating to religion more than to civil administration; so also in Neh 12.31, his seating of the princes for the procession.

(6,§6) *Is "cupbearer" favorite or chamberlain ?*

If we can try to put from our minds all preconvictions or foreseeing of what is to come later, and simply allow the Hebrew words of the first chapters of Nehemiah to evoke in our minds the "Sitz im Leben" which they spontaneously suggest, it would be something like this.

When the Persian potentate took his meals, he was served by deft and agreeable retainers. The pouring of his wine especially, as preserved in a long tradition of Persian poetry, was assigned to a sympathetic and generally youthful favorite who would have to lend an ear often and long while the noble diner was in his cups[34]. Nehemiah was the man -- or boy -- who actually poured the wine for the king's meals (Neh 2.1), not merely the holder of some title of dignity as 1.11 might suggest. There is no indication that he had any function, position, or influence apart from this.

His conduct in the Susa crisis will have to be described as calculated pouting. He received word of some setback among his kinfolk in Jerusalem[35]. He gave no sign of concern about it at all before ‖398‖ the King. Privately he wept and prayed, then cunningly made his plans. For several months [December (Neh 1.1) to April (2.1)] he bided his time. Then at an opportune moment, doubtless when wine or weariness had made the sovereign unusually sympathetic and chatty, Nehemiah "put on an act". For the first time he allowed the King to see him sad; so sad in fact that an inquiry followed. Then "with trepidation" (Neh 2.2) the cupbearer unburdened himself.

The proposal of this pampered stripling was nothing less than that he should be empowered to rebuild and fortify a metropolis as ancient and turbulent as any in the world.

---

34 On the *Saki* of the poetic tradition reflected in the Rubaiyyat of Omar Khayyam, see R. NORTH, *Guide to Biblical Iran*. 1956, 74.

35 In the most recent survey of the enigma of this "fire destroying Jerusalem's gate", J. MORGENSTERN, in *Hebrew Union College Annual* 27, 1956. 173, and 31, 1960, 16, concludes more enigmatically than ever that the disaster occurred in 485 B.C., which is probably long before Nehemiah's birth. More plausibly V. PAVLOVSKÝ (→ n.31), *Biblica* 38, 1957, 446, connects this disaster with an early effort to rebuild the wall shared by Nehemiah's brother.

And to this audacious plan the King's only reaction -- "while the Queen was sitting beside him" (Neh 2,6) -- was "How soon can I have you back with me ?"   From this verse some commentators conclude that Nehemiah was a favorite of the Queen, and that to her unspoken plea the granting of this request was due. Doubtless the passage implies he was someone's favorite, but more likely the King's.

As against all this, if we know in advance that Nehemiah at some time in his life became *pehâ,* whether after some years or especially if at once, then it becomes natural to read back into these first chapters some different overtones. And in fact the term "cupbearer" is, like so many other terms for far-reaching administrative functions, a mere metaphor borrowed from services to the King's person which were intimate and lowly but for that very reason betokened his supreme confidence in the one who exercised them.

In this sense, not unreasonably, Albright claims that the "wine-pourer" was the equivalent of Chamberlain; and like that official (originally "harem-keeper") was a eunuch, which we know as a title of honor for a Minister of State in Acts 8.27[36]. *Eunoûchos* is in fact the Greek rendition of "pourer", *mašqeh*: a copyist's fairly obvious interpretive correction of *oinochóos.* Whether or not Nehemiah's title was "eunuch" or its equivalent, the dynamic and even booming manner of acting which he shows throughout his memoirs is not exactly what we would expect of a real eunuch.

Our own conclusion is plainly that he was the King's "youthful favorite" or page. As such, he naturally shows up in Judah surrounded ||399|| by an aura of prestige. Before we can evaluate the reaction of local dignitaries there, we must first regulate the status commonly assigned to one of them.

(6, §7) *Was Sanballat governor ?* My [Jerome[1]] Chronicles-Ezra commentary fell into the trap of acknowledging without further inquiry that the prime adversary of Nehemiah was governor of Samaria. He is the same governor as the one mentioned in an Elephantine papyrus [*ANET* 492], Ginsberg's footnote to the passage confidently asserts[37]. But this Sanballat

---

36 W.F. ALBRIGHT (→ n.31), *Biblical Archaeologist* 9, :946, 11.

37 H.L. GINSBERG, in J.B. PRITCHARD, *ANET* (→ n.4); R. NORTH, "Chronicles; Ezra, Nehemiah" in *Jerome Commentary*[1], Englewood Cliffs N.J., 1968, 434 (= I, §102, §105).

was in office in 408 B.C., thirty-seven years after Nehemiah[38]. And in fact the recent discovery of papyri some ten miles east of Shiloh shows a governor of Samaria named Bananiah from 350 B.C., a full century after Nehemiah's collaborator; from which we are invited to reevaluate the likelihood of officials' names recurring in later connections[39]. Rowley handily disposes of Torrey's conclusion that Nehemiah really functioned under Artaxerxes II from 384 to 372[40]. He goes on to show that the matrimonial connections of the biblical (and ? Elephantine) Sanballat are too similar to those recorded by Josephus as contemporary of Alexander to allow us to think that two separate historical personages are meant[41]. ‖400‖ Really that article never poses the question of whether the biblical Sanballat

---

38 E.A. COWLEY (→ n.4), *Aramaic Papyri*, 1923, 110, regarding line 29 of papyrus 30, admits that the Sanballat of Nehemiah is not called *pehâ*, but sees no difficulty in his still being in office some 37 years after Nehemiah's first clash with him. His further claim that it is "desperate" to suppose identical matrimonial-alliances of two separate Sanballats is not based on Elephantine at all, but on data of Josephus irrelevant even as emended. There is in fact a "Shelemaiah son of Delaiah" in Neh 6.10 but he is "hired" (by Sanballat, Neh 6.12), not related to Sanballat, who in the Elephantine papyrus is father of both Delaiah and Shelemaiah.

39 Frank M. CROSS, *The Discovery of the Samaria Papyri*, in *Biblical Archaeologist* 26, 1963, 110-121.

40 C.C. TORREY, *Sanballat "the Horonite"*, in *JBL* 47 (1928) 380-389. Torrey takes for granted that anybody named Sanballat can only be a *pehâ*, all the more so as there were at least two Samaria governors attested by that name (his p.381), but with questionable reliance on Josephus he goes on to theorize that Nehemiah himself must have functioned under Artaxerxes II sixty years after 444 B.C.

41 JOSEPHUS FLAVIUS, *Antiquities* 11 (302), 7,2, describes how a Sanballat whose daughter was the wife of the brother of the high priest Jaddua was made satrap of Samaria by Darius "the last" (= Codomannus 338-331). Editor R. MARCUS in an appendix to the Loeb Library Josephus VI, Harvard 1937, 499, explains that by emending Jonathan ben-Joiada of Neh 12,11 to Johanan as in 12,12 we get that "one of the sons of Joiada" was himself married to Sanballat's daughter in Neh 13.28, whereas in Josephus her husband is brother rather than (grand-) son of a high priest, but son of Jonathan. Either the matrimonial details furnished by Josephus are totally unreliable, or else, even if we overlook that fact that he is 100 years too late, the details which he furnishes are reliable and therefore cannot fit the Sanballat of Nehemiah. Reliable or not, what he really proves is that the names involved are as common as Schmidt, Jones, and Kelly.

is a governor or officeholder at all[42]. A later article shows that his preoccupation about date leaves undisturbed his conviction that Nehemiah's Sanballat was in fact a governor[43]. But a rexamination of all the passages relative to authority now reveals that no such title or functions are attributed to any Sanballat in the Ezra-books at all.

Sanballat first appears in Neh 2.10 as a villager of (Beth-) Horon on the westerly border between Judah and Samaria. He is enraged at the fact that Nehemiah has presented his credentials to the unnamed and plural governors (*pahawôt*) of Eber-Nahar. In Neh 2.19 he and his associates recur without title, in the rather plebeian role of deriding Nehemiah's work. In the Hebrew texts Neh 3.33 and 4.1 (Greek 4.1,7), Sanballat is again enraged, and again without title or authority as also when he is cursed by Nehemiah, 6.14. Finally in 13.28 it turns out that Sanballat too is related by marriage to the Judah community, no less than his henchman Tobiah of whom this was narrated already in Neh 6,17f and in 13,4.

What is there then but a name ? We can only tremble at the thought of future "historians" assuming that anyone named Johnson in Texas between 1866 and 2066 is the president who sent troops into Santo Domingo. What we really learn from the Josephus and Elephantine parallels is that Sanballat is a common and frequently attested name. ‖401‖ It is a Babylonian name, but since it is provably borne by governors of Samaria, common-sense would lead us to expect that some of the courthouse-clerks' new babies would be thus named. Only in the assumption -- tacit with most commentators today -- that Nehemiah and Sanballat are somehow on a footing of equality, can the various maneuvers between them be explained. If Nehemiah is *pehâ*, then there is point in supposing that Sanballat is also. Nothing in the portrayal of Sanballat leads us independently to suppose this.

The prevailing consensus about Sanballat's governorship further trapped my commentary into maintaining that the artistry of this literary

---

42 H.H. ROWLEY, *Sanballat and the Samaritan Temple*, in *Bulletin Rylands*, 38, 1956, 172, makes his own the judgment of Cowley that the similarities of in-laws are too detailed to be coincidental. But he glides over the fact that for Cowley part of the inescapable convergence lies in the fact that both Elephantine and Nehemiah Sanballats are governors, which is not a datum. At any rate, the conclusion of Rowley's whole article is that Josephus cannot be taken as reliable. Thereby falls out the whole basis for taking the (emended) matrimonial alliance of a governor Sanballat living in 340 B.C. as middle term for identifying a governor Sanballat of 408 with a Sanballat of 445 not attested to be governor.

43 H.H. ROWLEY, *The Samaritan Schism in Legend and History*, in *Israel's Prophetic Heritage*, New York, 1962, 217.

compilation about Nehemiah lies partly in showing him as surrounded by enemies on the borders of Judah to the north, east, south, and west: Bethoron-Samaria, Ammon, Arabia, and Ashdod (Neh 4.7). Re-thinking the matter in the light of the *facts*, one must be struck by the extent to which Nehemiah's enemies are "they of his own household" (Mi 7.6; Mt 10.36).

The two principal foes are married to Jerusalemites. Also, Ashdod is a name connected with, and perhaps even generalized for, sons of illegitimate union: Zech 9.6; Deut 23.3. Any American knows how easy it is to vilify home-town or next-door neighbors by a slurring name of "foreigner" based on racial origins: "what would you expect from a mick or a spic or a limey or a dago ?" (Glossary: Irish, Spanish, British, Italian).

It would go beyond our present goals to cudgel the fact obvious in Neh 6.14-18 that Nehemiah's hostilities are far more purely personal grudges than the noble crusades for God and country which he made them out to be. But we must emphasize that the term "Samaritan" was already recognized to be applied in the Ezra-books to unloved collaborators of the foreign regime, not only officeholders, but particularly the "little people", *'am hā-āres*[44]. It now appears that Nehemiah's challengers must all be placed in the latter category, but within Judah itself.

One thing is clear, that they are YHWH-worshipers as truly as himself, though doubtless with forms and modalities less commendable ‖402‖ than his. This is the view of Professor Rowley, who adds, "There is more reason to question the racial purity of the people of Jerusalem than those of Samaria"[45]. Sooner or later we will have to reckon with the extent to which Nehemiah's frantic insistence on "purity of blood" is a germ of racist supremacy. In a recent Dutch commentary his policy is piquantly called "apartheid"[46]. There is nothing contrary to our respect for the sacred books in inquiring whether even as noble a character as Nehemiah may have been

---

44 By this term we understand: *a*) not "foreign-born landowners", as A. ALT, refuted by GROSHEIDE (→ n.25), *Gereformeerd Theologisch Tijdschrift* 54, 1954, 67 ; *b*) not former poor Judean *dallat hā-āres* enemies of the Deuteronomic movement, whom the Babylonians favored by furnishing them with land, as E. JANSSEN, *Juda in der Exilzeit*, Göttingen 1938, 49 & 121; but *c*) people of Judah who were employees or collaborators of the Samaria-based Babylonian/Persian regime, as D. ROTHSTEIN, *Juden und Samaritaner*, Leipzig 1908, 28 & 41.

45 ROWLEY, *The Samaritan Schism* (→ n. 43), 1962, 222.

46 J. DE FRAINE, *Esdras en Nehemias*, in A. VAN DEN BORN, *De boeken van het Oude Testament* V/2, Roermond, 1961, 82; an even stronger branding of racism is cited from G. KITTEL, *Das Konnubium mit den Nichtjuden*, 1937, 30, in RUDOLPH, *Esra* (→ n.10) 1949, 89.

partially motivated by a racial rather than a purely religious commitment, and as such run counter to the deeper and more enduring trends of Judeo-Christian revelation[47]. But we may apply also to Nehemiah what Rowley again tellingly observes, "From our safe distance it is easy to criticize Ezra for his intolerance; but it may well have been that but for that intolerance Judaism would have faded away, leaving as little mark on the course of the world's religious history as the Samaritans have done"[48].

(6, §8) *What is Nehemiah's relation to local officials in Judah and Samaria ?* With regard to plainly Persian officials, when once the Sanballat myth is exploded, there is nothing to say except with Neh 2.9 that Nehemiah's credentials were presented amd acceptable to all Persian officeholders.

Within the Jewish community itself, Nehemiah deals conciliatingly with *s^egānîm* and *hōrîm* (2.16b; 4.8H; 5.7), less tranquilly with *s^egānîm* alone (2.16a; 13.11) and *hōrîm* alone (13.17).

Segen or *sāgān* occurs only in the plural, and apart from these contested passages where it is counterpoised to Nehemiah's allegedly-*higher* authority, implies a vague local or military jurisdiction in Ezek 23.6 and Jer 51.28, always flanking *pāhôt*. In Is 41.25 and the Akkadian *šaknu*, it more clearly indicates true local jurisdiction. The *s^egānîm* occur also in Ezra 9.2 in parallel with *śārîm* as chief offenders among the racial integrationists.

‖403‖ *Hōr* is a word common in Aramaic, Arabic, and modern Hebrew, with the sense of "freeborn, freedman". In few preexilic passages like 1 Kgs 21.8 (in parallel with the elders, *z^eqēnîm*), and Isa 34.12 (in parallel with princes, *śārîm*) it seems to mean "the nobles", which is the customary and acceptable rendition in Nehemiah.

Significantly perhaps, *s^egānîm* and *hōrîm* are the only terms indicating some kind of Jewish commmunity authority either inferior or superior to Nehemiah's own. In the chapters of Nehemiah where it is rather Ezra's activity that is proximately or possibly in question, we find other terms, "princes of the town or state of Judah", *śārê ha'am* 11.1; *śārê ha-medînâ* 11.3; *śārê y^ehûdâ* 12.31 (to which may be added the fort-commandant *śar ha-bîrâ* of Neh 7.2, and Ezer ben-Jeshua the *śar* of Mizpah in 3.19).

---

47 Some incidental aspects of this problem are noted by G. AHLSTRÖM, *Aspects of Syncretism in Israelite Religion*, Lund, 1963; and W. BRAUDE, *Jewish Proselyting* (sic!), Providence, 1940.

48 ROWLEY, *Sanballat* (→ n.42), in *Bulletin Rylands* 38, 1956, 198.

There are also "patriarchs", *râšê hā-ābôt* (8.13) with their *pāqîd* or "superintendent" Zabdiel in 11.13. In Ezra's own more identifiable memoirs we find him dealing largely with *śārîm* (Ezra 9.1 f; in association with "elders and judges" in Ezra 10.14) and *râšê ābôt* (Neh 8.13; but in 8.9 there is strangely no mention of *peha, śārîm, sᵉgānîm, šōpᵉtîm, zᵉqēnîm,* or *hōrîm*).

To advert briefly to the pre-Ezra parts of Ezra, the *râšê ābôt* seem to share whatever authority Zerubbabel has in 2.68; 4.2f. Sheshbassar as a "prince" in 1.8 is *nāśî* not *śar,* and "for" not "of" Judah. Neither Sheshbassar nor Zerubbabel is mentioned in Governor Tattenai's report as exercising any authority or leadership in the Judah community, but are only "the strong-men among their chiefs", *gubrayyā' dî bᵉrāšêhôm* (5.10; cf. 5.8). No title at all is given to either Zerubbabel or Jeshua in Ezra 2.2; 3.1; 5.2; in 4.3 they are associated with "the rest of the fathers", *šᵉ'ar hā-ābôt.* Jeshua is a priest; he precedes in 3.1; and he supervises in 3.9.

We remarked above that Nehemiah never commands the leaders with whom he is associated, but deals "conciliatingly" with them. A better word would have been "jockeyingly". He pleads, fawns, sputters, rants, or quarrels with skilful adaptation to whatever the situation demands[49]. And this is by no means incompatible with his being a top superior possessed of full authority. The geniality and "human relations" insight in Nehemiah's leadership are shown by recent sociological studies to be the most efficient ways of exercising jurisdiction and highest authority. But these tricks are also notably compatible with -- and, alas, more commonly found in -- contractors ‖404‖ and merchants who have a job to get done and want it to be finished off with as little friction as possible. This is what we find to be the case with Nehemiah, since he never invokes any other kind of authority, and deals with people whose titles are for the most part more authoritative than his own.

7. *Conclusions.*

1. Nehemiah was not governor. The only passage in which *peha* is applied to him is Neh 5.14, a corruption, perhaps for *bāhem,* "among them". *Tiršātā'* is a title of honor, "Excellency".

2. Sanballat was not governor. Officeholders of this name in Josephus and the papyri were 35 to 100 years after him, and attest the

---

49 A. GELIN, *Le livre d'Esdras et de Néhémie,* Paris, 1960, 23f.

frequency of this name. He and Nehemiah's other hecklers were probably
Judeans, nicknamed contemptuously according to their racial descent.

3. Nehemiah in his youth was a page, and in Judea was a
building-contractor. The only authority he is shown exercising among the
Judean *sᵉgānîm* and *hōrîm* is that of his genial persuasiveness, backed by
"friends in the capital".

4. Ezra has no title other than priest and writer, and no mission
other than to exercise his religious calling freely in accord with his
conscience and his special talents.

5. Neither Ezra nor the temple-builders with Zerubbabel were
allotted an unlimited expense-account by the Persian regime; there is no
cogent proof that they were allotted anything other than patron-donations, tax
exemption, and special ration coupons.

6. As a subject receiving encouragement in normal religious
activities from his own sovereign, Ezra can scarcely be compared to an
authority negotiating a Concordat in virtue of his simultaneously religious
and political sovereignty.

6

Ezra and the Origins of our Bible

1. Link with what precedes

a) Doubtless unexpectedly, this last essay is presented as a direct lineal sequence of the first. Our research on Medicine revealed that in the Bible there is no word for brain; and that the *lēb* generally rendered "heart" refers more generally to the inner organs of cognition, will, and subconscious body-control: loosely located within the stomach-area. In fact, the Bible has no word not only for brain nor for heart (as now understood), but also not for nerve or lung, nor indeed for spoon or comb known from excavation, or many other words needed for daily communication.

This fact has served as one of several scholars' extremely varying approaches all leading to the conclusion that Biblical Hebrew was never a "used" language, a means of social communication, but was "invented" by selecting or recombining elements of the environing dialects. How or when this took place is either bypassed by these various approaches, or is loosely linked with "Ezra's Torah" (Neh 8,2). The omission of any Ezra flanking Nehemiah in Sirach 49,13 is for some an indication that the Bible-compilation took place after 130 B.C.E.

Under the name "Ezra" is sometimes vaguely understood the doubt-less large group of anonymous scribes in that "Persian" era who helped in the definitive compilation of the Pentateuch or our whole Hebrew Bible[1]. Quite recently there has been a very strong tendency to link the activity of "Ezra" and its Torah-connections to the sociopolitical conditions in Judah due to strong Persian dominance there and the threat to Persia of coastal Dor, which precisely around 458 had become a colony of Athens and base of its fleet in support of Egypt's revolt against Persia.

---

1 Daniel L. (CHRISTOPHER-) SMITH in his translator's-preface to J. WEINBERG, *Citizen-Temple Community* (*JSOT* supp. 151, 1992) 14: "Most modern critics date the final composition (and an increasing number the very writing) of the Bible in the post-exilic era."

These are the problems which will have to be considered in endeavoring to complete our survey by examining or supplying the "how?" and "when?" of the varyingly-alleged "invention" of Biblical Hebrew.

––––––

b) To "clear the deck" of material extraneous to this discussion, we have felt it necessary to premise (essay 5 above) our position with regard to the commonly presumed political links of Nehemiah or even of Ezra with the local administrative apparatus of the Persian government[2]. As noted above, our concern there is with what the Ezra-books actually *say* (or in some few cases what options are open for the emendation of admittedly corrupt terms).

We may admit that upon carefully scrutinizing and reprinting the article, we had a twinge of regret at what seemed to be an overall negative and deconstructive sound. It is true that we often used for Nehemiah highly favorable qualifiers like genial, dynamic, successful, and deeply religious (but not "boisterous"; nor as Eskenazi "demanding, heavy-handed; belligerent"[3]; nor "egoentric"[4]; and certainly not as Clines: "a liar ... out to persuade his readers of his importance, his selflessness, his energy"[5]). But our article was not written to *prove* all the good things to say or think about Nehemiah.

The case of Ezra was less disturbing, since he is fairly presented as an "unassuming" biblical scholar, ready to preach in public when needed or

––––––––––––––––––

2 Peter FREI, "Das Beglaubigungsschreiben Esras", p. 51-61 of his 80-page updating of "Zentralgestalt und Lokalautonomie im Achämenidenreich" in his (with Klaus KOCH) *Reichsidee und Reichsorganisation im Perserreich* (*OBO* 55; Fribourg/Göttingen ²1996, Univ./Vandenhoeck) 55f confronts the recent denial of authenticity in the Artaxerxes decree(s) and especially their huge donations, by A.H.J. GUNNEWEG, *Esra* (KommAT 19/1, Gütersloh 1985).

3 Tamara C. ESKENAZI, *In an Age of Prose: a Literary Approach to Ezra-Nehemiah* (SBL monograph 36, Atlanta 1988) 145 f.

4 Robert P. CARROLL, "Coopting the Prophets: Nehemiah and Noadiah", in Fest. J. BLENKINSOPP, *Priests, Prophets and Scribes* (→ ftn. 11), ed. E. ULRICH, *al.* (*JSOT* supp. 149; Sheffield 1992, 87-99) p. 92.

5 David J.A. CLINES, "The Nehemiah Memoir: the Perils of Autobiography" in his *What Does Eve Do to Help ? and Other Readerly Questions to the Old Testament* (*JSOT* supp. 94 (Sheffield 1990, 124-164) p.126; and yet his p. 144, amid many examples of "utterly unreliable texts" cites as fully reliable the "attack of one provincial 'governor' upon another"; so also p. 158.

just by his penitential actions[6]: though we will take note of a tendency to push him more to the political forefront in current scholarship.

Regarding Nehemiah, our article was not written to prove anything *bad* about him, unless it might be that some readers would be led to feel that his unusually authoritative and forceful personality made people *think* that he held some governmental or other office higher than was really the case -- and that he may well have recognized this fact and utilized it towards attaining his altogether admirable goals. Specifically the article was not written to prove that Nehemiah was *not* governor (though that also would not be anything bad about him), but rather to show the dubiousness of the (at most three) brief texts which are adduced to prove that he *was*.

What we really set out to prove was that the universally (though expressly with perplexities and misgivings) admitted governorship of Nehemiah was based on these defectively-transmitted texts, whose emendation left a free option both for those who already firmly believed that he was governor (*peha*), and for those (if any) who found this nowhere clearly stated in the two inadequately-attested mentions of *tiršātā'*, or in the rest of the text of the Ezra-books (or elsewhere, as it happens).

Nehemiah's own words in 5,14 RSV are: "I was appointed to be their governor". In Hebrew this is rather "he (or Someone) commanded me": tolerable as a kind of passive, though surprising if the real subject was the Great King Artaxerxes. But the real crux is *peham*.

It may well be admitted from the start: first, that *peha* really means governor, though all commentators show dismay that (though in Haggai 1,1; 2,2 for Zerubbabel) it is never used in the Ezra-books for Sheshbassar, Zerubbabel[7], Sanballat, or Nehemiah at his arrival[8]; only for Tattenai in

---

6 Aage BENTZEN, "Esras Persönlichkeit", *Studia Theologica* 2 (1948) 95-98: not "passive".
-- Jesús GARCÍA TRAPIELLO, *La autoridad política en la Biblia; origen y desarrollo en el Antiguo Testamento* (*BAC* 1997) on p. 192 unusually claims that Ezra 7,26 "converts the traditional law of YHWH into a State law", and his index of "personages having political authority" includes Ezra but not Nehemiah (there is no chapter on either).

7 Sara JAPHET, "Sheshbazzar and Zerubbabel against the Background of the Historical and Religious Tendencies of Ezra-Nehemiah", *ZAW* 95 (1983) 218-229; H.G.M. WILLIAMSON, "The Governors of Judah under the Persians", *Tyndale Bulletin* 39 (1988) 59-82.

8 Tamara ESKENAZI, *In an Age of Prose* (→ ftn.3) 140: "The reader [of Neh 5,14], surprised that Nehemiah had been appointed governor, wonders whether Artaxerxes also would be similarly surprised"; Thierry PETIT, "L'évolution sémantique des termes hébreux et araméens

construct-state Aramaic *pahaṭ*[9] (Ezra 5,3; 6,6); and secondly, that *peha* is a sufficiently unusual Hebrew form to render its grammatical variations difficult.

Nevertheless *peham* in Neh 5,14 is generally admitted to be a corrupt form. Part of the problem is that in his whole career of twelve years rife with bureaucratic disputes *peha* has never yet been said of him.

More to the point, Kittel-Kahle *Biblica Hebraica* proposes *pehātām* as a queried emendation to correspond to the LXX *eis árchonta autôn*. But why "*their* governor in Judah" instead of "*your* governor"? My article proposes as the option open to those who find Nehemiah as *peha* nowhere else in the Ezra books some alternative emendation (*bahem* is mentioned as a possibility, but *bakem* is just as easy, "yours" instead of "theirs"). Though we could not blame reluctance to accept an emendation unsupported by the Septuagint, it does in fact have some similarly small variants in the Ezra-books.

But *peha* is claimed to be applied to Nehemiah not once but *three* times, again here and once in 5,18, both in the phrase "bread of the *peḥah*", but both negatively, "which neither he nor his brothers ever ate". (Despite the plural, there is a kind of echo here of Nehemiah's brother Hanani who in 7,2 would replace him: as *peha* not said, though a segment of the commentators claim that at his unnoticed return Nehemiah "took back" the governorship.) The "governor's bread", which I was content to leave as a generality for "high-quality food", has now been preempted as a technical term for "royal taxation"[10].

---

phh et *sgn* et accadiens *pāḫatu* et *šaknu*", *Journal of Biblical Literature* 107 (1988) 53-67. -- Sean E. MCEVENUE, "The Political Structures in Judah from Cyrus to Nehemiah", *Catholic Biblical Quarterly* 43 (1981) (353-) 364 defends the Galling-Alt view that Judah as just an appendix to Samaria did not have its own governor, against G. WIDENGREN in *Israelite and Judaean History* (ed. J. HAYES & J.M. MILLER (London 1977) 510f, stressing *m^e dînâ* and Morton SMITH's defense of Neh 5,15 as "The former governor who was before me".

9 Joseph FLEISHMANN, "The Investigating Committee of Tattenai: the Purpose of the Investigation and its Results", *Hebrew Union College Annual* 66 (1995) 81-103 on Ezra 5,1-6,15.

10 Joel WEINBERG, *The Citizen-Temple Community* (→ ftn.1), tr. Daniel L. (CHRISTOPHER-) SMITH (*JSOT* supp. 151, Sheffield 1992) 21 translates *leḥem ha-peha* as "taxes-in-kind" (which would then have to be changed to silver as the only tax-revenue acceptable in Persia). But the term for "King's Tax" is held to be rather *middat ha-melek* as Neh 5,4, and the

Neh 8,9, and less clearly 10,2H, are the only places where Nehemiah is named alongside Ezra, and therefore (as is highly questionable) contemporary to him[11]. In 8,9 we have "Nehemiah, he (was) the *tiršātā'* " and in 10,2H (without repeating Ezra's name from 32 verses before in the present ill-localizable text) "on the seals (i.e. among the signers was) Nehemiah the *tiršātā'* ". In Kittel-Kahle the *tiršātā'* is bracketed both times as not in the Greek. The term is taken by some to mean "governor", by others more vaguely "Excellency"; it occurs otherwise only in the doublet-list Ezra 2,63 = Neh 7,65 (RSV "governor") as the unnamed authority who provisionally forbade the eating of priestly food until genealogy could be proved (and in Neh 7,69 as donor).

A 2000-year exegetical consensus was split right down the middle when A. van Hoonacker from before 1890 proposed that Ezra came only *after* Nehemiah, under Artaxerxes *the Second* in 398. This bombshell was considered constructive, not negative, even by its adversaries in the immense paper-war which followed[12]. Finally a *via media* was offered in a

---

"widely admitted" claim that the imperial tax had to be paid in silver only is denied, by Kenneth G. HOGLUND, *Achaemenid Imperial Administration in Syria-Palestine and the Missions of Ezra and Nehemiah* (SBL diss. 125, Atlanta 1992) 235, citing Christopher TUPLIN, "The Administration of the Achaemenid Empire", in *Coinage and Administration in the Athenian and Persian Empires*, ed. Ian CARRADICE (*BAR*-Int 343; Oxford 1987) 113. Hoglund p. 224 on "garrison" implying revenue collection favors "(Pierre) BRIANT's thesis" with no footnote: perhaps *Rois, tributs et paysans* (Paris 1982) or (ed. with Clarisse HERRENSCHMIDT), *Le tribut dans l'Empire perse* (Table Ronde 1986; Paris 1989, Sorbonne).

11 Judson R. SHAVER, "Ezra and Nehemiah: on the Theological Importance of Making them Contemporaries" in Fest. J. BLENKINSOPP, *Priests, Prophets and Scribes: Essays on the Formation and Heritage of Second Temple Judaism*, ed. E. ULRICH, al. *JSOT* supp. 149, Sheffield 1992; 76-86) p. 84 against Blenkinsopp (Ezra-N 1988, p.65 & 205) and partly supporting B. CHILDS, *Introduction to the OT as Scripture* (Philadelphia 1979, Fortress) p.631. -- Also in the Blenkinsopp Festschrift, James C. VANDERKAM, "Ezra-Nehemiah or Ezra and Nehemiah ?", 55-75 holds against ESKENAZI two independent books.

12 The traditional priority of Ezra was defended especially by H.H. ROWLEY, "The Chronological Order of Ezra and Nehemiah", in I. GOLDZIHER *Memorial I*, ed. S. LÖWINGER & J. SOMOGYI (Budapest 1948, Globus) 117-149 [= Rowley's *Servant of the Lord* (1965) 135-168]; and now with a high-priestly chronology from "papponymy" in the newly-available Daliya papyri: F. M. CROSS, "A Reconstruction of the Judean Restoration", *Journal of Biblical Literature* 94 (1975) 4-18. See also C.G. TULAND, "Ezra-Nehemiah or Nehemiah-Ezra ? an Investigation into the Validity of the Van Hoonacker Theory", *Andrews University Seminary Studies* 12 (1974) 47-62.

conjectural emendation of 7th to 37th year of Artaxerxes (I) in Ezra 7,7, which would salvage the contemporaneity of Ezra and Nehemiah *tiršātā'*, indicated only and with controverted textual basis in Neh 8,9; 10,1.[13] This compromise has been widely accepted chiefly on the authority of Rudolph and Albright[14]. But it is firmly rejected in favor of 398 by Cazelles and Widengren[15]. This continuing controversy is of relevance here only as stressing the legitimate option between emendations: 37th in Ezra 7,7 or excising Nehemiah (with or without irrelevant *tiršātā'*) in Neh 8,9; 10,1.

c) We may be pardoned for having reprinted our essay here, partly because it appeared in a rather inaccessible Festschrift, and partly because it has nevertheless been cited more than our usual fate: generally without comment, never with acceptance. But David Noel Freedman and his fellow-editors have generously granted my day in court with the *Anchor Bible Dictionary*[16]. It is true that in the pages after my Ezra article another by Klein states that "North's severely negative view is refuted" in another survey by Klein[17]. With such a reaction I already had to express above my regretful agreement. Naturally his fair and courteous half-page does not reject *everything*, especially about Ezra; but I may regret also that he does not note

---

13   Aaron DEMSKY, "Who Came First, Ezra or Nehemiah ? The Synchronistic Approach", *Hebrew Union College Annual* 65 (1994) 1-20: contemporaneity can be saved by recognizing the use of two different calendars in the text. In "Who Returned First, Ezra or Nehemiah ?", *The Bible Review* 92,8 (1996) 23-33, Demsky specifies that Nehemiah, in the Babylonian month-system, preceded Ezra (Judah month-system) by only 2½ years.

14   W. RUDOLPH, *Esra und Nehemiah* (HAT I/20, 1949) 71; W.F. ALBRIGHT, "A Brief History of Judah from the Days of Josiah to Alexander the Great", *Biblical Archaeologist* 9 (1946) 13, renouncing *JBL* 46 (1921) 21; V. PAVLOVSKÝ, "Die Chronologie der Tätigkeit Esdras. Versuch einer neuen Lösung", *Biblica* 38 (1957) 257, 448. -- The original compromise-proposal for Ezra 7,8 was 27th; but it was quickly bypassed in favor of 37th.

15 Henri CAZELLES, "La mission d'Esdras", *Vetus Testamentum* 4 (1954) 113-140; Geo WIDENGREN, "The Persian period, 2A. The Chronological Order of Ezra and Nehemiah" in *Israelite and Judaean History, ed.* J.H. HAYES, J.M. MILLER (London 1977) (503-) 509.

16 R. NORTH, "Ezra (Person)", "Nehemiah (Person)", "Palestine: Postexilic Judean Officials", *AnchorBD* (NY 1992, Doubleday) 2, p.726-8; 4, p. 1068-71; 5, p.86-90.

17 Ralph W. KLEIN, "Ezra-Nehemiah, Books of", *AnchorBD* 2,735; and "Ezra and Nehemiah in Recent Studies", in Fest. G.E. WRIGHT, *Magnalia Dei: the Mighty Acts of God* (ed. F. CROSS; NY 1976, Doubleday; 361-376), p.365.

that the *pehām* on which he relies is generally admitted to be a form in need of emendation; the issue at stake was the legitimacy and freedom of option between alternative emendations in two texts.

d) In what follows we will try to discover what would be a possible *when* and *how* for the variously-claimed "invention of Hebrew" and compilation of our Bible in that language. We will first reexamine all we can know of the "Torah of Ezra" in his canonical books. Then we will consider the Greek First Esdras (apocryphal Third Ezra) and Josephus Flavius' exposition of it.

Next we will study the political situation in Persian Palestine which has recently been claimed to furnish indications of Ezra's activity not specified within canonical Ezra-Nehemiah. We will give consideration to Nodet's focus on Ezra and Nehemiah in a study really showing from Maccabees that our "Pentateuch *with sabbath*" is of origin four centuries after Ezra.

Naturally we must study apart the origins and history of medieval Jewish glorifications of Ezra's compilation of more than just the Torah, and their repercussions in Christian exegesis. Finally we will follow up the hint of Sirach that Ezra was uninfluential or unknown in 130 B.C., which some interpret to mean that only after that period our Bible was compiled by an activity linked to an Ezra who had existed only in some obscure way ("not at all", some say).

Our aim is *not* to prove or support any of the varying claims that Hebrew was a language never in daily-life use but "invented" for the compilation and preservation of our Bible. We aim rather to supply what we find missing in these contentions, "when" and "how" such a momentous event *could* most likely have taken place. Needless to say, *positive* indications will be hard or impossible to find; but it is relevant to show the *compatibility* of some life-situation(s) with the claim. Possibly it would be wiser to say "when and how its realization would have been least unlikely".

2. The "Torah" of Canonical Ezra and Assistant-Scribes

a) The principal text is Neh 8,1-3, "All the *'am* as one man ... said to Ezra the *sōpēr* to bring the *sēper* of the *tôrâ* of Moses, which YHWH commanded to Israel; and Ezra the priest brought the *tôrâ* before the *qāhāl* man and woman alike .. and he read in it at Watergate Square[18] from dawn until midday .."[19].

Then comes a list of six standing at his right and seven at his left (Neh 8,4). But only with Neh 8,7 comes, first a list of thirteen names all different except Maasseiah, then "*and* (H with justifying note; not in RSV attributing it to Vg 1 Esdras 9,48) the Levites explaining to the people (*mēbînîm hā-'am lᵉ-*) the *tôrâ* as they stood there (*wᵉ-hā-am 'al 'omdām*). The "explaining" is often claimed to consist in translating into popularly-used Aramaic the text which Ezra was presumably reading in Hebrew; but we may just as legitimately say that they gave in the dialect(s) of local use a paraphrase emphasizing chiefly the parts most relevant to the people's moral and ritual obligations.

"And *they* (8,8H noting 'he' as conjectural) read in the book, in the *tôrâ* of *Elohîm*, with explanation (*mᵉporaš* "being explained"; RSV "clearly"), and bringing insight (*wᵉ-śôm śekel*), for they (RSV 'the people' with H conjectured 'it/he') had understanding in the reading". This is followed immediately (Neh 8,9) by "And Nehemiah he (who was) *tiršātā'*, and [all bracketed in H as not in LXX] Ezra the priest the *sopēr*, and the Levites explaining to the people, said:" -- strangely nothing on fidelity to Torah, but only a warning not to mourn or fast but only to rejoice; so also the Levites (repeated) in Neh 9,11. Then in 9,13. "On the next day the heads of the [without *battê* 'houses of' as RSV] fathers for all the *'am*, [then not 'with' as RSV] the priests and the Levites gathered to Ezra the *sopēr*, and (H notes omitted in LXX Vg) to study (*haśkîl*) the matters (*dibrê*) of the Torah."

The above passages will serve also as basis for the "school of scribes" generally assumed to have assisted Ezra (doubtless already in

---

18 WILLIAMSON's *Word Commentary* p. 287 on Neh 8,1 (& 3,26) locates this Watergate reading-site *outside and facing* the Temple wall, citing prominently "In the choice of site we have Ezra's deliberate proclamation that the Torah was greater than the Temple and its sacrifices, indeed that the Torah as such was above anything it might contain" from H.L. ELLISON, *From Babylon to Bethlehem* (Exeter 1976, Paternoster) p.47 (xix) & his "The Importance of Ezra", *Evangelical Quarterly* 53 (1981) 48-53.

19 In the Ezra performance of Neh 8 "oral and literate aspects of culture intertwine", says Susan NIDITCH, *Oral World and Written Word* (Louisville 1996, Westminster-Knox) p. 105 & 134. --Dwight R. DANIELS, "The Composition of the Ezra-Nehemiah narrative", (also ed.) Fest. K. KOCH, *Ernten, was man sät* (Neukirchen 1991; 311-328) p.327 claims that Neh 8-11 (+ dubia) constitutes a third source differing from Ezra 7-10 and Neh 1-7 (+ varia); note also Shemaryahu TALMON, "Esra-Nehemia, Historiographie oder Theologie ?" in his *Israels Gedankenwelt* (Neukirchen 1995) 218-240.

Babylon[20]) in his "study and explanation of the Torah", whatever or wherever that was. But first we must survey the many insistent views as to what exactly is meant by "Torah of Moses" here. And first of all, this noun from *yārâ* is not properly "Law" in a pejoratively "legalistic" sense[21], but "teaching, guidance": in practice reserved for the guidance (including virtually all the activities or traditions) of Moses which we find in the Pentateuch.

    b) The word Torah (of Ezra) counted 8 times in Neh 8 cited above, occurs further in Neh 9,3.29, introducing or in a "public prayer" by Ezra (Neh 9,6), summarizing Israel's history not disapprovingly through Sinai, but quite reproachfully in verses 16-37[22]. The final verse 38 (to improve things) abruptly proposes a covenant to be signed. This chapter 9 is regarded plausibly by many but not by all as continuing chapter 8. But the verse abruptly proposing a covenant in our Neh 9,38 is Neh 10,1 in the Hebrew; and in 10,2 (our 10,1) is signed not by Ezra at all, but by Nehemiah (*tiršātā'*, bracketed in H as not in LXX) and a long long list of others.

    This Neh 10 further uses *torâ* in the Hebrew verses 29, 30, 35, 37

---

20 Though with no special attention to scribal activity, the highly original and up-to-date essay of Gianluigi PRATO, "Babilonia terra d'esilio e centro propulsore dell'ebraismo. Un fenomeno di dissociazione valutativa", in Fest. C.M. MARTINI, *La parola di Dio cresceva (At 12,24)*, ed. Rinaldo FABRIS (RivB supp. 33; Bologna 1998, Dehoniane; 57-76) strongly hints that the whole of Israelite history was *composed* in the era of "return to Judah", not only from Babylon where Judahites had been quite comfortably installed both before and during the "exile", but also from Egypt (the so-called "first" Exodus really contemporaneous! p.74); and the goal of writing this history was to make clear "behind the screen of Persian rule in Judah" (p.65) the shape which Jewish life had really been developing in Babylonia -- a goal notably different from Davies' above-noted (p. 96) "writing of history from scratch" to aggrandize salaried scribes and their Persian-enforced creation of a new "Judahite" identity for forced immigrants from many or any lands, hardly any if any "returnees to Judah" at all.

21 K. G. HOGLUND, *Achaemenid Imperial Administration* (1992) 226 says that Ezra 7,10 shows "the largely legal character of the mission". But see "Die Unterweisung im Gesetz" in Joachim BECKER, *Esra/Nehemia*: Neue Echter-Bibel (Würzburg 1990) p. 88; and Moshe GREENBERG, "Three Conceptions of Torah in the Hebrew Scriptures", in the *Festschrift R. Rendtorff* (Neukirchen 1990) 365-378.

22 Maurice GILBERT, "La place de la Loi dans la prière de Néhémie 9", in Fest. H. CAZELLES, *De la Torah au Messie*, ed. M. CARREZ (Paris 1981; 307-316), p. 315: Other biblical confessions speak of sins against YHWH rather than against Torah; here in verse 29 the Prophets have tried to draw the people back to Torah.

(our 28 ..) for specific details commanded; thus also Neh 12,44 [and 13,(?1.)3 below]. In Ezra 3,2 it is in relation to Jeshua. But in Ezra 7,6.10 it is used for Ezra himself more or less as in Neh 8.

In Ezra 10,3 very significantly we have precisely what is missing to avoid the abruptness after Neh 9,37 and 10,1H (= our 9,38): Shecaniah proposes to make then and there a *covenant* for the better observance of Torah[23]. But this proposal is specifically in view of the prevalence of mixed marriages announced to Ezra by unnamed authorities in Ezra 9,1; provoking his violent reaction in Ezra 9,3; but then in Ezra 9,6-11 a calmer public prayer addressed to God (much as in Neh 9,5-39); and In Ezra 9,12-15 is outlined a methodical program (with brief shifts from second person singular for God to plural for the offenders in verse 12 and first person plural in verse 13 and 14).

Thus this proposed covenant is not so much related to Neh 10,1H as to Neh 13,25. In 13,1 anonymously there had been "read in the *book* (+ LXX 'of the Torah') of Moses" that the *qāhāl* should admit no one of Moab (Num 22,3) or Ammon"; and "upon hearing the *torâ*" they (also anonymous; LXX passive) separated *every* 'mix' (Neh 13,3 '*ēreb* = 'alien' ? or 'foreign spouse'); nevertheless in Neh 13,22-27 Nehemiah reacts violently against some who had spouses of Ashdod[24], Ammon, or Moab, "pummeling them and pulling their hair" and forces them to an oath (Neh 13,25 = ? covenant). All these occurrences of a Torah covenant/oath are immensely disputed as to the chronology of Nehemiah himself or in his relation to Ezra, but we must bypass this as really adding nothing to what is meant by "Ezra's Torah".

c) But of further importance for determining the Torah-activities of Ezra is *dat* in Ezra 8,36 (a single occurrence as against some 20 in Esther), plus Ezra 7,12.14.21.25.26 in the cited Aramaic letter of Artaxerxes (and 8 times in Aramaic Daniel). Though *dat* is the modern Hebrew word for "religion", it seems to be a Persian loan-word for decree ("law for a special

---

23 Dennis J MCCARTHY, "Covenant and Law in Chronicles-Nehemiah", *Catholic Biblical Quarterly* 44 (1982) 23-44; F. Charles FENSHAM, "Covenant, Promise and Expectation in the Bible", *Theologische Zeitschrift* 23 (1967) 305-322 & *The Books of Ezra and Nehemiah*: NICOT (Grand Rapids 1982, Eerdmans).

24 André LEMAIRE, "Ashdodien et Judéen à l'époque perse: Ne 13,24" in Fest. É. LIPIŃSKI, *Immigration and Emigration within the Ancient Near East* (Orientalia Lovaniensia Analecta 65, Louvain 1995) 153-163.

situation"; thus in Ezra 8,36)[25]. In the Aramaic letter it seems to mean a more generalized "Law" (of the Eloh of heaven) equivalent to *torâ*.

Special attention is merited by Ezra 7,14, the law (of Ezra's God) which is in Ezra's hand, and the variant 7,25, the wisdom of Ezra's God, also in Ezra's hand[26]. Though "in your hand" in itself may well mean "at your disposition, available to you", still in our discussion of what exactly "Ezra's Torah" means, it might seem more obvious to take it as "a copy or scroll", perhaps even a "master-scroll" of the Torah which Ezra is concretely carrying[27].

----

d) From all these textual data, what conclusion is to be drawn as to what ultimately was the contents of "his" Torah which Ezra read to the people, studied, and used as the basis of his reforms ? There are four principal possibilities[28]. i) The Pentateuch or much or most of it as we know it in our Bibles; ii) Deuteronomy alone[29]; some say the deuteronomic code,

---

25 Rolf RENDTORFF, "Esra und das 'Gesetz'", *ZAW* 96 (1984; 165-184) p.166: *dat* in Ezra 7,12 is a *royal* law, wrongly presumed equal to *torâ* of Neh 8; p.172, Ezra was an *official* sent to *investigate*; p.179, his role in Neh 8 is entirely different.

26 Peter FREI, "Die persische Reichsautorisation [Esra 7,12-26; Neh 11,23f], ein Überblick", *Zeitschrift für altorientalische und biblische Rechtsgeschichte* 1 (1995) 1-35; further 36-46, Josef WIESEHÖFER, & 47-61, Udo RÜTERSWÖRDEN. -- On the villages in the Nehemiah passage, see Pierre BRIANT, "Villages et communautés villageoises d'Asie achéménide et hellénistique", *JESHO* 18 (1975) 165-188.

27 The book with the Law of Moses "was certainly a papyrus roll which Ezra had brought from Babylon", says Werner DOMMERSHAUSEN, *Im Schatten des Tempels: Esra, Nehemia* (Kl.Kommentar AT 8; Stuttgart 1974) p. 41, though papyrus is normally found in sheets, and rolls or scrolls are made of skins.

28 (J.M. MILLER -), John H. HAYES [sole author of Persian era ch.14 (p.20)], *A History of Ancient Israel and Judah* (Philadelphia 1986, Westminster) 473; Derek KIDNER. *Ezra and Nehemiah* (Tyndale OT, Leicester 1979) 158-164 Appendix: Ezra's Book of the Law.

29 Only Deuteronomy; no narrative material: U. KELLERMANN, "Erwägungen zum Esragesetz", *ZAW* 80 (1968) 273-385, rejected In WILLIAMSON's *Ezra-Nehemiah* (1985) p. xxxvii. -- Now Frank CRÜSEMANN, *The Torah: Theology and Social History of OT Law* (Kaiser 1992), tr. Allan W. MAHNKE (NY 1996, Fortress) holds that a "Torah given on Sinai" was a post-deuteronomic innovation; our Pentateuch is a compilation of originally competing legal corpora, produced in the context of Persian governmental authorization by a coalition of debtors and priests.

but not commonly what has been known since Noth as the "deuteronomist history"[30]; iii) P alone, the priestly Pentateuch framework (which by many is maintained to be the specific contribution of Ezra) including H(oliness-Code)[31]; iv) none of the above, but an otherwise-unattested collection of laws similar to those in various places of our Bible[32].

The first of these options, the Pentateuch, is more suited than the others to the search for a "when and how" of a compilation of the Bible (in a new language). But we must not leave out of account Mowinckel's insistence that it was not a law "promulgated" by Ezra or "new" in Judah. We may admit, however, that the some-six hours of Ezra's reading in Neh 8,3 was not long enough to read the *whole* Pentateuch; "selected parts" can suffice for our purpose.

A more grave objection remains. Within the domain of historico-critical exegesis (as distinct from medieval teachings) no one seems to have raised the question of whether "Ezra's Torah-study" may have included *more* than the whole Pentateuch. Also never considered is the possibility that the D of the Pentateuch might have trailed along the whole of Noth's deuterono-mist (indeed Sacchi in a Rome lecture claimed that if you go backward from 2 Kgs 15,30 you find no real break in narrative-development until Gen 1,1!).

---

30 D + E, according to H. CAZELLES, "La mission d'Esdras", *Vetus Testamentum* 4 (1954; 115-140) p.139; "in 398 the Persian court, having lost Egypt, in order to use the Palestine Jewish Community as it had used Elephantine, gives full power to a priest, Ezra". -- D. KRAEMER, "On the Relationship of Ezra and Nehemiah" [competing candidates for the role of founder of Judaism], *JSOT* 59 (1993; 73-92) p. 87: Ezra's view of the Torah in Nehemiah differs radically from his view in the Ezra-book.

31 Sigmund MOWINCKEL, *Studien zu dem Buche Ezra-Nehemiah, III. Die Ezrageschichte und das Gesetz Moses* (Norsk Videnskaps Akademi 2/7, Oslo 1965) p. 126, not a hitherto unknown law compiled by Ezra; but (p.140) the Pentateuch, including D, P, and H, as known and followed already in Judah, but not identical in every detail. -- Klaus KOCH, "Ezra and the Origins of Judaism", *Journal of Semitic Studies* 19 (1979; 173-197), p.180, "*None* of the allusions in the Ezra record fit entirely any of the laws of the canonical Torah"; (p.181) Ezra's law was not a new one but included P; the author was not Ezra but a powerful pressure-group.

32 So C. HOUTMAN, "Ezra and the Law: Observations on the Supposed Relation between Ezra and the Pentateuch", in 1980 meeting. *Remembering All the Way, Oudtestamentische Studiën* 21 (1981; 90-115) 109, following B.D. EERDMANS, "Ezra and the Priestly Code", *Expositor* 7/10 (1910) 306-326; and G. HÖLSCHER, *Die Bücher Esra und Nehemia*[4] (HSAT: Tübingen 1923) 501; 542. -- See now David M. CARR, "Controversy and Convergence: Recent Studies on the Formation of the Pentateuch", *Religious Studies Review* 23 (1997) 22-32.

Further there might be question of Chronicles, so involved with both this deuteronomist Pentateuch and (for some still) with Ezra-Nehemiah. The Psalms at any rate would seem relevant[33]. There is possibility of some early Proverbs. All this more than doubling the volume of "Ezra's Torah" is not intended as a *reductio ad absurdum*, because precisely *all* these are tacitly envisioned in every one of the "invented language" approaches surveyed above and vaguely linked with the Ezra-era ("his 'changing the style of writing' (*b. Sanh.* 21-22) may owe as much to later tradition as to biblical interpretation"[34]). Davies (p. 97 above) perforce adds even the whole massive Prophets corpus, though in a section apart.

Is this to say that thus the Ezra-school compiled our whole Bible ?[35] Such was in fact a Renaissance view which we will examine presently. As for Qohelet and Daniel, now held to be of Hellenistic origin, and the Ezra-books themselves along with Job, in a modern critical outlook they will either suggest that the compilation attributed to Ezra really originated two centuries later, or at least will certainly call for some explaining apart.

----

e) As noted above, in Neh 8,4-7 the three lists of names of those closely associated with Ezra in his presentation of the Torah would seem to

---

33 Samuel E. BALENTINE, "The Politics of Religion in the Persian Period", Fest. Rex MASON, *After the Exile*, ed. John BARTON & David J. REIMER (Macon GA 1996; 129-146) p.133 & 139, in developing his claim that the biblical people in realistic awareness of Persian power had to create for itself an entirely new life-style, emphasizes the Psalms as a large component of their new piety. -- Erich ZENGER, "Der jüdische Psalter -- ein anti-imperiales Buch ?", in *Religion und Gesellschaft. Studien zu ihrer Wechselbeziehung in den Kulturen des Antiken Vorderen Orients*, ed. Rainer ALBERTZ (1995 Münster AZERKAVO meeting: *AOAT* 248, Münster 1997; 95-108) p. 96 "The Psalms can be called the prayerful making one's own of the Torah and the Prophets"; p. 104, "In the first psalm cannot be missed the allusion to Dt 17,14-20 describing the ideal king as 'scholar of the Torah'".

34 H. G. M. WILLIAMSON, "Ezra and Nehemiah, Books of", *Dictionary of Biblical Interpretation* 1, ed. John H. HAYES (Nashville 1999, Abingdon) 376.

35 "After the catastrophe of 587 B.C.E., Israel compiled, edited, and used the Scriptures. As far as we know, the composition of the Hebrew Scriptures was the first tentative act to build a whole community around the written 'Word of God' ... from the collaboration of a class of scribes and interpreters", says Erhard S. GERSTENBERGER, "The Religion and Institutions of Ancient Israel: Toward a Contextual Theology of the Scriptures", in Fest. Gene TUCKER, *OT Interpretation, Past, Present, and Future*, ed. J. MAYS (Edinburgh 1995; 261-276), p.273.

indicate "scribal assistants", chosen not merely as competent "explainers" or Aramaic paraphrasers for here and now, but because they had been intimately involved for a long time in Ezra's own procedures in his study and use of the Torah[36]. It may be cautiously added that *if* Ezra's work was really the uniting together of various scroll-fragments and supplying from oral traditions the connectives or transitions which were lacking, then his "school of scribal assistants" may or must be assumed to have had a fairly large part in the process. But that is a very big "if", and in trying to justify this view as already cited from Jerome and Bellarmine, we will have to face the relevance of Third Ezra and Josephus, and then make some effort to sift out the grain of truth in the heroically large role assigned to Ezra by medieval Judaism.

3. Third Ezra and Josephus

a) In the Septuagint the four books about Ezra have in first place what it calls First Esdras (Esdras-*a*'), nowadays usually Third Ezra following the Vulgate. It is a longer narrative, from brief mention of Josiah to a long fictionalized story about Zerubbabel, then a full account of Ezra as in canonical Ezra plus Nehemiah 8. Hanhart's edition of Septuagint Esdras I

---

36 Some fresh observations on the relation of scribes to *libraries* emerge in Thomas L. THOMPSON, "Text, Context and Referent in Israelite Historiography", in *The Fabric of History: Text, Artifact and Israel's Past*, ed. Diana V. EDELMAN: *JSOT* supp. 127 (Sheffield 1991; 65=92) p.78, citing E.A. KNAUF ("*Midian*") to whom is due also the preceding p.26-64, "From History to Interpretation". -- Cristine SCHAMS, *Jewish Scribes in the Second-Temple Period* (diss. dir. M. GOODMAN): *JSOT*.s 291 (Sheffield 1998) [mentioning on p.32 A. SALDARINI, *Pharisees, Scribes and Sadducees* (Edinburgh 1989, Clark) as the best of many studies so far]: only pp. 46-59 on Ezra-Neh, mostly on the narrative "history", dubiously reliable according to L.L. GRABBE, "Reconstructing History from the Book of Ezra", in *Second Temple Studies I*, ed. P. DAVIES (*JSOT*.s 117, 1991) p.104. -- R.H. PFEIFFER, "Ezra / Ezra and Nehemiah", *Interpreter's Dictionary of the Bible 2* (Nashville 1962, Abingdon; 214-9) 219: Ezra was really the first of the scribes, a group known only after 400 to the Chronicler ['whose authorship of Ezra is now certain', p.218 now outdated; not really rectified in the Supplement vol. 5 (1976) 156-8 "Chronicles, 1. The question of unity: I-II Chronicles, Ezra, Nehemiah" by P.R. ACKROYD, nor in 317-328 "Ezra and Nehemiah" by S. TALMON, who at least mentions in his bibliography S. JAPHET, "The Supposed Common Authorship of Chronicles and Ezra-Nehemiah Investigated Anew", *Vetus Testamentum* 18 (1968) 330-371]. But some "rearrangements" will prove needless if Ezra-N is seen as the conclusion of Chromicles, still insists A.H.J. GUNNEWEG, "Zur Interpretation der Bücher Esra und Nehemia. Zugleich ein Beitrag zur Methode der Exegese", *VTS* 32 (1981) 146-161.

gives this table of correspondences[37]:

1,1-55 = 2 Chr 35,1-36,21	3,1-5,4 [unused]
2,1-3 = Ezra 1,1-3 (= Chr)	5,7-70 = Ezra 2,1-4,4
2,4-14 = Ezra 1,4-11	6,1-9,38 = Ezra 5,1-10,44
2,15-35 = Ezra 4,7-24	9,37-55 = Neh 7,72-8,12

Third Greek Esdras corresponds to canonical Nehemiah, while Fourth Esdras is an apocalypse from some centuries later. Both First and Fourth Esdras are given as an appendix in some editions of the Vulgate, though not considered even deuterocanonical[38].

b) Eskenazi maintains that Third Ezra was put together, but as an independent work, by the Chronicler from already existing canonical Ezra and Nehemiah, in order to adjust their theology to his own[39]. The lengthier study of Pohlmann seems to make out that Third Ezra, without its beginning and ending which have been lost, was put together from Ezra-Nehemiah (with editing) as the original conclusion of Chronicles[40]. In his self-defense against these views (Eskenazi only in a late-coming footnote), Williamson maintains as the *only* alternative that Third Ezra is practically complete as it stands, and drawn from Chr-Ezr-Neh[41].

But perhaps because Josephus Flavius follows (except occasionally) Third Ezra, some maintain that our canonical Ezra and Nehemiah (= LXX Second and Third Esdras) are summarized and adapted from Third Ezra (=

---

37 Robert HANHART, *Esdras I*: Göttingen 1993, p. 54 [his *Esdras II* (1993) includes the canonical Ezra and Nehemiah in 23 chapters].

38 Jacob M. MYERS, *1 and 2 Esdras*: Anchor Bible 42 (Doubleday 1974) gives a translation and commentary on Third Ezra (along with Fourth Ezra = 2 Esdras), distinct from his commentary on *Ezra and Nehemiah*: Anchor Bible 12, 1965.

39 Tamara C. ESKENAZI, "The Chronicler and the Composition of 1 Esdras", *Catholic Biblical Quarterly* 48 (1986) 39-61. The French text of M. CARREZ, "1. Esdras Septante" in *Revue d'Histoire et de Philosophie Religieuses* 74 (1994) 11-42 holds it is based on canonical Ezra-Neh where these existed in Hebrew.

40 K.-F. POHLMANN, *Studien zum dritten Esra. Ein Beitrag zur Frage nach dem ursprünglichen Schluss des chronistischen Geschichtswerkes* (*FRLANT* 104, Göttingen 1970, Vandenhoeck & Ruprecht) p.72.

41 H.G.M. WILLIAMSON, "The Problem with First Esdras", in Fest. Rex MASON, *After the Exile*, ed. J. BARTON & D.J. REIMER (Macon 1996, Mercer Univ; 201-216) p.231.

First Esdras). This is the view of Sacchi, whose informative exposition we may thus summarize.

c) Third Ezra must have been written after Chronicles but before the Ezra parts of Nehemiah. These in turn precede Josephus, because from them he draws the view of Ezra and Nehemiah collaborating, but he innovatingly imputes to them a similar ideology. Third Ezra takes its start from 2 Chronicles Josiah, not from his covenant 34,11-43 but from his immediately following Passover (35,1)[42].

Third Ezra never uses the word covenant (*bᵉrît* in 8,90, though taken over in canonical Ezra 10,3, means "oath"), but aims to show the continuity of the true cultus from Josiah through Zerubbabel's (famous "Truth prevails" contest and) Temple to Ezra. Third Ezra has in common with Nehemiah only xenophobia, not Temple and Law of a Deuteronomic lay and covenant Judaism. In both Third Ezra and canonical Ezra the figure of Ezra represents rather the P-strand emphasis on cultus.

Thus Third Ezra (and presumably the Nehemiah memoir -- (? including chapters 8 f) -- must have been written before Maccabees during a period when Ezra could fall into oblivion because his work was merely an *esasperazione* of Nehemiah's (p.469). Sacchi does not seem to hazard date-parameters for canonical Ezra other than that he had become important as making the "absolute value of the Law autonomous vis-à-vis the State" so that numerous apocrypha appeared under his patronage in the 1st-2d centuries C.E. Perhaps thereby Sacchi wished tacitly to leave room for aspects of the "Ezra never existed" view of Garbini (below), with whom he had said he was in partial unspecified agreement.

d)   The relevance of Josephus Flavius has often been treated separately. A separate Josephus portrait for Ezra has been given by Feldman[43].

---

42 Paolo SACCHI, "La questione di Ezra", in Fest. A. VIVIAN, *Wᵉ-zo't lᵉ-Angelo, raccolta di studi giudaici*, ed. Giulio BUSI (AISG Testi e Studi 11; Bologna 1993; 461-470) p. 465.

43 Louis H. FELDMAN,"Josephus' Portrait of Ezra", *Vetus Testamentum* 43 (1993) 190-214: Josephus diminishes Ezra's importance; his mission is chiefly a political support of the Persians in view of the Delian threat; but to Ezra 7,26 is added in Ant 11,30 the interesting observation that "ignorance of the law is no excuse." -- Lester L. GRABBE, "Josephus and the Reconstruction of the Judean Restoration", *Journal of Biblical Literature* 109 (1987) 231-246: reserves on CROSS (ftn. 12), revision of the high-priest list from newly-found inscriptions.

It is only from Josephus, whether from sources or from his own pious imagination, that we learn anything at all about the later career and death of an Ezra serenely conscious of having done his duty and accomplished his mission[44].

Many researchers maintain, however, chiefly from a comparison with the bombastic successes of Nehemiah, that Ezra is hinted in the canonical books to have really failed in his goals and therefore to have fallen quietly into a deserved oblivion. (Even Nehemiah is claimed to have been not so successful as he shows himself: to the extent that his "Babylon vacation" of Neh 7,1 was really a "diplomatic recall" to Susa to render an account of why he had failed to serve Persian interests adequately.)

Feldman tends to stress that Josephus indicates his own viewpoint more by what he omits than by that he adds; so far forth, not much help can be expected from him in expanding our view of what Torah may have meant as "utilized" in the time of Ezra. But the researches to which we now turn often find some detail in Josephus to press in favor of their own thesis.

4. "Proxy-data" as to What was Really Happening in Judah

a) "So little is known about the social and historical background of the early Second Temple period that many scholars have recourse to ideologically constructed social structures often drawn from the classical world. This technique involves using what is sometimes called 'proxy-data'"[45]. In fact, perhaps more recently, many contributions deplore the one-sided use of the

---

44 *Antiquities* 11,158. "He was buried with great magnificence in Jerusalem", Ralph MARCUS gives in his Loeb translation (Harvard 1966 = 1937) vol.6, p.391; but his note adds that Ezra died in Persia according to GINZBERG's *Legends of the Jews*, vol.4, p.358 & vol.6, p.446. -- Of Nehemiah *Ant.* 11,183 says only "he died at an advanced age .. and left the walls of Jerusalem as his eternal monument"; but on Nehemiah's "recall" to Susa to justify his failures, see Kent H. RICHARDS, "Re-Shaping Chronicles and Ezra", in *Gene M. Tucker Festschrift*, ed. J.L. MAYES (→ ftn. 36 above; Edinburgh 1995, Clark; 211-224) p. 220.

45 Robert P. CARROLL, "Textual Strategies and Ideology in the Second Temple Period", in *Second Temple Studies 1. Persian Period*, ed. Philip R. DAVIES (JSOT supp.117; Sheffield 1991; 108-124) p. 109 and note 1, citing H. KREISSIG 1978, H.G. KIPPENBERG 1978 and ed. 1977; G.E.M. DE STE CROIX 1981; and adding in the next note "This is not the place for a critique of 'proxy-data' and the Marxian approaches to biblical studies".

readable and easily-accessible classical data as against computerized geo-archeology[46].

The flood of new books and collections favoring for Ezra-era Judah a more socio-economic approach, drawing in more largely the Persian power-centers and coastal satrapies, seems to bear largely the imprint of Tamara Eskenazi, though she herself points to Ackroyd as the pioneer[47]. More commonly perhaps that title is accorded to Weinberg for his "Citizen-Temple Community"[48]. Eskenazi's doctorate describes how the *people themselves*, not any cultic or political officials, really initiate and carry through the reforms indicated in Ezra-Nehemiah[49]. Thus we have in her work both a truly sociological orientation (perhaps paradoxically subtitled "a literary approach") and its quite-original application in a concrete case, the breakthrough of democracy. This is also, cautiously in accord with its Soviet background, the drift of Weinberg's citizen-temple community. A place apart

---

46 Josette ELAYI and Jean SAPIN, "Reading the Textual Sources Another Way", in their *Beyond the River; New Perspectives on Transeuphratene* (1991; tr. J. Edward CROWLEY: JSOT supp. 250, Sheffield 1998; 97-109; p.107: "Scribes like Ezra were additive. recapitulative"); p. 101 twice praises the *access* of CTESIAS to both Tyrian and Persian archives [though whether and how he ever *used* this access is usually judged negatively]. To the objection that classical sources have been used up dry, on p. 102 is cited P. BRIANT, *Rois, tributs et paysans* (Paris 1982) p.491: "It is sometimes not so much the sources themselves as the ability of the historians to ask questions that is threatened by exhaustion". See now Briant's *Histoire de l'Empire perse de Cyrus à Alexandre* (Paris 1996, Fayard).

47 Tamara C. ESKENAZI. "Current Perspectives on Ezra-Nehemiah and the Persian Period", *Currents in Research, Biblical* 1 (1993; 59-86) p.60: Peter R. ACKROYD, "A Subject People: Judah under Persian Rule" (1984) in his *The Chronicler in his Age* (JSOT supp. 101, Sheffield 1991; 188-238); his p. 200 notes that biblical-era Persia was not all-and-only good, nor Babylon all bad; and p. 283 protests against regarding a Torah-oriented community as thereby "legalistic". On F. M. CROSS, "Reconstruction" see ftn. 12 above.

48 Joel WEINBERG, *The Citizen-Temple Community* [→ ftn. 10 above: 7 articles from 1972-7], tr. Daniel L. (CHRISTOPHER-)SMITH: *SOTS* supp. 151. Sheffield 1992. Compare Edward LIPIŃSKI, ed., *State and Temple Economy in the Ancient Near East* I-II (Orientalia Lovaniensia Analecta 5 (Louvain 1979, Univ.); Pauline A. VIVIANO, "Ezra and Nehemiah in Sociological Perspective", *The Bible Today* 37 (1999) 207 f.

49 Tamara C, ESKENAZI, *In an Age of Prose; a Literary Approach to Ezra-Nehemiah:* SBL Monograph 36. Atlanta 1988, Scholars. -- A similar view seems to underlie the explanation of single relevant verses in the earlier H.G.M. WILLLIAMSON, *Ezra, Nehemiah* (Word Biblical Commentary 16, Waco 1985) e.g. p.288. Both authors maintain that Ezra-Nehemiah are a single unit not due to the Chronicler.

should be reserved for the massive compilation of the several-years' Groningen seminar[50].

"Now for the first time we have two distinct groups [indigenous/ returnees] both claiming to be the genuine heirs of the Israel destroyed"[51]. This raises the everlasting question of whether the indigenous are really the *'am hā-āres,* "the people of the land", and whether they are really landless expropriates after a Persian land-handout to the returnees[52]. Do these really henceforth constitute "classes" in a class-struggle?[53]   We have here a striking example of social change to be coped with[54].   And it is also a challenge to the functioning of a new style of empire[55].

But in many of the articles and compilations of this sort, the emphasis seems to be on repeating again and again from every angle the legitimacy of the socioeconomic-geophysical orientation. A new and original

---

50 Heleen SANCISI-WEERDENBURG & Amélie KUHRT, eds., *Achaemenid History*, especially 6. *Asia Minor and Egypt; Old Cultures in a New Empire*, Leiden 1991.

51 J. BLENKINSOPP, "The 'Servant of the Lord' in Third Isaiah: Profile of a Pietistic Group in the Persian Epoch", in *"The Place is Too Small for us": the Israelite Prophets in Recent Scholarship*, ed. Robert P. GORDON (Winona Lake IN 1995, Eisenbrauns; 392-412) p. 394 on Ezra 9 f. -- More general: E.J. HOPPE, "The Restoration of Judah" & Rachel DULIN, "The Leaders of the Restoration", *The Bible Today* 24 (1986) 281-6 & 287-291.

52 D.J. SMITH, "A Materialist Theory of the Post-Exilic *bēt ābôt*", in his *The Religion of the Landless; the Social Context of the Babylonian Exile* (Bloomington IN 1989, Meyer Stone) p.116. -- R. CARROLL's "Textual Strategies" in *Second Temple Studies* 1 cited above (ftn. 45; 1991) p. 115 f singles out Jer 32 rebuying his own land as a "textual strategy", helping to enforce the [returnees'] ideological claim to land [given by Babylon in 587 to the poor left in Judah]; similarly Lev 25,23, "the land is YHWH's". -- H. KREISSIG, *Wirtschaft und Gesellschaft im Seleukidenreich: Die Eigentums- und die Abhängigkeitsverhältnisse* (Berlin 1978, Akademie).

53   H.G. KIPPENBERG, *Religion und Klassenbildung im antiken Judäa.   Eine religionssoziologische Studie zur Verhältnis von Tradition und gesellschaftlicher Entwicklung* (Göttingen 1978, Vandenhoeck) and ed. *Die Entstehung der antiken Klassengesellschaft* (Frankfurt 1977, Suhrkamp). -- Less proximately, G.E.M. DE STE CROIX, *The Class Struggle in the Ancient Greek World* (London 1981, Duckworth).

54 K. TOLLEFSON, "Nehemiah, Model for Change Agents; a Social Science Approach to Scripture", *Council for the Study of Religion* 15 (1986) 124 f.

55 N.S. EISENSTADT, *The Political Systems of Empires*; NY 1963, Glencoe Free Press. -- M.A. DANDAMAEV, *A   Critical History of the Achaemenid Empire*; Leiden 1989, Brill; Heidemarie KOCH, *Achämeniden-Studien*; Wiesbaden 1995, Harrassowitz.

application to some concrete case is rare, except sometimes aiming at refutation of Weinberg[56]. Even the Ionic revolt and Udjahorresnet offered as "new light" on the Ezra-book data have really been with us for a good while[57]. Of course it is natural that each separate author should wish to justify fully her or his own methodological position before hoping to get around eventually to concrete cases[58].

  b) We must recall here that we are seeking here not such "proxy-data" as are applicable to *any* concrete case of the Persian period, but only what would seem to indicate a likely or likeliest time and place for the alleged putting of our Bible into an "invented" language. Philip Davies subscribes fully (though briefly and only on the basis of Knauf) to this occurrence, as a relatively small part of the socioeconomic importance of scribal activity in the Persian period. In fact his scribes salaried by and in the interests of the Achaemenid regime invented not only Biblical Hebrew as a language, but also the whole of "Israel's history" which had really never existed[59].

---

56 We may add Paul L. REDDITT, "The Postexilic Community during the Persian Period", in his "Nehemiah's First Mission and the Date of Zechariah 9-14", *Catholic Biblical Quarterly* 56 (1994; 664-678) p. 670; and Ira SHARKANSKY, *Israel and its Bible: a Political Analysis*: Garland Social Sciences 1031, NY 1996:

57 On the ill-starred Inarus → p. 157-9 below. -- Joseph BLENKINSOPP, "The Mission of Udjahorresnet and those of Ezra and Nehemiah", *Journal of Biblical Literature* 106 (1987) 409-421 [F.K. KIENITZ, *Die politische Geschichte Ägyptens 7.-4.Jh.* (Berlin 1953, Akademie) 61: Udja-Hor came from Elam to restore Egypt's temples]. -- M. HELTZER, "Nehemiah 11,24 and the Provincial Representative at the Persian Royal Court" [Petahiah compared to Udjahorresnet and the Greek Histiaios Arlissis], *Transeuphratène* 8 (1991/4) 109-121; see also his "The Social and Fiscal Reforms of Nehemiah in Judah and the Attitude of the Achaemenid Kings to the Internal Affairs of the Autonomous Province", *Apollinaris* 62 (1989) 335-355.

58 In Philip R. DAVIES, ed., *Second Temple Studies I. Persian Period* (*JSOT* supp. 117, Sheffield 1991) half the essays are a critique of the others; notably trenchant is Peter R. BEDFORD, "On Models and Texts" 154-162; p. 155 on (proxy-text) evaluating of the Jerusalem Temple from temples of the period elsewhere. -- More concrete cases, though (except GRABBE) not very relevant to our present search, are in ESKENAZI & Kent H. RICHARDS, eds., *Second Temple Studies 2. Temple Community in the Persian Period* (*JSOT* supp. 175, 1994).

59 Philip R. DAVIES, *In Search of "Ancient Israel"* (JSOT supp 148, Sheffield 1992) ch.6, p.94-112, "Who Wrote the Biblical Literature. and Where ?", and ch.7, p.113-133, "How was the Biblical Literature Written, and Why?", set forth briefly above on p. 95-98. Perhaps more relevant to the present generalized setting is his ch.5, "The Social Context of the Biblical

As we noted above, Davies presents this part of his book not as a "working hypothesis" but simply as a "heuristic narrative", but it is hard to escape the conviction that for him this is pretty much the way things really happened. At any rate his observations about vigorous scribality amid a negligibly tiny reading public form a legitimate part of the "proxy-data" which we are trying to find out how to incorporate into our search. But be it noted that we are seeking, not by any means materials either to defend or to attack his "un-hypothesis", but rather what is relevant to *any* of the very diverse approaches outlined above toward putting into an "invented" language an *existing* history, whether completely or only fragmentarily already written or still partly oral.

An immense expense and Persian government intervention would have been required for the training and salary of the many schools of scribes needed to create from scratch a five-to-ten century history for the forced immigrants, not all ("if any", Davies queries) Judeans from Babylonia, into whom the regime wished to instill a sense of century-old identity and unity -- even apart from using a newly-created language for the purpose. This latter job alone could have been done much more easily and cheaply by a small Ezra synagogue-school type of scribes, especially if there was question at first only of the Torah, with the Psalms and other Writings and Prophets continuing on, possibly even for a century or more.

Amid the flood of far more generalized Persian-era data which we have tried to survey above, Davies undoubtedly plays a much more important role than we have been able to indicate. For one thing, he is co-editor of the thriving *JSOT* supplements in which have appeared cited works of Weinberg, Eskenazi, and others. For another, he has written numerous articles not

---

Israel" which is really an effort to retrieve the earliest occurrence of the name and the polity "Israel" as they were perceived in the living-conditions of the Ezra-era when their history is claimed to have begun.

-- Note now Keith W. WHITELAM, *The Invention of Ancient Israel: the Silencing of Palestine History* (NY 1996, Routledge) and its review by N.P. LEMCHE, *Scandinavian Journal of the OT* 10 (1996) 88-114; and p. 3-15 there, Thomas M. BOLIN, "When the End is the Beginning: the Persian Period and the Origins of the Biblical Tradition".

-- Further Iain W. PROVAN, "Ideologies, Literary and Critical Reflections on the History of Israel", *Journal of Biblical Literature* 114 (1995) 585-606, on T. THOMPSON [reply "A Neo-Albrightian School ?" p.683-698] and Davies [from whose *Search* p.13 is accepted on p. 599, "No history is ever an innocent representation of the outside world"] p. 699-705.

mentioned here but relevant to our theme[60]. Indeed he has been interviewed and cited as spokesman for the reductive biblical history school hitherto linked chiefly to the names of Lemche and Thompson. So it must come as a surprise that we have so far found nothing in other writings of Davies which help much toward *our* inquiry as distinct from his *Search for "Ancient Judaism"*.

c) "The composition of the *Jehuda* Torah and Persian politics" is the highly relevant title of the third chapter in Blum's recent momentous work on the Pentateuch[61]. "Ezra's pentateuch", Persian-promoted (Ezra 7,25), basically the unified liberation-story of Ex-Num, ended up as a compromise between a heavily lay-edited D tradition (with scarce mention of the J or E which it largely included); and a strong but inner-conflicting P counter-affirmation of priestly privileges. (Other insertions were made still later, such as Lohfink's "God your healer", Ex 15,26, our p.32 above).

Following Blum faithfully, but in the perspective of a whole history of Israelite religion from the origins to the Maccabees, is Albertz' ch.5.31, "The canonization of the Torah and the Persian imperial organization". He fully accepts Frei's "imperial authorization" (p.136 ftn.2 above) confirmed by the Xanthos inscription, as basis of the Ezra Torah-imposing mission, "even if the so-called Ezra decree is hardly authentic in the form which has been handed down to us"[62].

The pre-priestly tradition or composition is called Deuteronomic (K^D, with little mention of J or E) as in Blum, and (allowing for Jeremiah and

---

60 Fortunately *not* relevant, but doubtless causing even his adherents to wince, is his "Life of Brian Research", in *Biblical Studies, Cultural Studies: Gender, Culture, Theory 7*, ed. J. Carol EXUM (*JSOT* supp. 266, Sheffield 1998) 400-414, in which he holds that the Monty Python film spoofing the life of Jesus is like Qohelet a countertext, and indispensable for a sound NT methodology. And now we read in Davies' "The Future of 'Biblical History'" [purporting to be an article of the year 2050], in *Auguries* (Sheffield Jubilee, ed. D.J.A. CLINES & S.D. MOORE: *JSOT* supp.269 (Sheffield 1998) (126-) 143, "The past of biblical studies, like its mother, Christian theology, is as a dominant and authoritative cultural voice in a world that was western."

61 Erhard BLUM, *Studien zur Komposition des Pentateuch*: BZAW 189 (Berlin 1990, de Gruyter) 332-360 [361-382, "Endgestalt" (361 & 144 on LOHFINK Ex 15,26)].

62 Rainer ALBERTZ, *A History of Israelite Religion in the Old Testament Period, 2. From the Exile to the Maccabees* [1992], tr. John BOWDEN (London 1994, SCM), p. 467, citing in Note 7 GUNNEWEG, *Esra* p. 129. Otherwise Moshe GREENBERG, "Three Conceptions of the Torah in the Hebrew Scriptures", *Fest. R. Rendtorff* (→ ftn. 87) 1990, p. 365-378.

Shaphan variations) "can well be connected with the council of elders or the lay commission formed from it" (p.469). "The most important preliminary decision taken by the lay theologians was their resolve to write a history of the early period of **Israel** and its origin" (p.471), beginning from Abraham Gen 12, and deliberately omitting creation traditions, "which were certainly to hand in their basic document" (p.472).

This new lay history, or rather this old document with newly composed history-additions (the whole of Gen 12-50) and suppressions, promptly became widely-enough diffused to constitute a challenge calling forth an equally-revised K^P or priestly alternative. This new P included the whole of Gen 1-11 to show that its concern was all mankind and not merely Israel.

Actually in the religious sphere there was fair convergence on basics like YHWH, Sinai, Decalogue, and even the towering authority of Moses (though P inevitably sought some suitable prominence for Aaron). Paradoxically the priests' main opposition lay in a democratic hostility to kingship (known to have made abusive decisions in the pre-exilic cult) and in a solidarity with the poorer and weaker elements in the population: as against the lay-commission's tendency to be dominated by the aristocrats, of whom a portion (not all) aimed to preserve land-laws fostering their own wealth.

Despite persisting divergences, it was possible to hammer out the compromise known as the Persian-authorized "Ezra's Torah". But many social tensions persisted in the community and are outlined by Albertz down to Maccabee times.

It cannot have escaped notice that this abundant "writing of Persian-authorized history in the Ezra-era" is an anticipatory echo of the Philip Davies view set forth above: except to the extent that for Blum and Albertz the writers are not "inventing" the whole of an unknown and largely unavailable history of "Ancient Israel", but rather making ample insertions or suppressions in some largely historical compositions. However, they too apparently did not hesitate to "invent" when the need arose: "the reform priests thought up a didactic story" Num 17,7b-10 (Albertz 2,488).

d) *The Inarus episode.* Among more general concrete cases, the one which has been most often stressed both by and before what is offered as a "New Quest" is the Persian government's concern against Judah being drawn into the Egyptian revolt. And nowadays it is Ezra rather than Nehemiah who, priest and scribe though he was, was sent by Artaxerxes (to head the "fact-finding mission" of Ezra 7,14) as a measure for tightening up firm controls of the loyalty of the returnees and other inhabitants of Judah[63].

The "proxy-data" which must serve as principal proof of this contention come and have much earlier come from an obscure historian named Ctesias. As we noted above, he is being praised for having had *access* to local and top-level archives; which is not the same as his having actually *used* them. We possess historical data from Ctesias (notably his Books 14-17) only in the form of summaries in Photius. Though often dismissed as unreliable, this information is considered by some even more helpful than Thucydides[64].

Egypt, as a principal component of the Persian Empire, was on the edge of revolt for some time[65]. Evidently the nearness of Judah and its bridge-road function made it likely to be drawn into the conflict, though there has been no general acceptance for Morgenstern's claim that Xerxes attacked Jerusalem in 485 B.C.E., or that this was the destruction of its wall described much later to Nehemiah by his brother (Neh 1,3)[66].

---

63 Othniel MARGALITH. 'The Political Role of Ezra as Persian Governor", *ZAW* 98 (1986) 110-112; Lester L. GRABBE, "What was Ezra's Mission ?", in *Second Temple Studies 2* (*JSOT* supp. 175, 1994; 286-299): he acts as independent of satraps and superior to governors. -- Not Ezra himself but the prior wall-building troubles in Ezra 4,7-23 are certainly related to the Inarus uprising according to Anson F. RAINEY, "The Satrapy 'Beyond the River'", in the short-lived *Australian Journal of Biblical Archaeology* 1,2 (Sydney 1969; 51-78) p. 62.

64 Joan M. BIGWOOD, "Ctesias' Account of the Revolt of Inarus", *Phoenix* 30 (Toronto 1976) 1-25; also 32 (1978) 15-41, "Ctesias as Historian of the Persian Wars" and 34 (1980) 195-107, "Diodorus and Ctesias"; R. HENRY, *Ctésias, la Perse, l'Inde. Les sommaires de Photius* (9 vol. 1959-1991) [Fragmente der griechischen Historiker 688]; Gerhard WIRTH, "Ktesias", *Der kleine Pauly* 3 (Stuttgart 1969, citing *RE* 11,2032 -2073) [*Der kleine Pauly* 4 (1972) 813-817, Konrat ZIEGLER, "Photios, Patriarch von Konstantinopel bis 886 / Die 'Bibliothek'], which epitomized 99 secular authors, 21 of them historians including Ctesias.

65 Edda BRESCIANI. "The Persian Occupation of Egypt", in *The Cambridge History of Iran II. The Median and Achaemenian Periods*, ed. Ilya GERSHOVITCH (1985) 502-528; A. ANDREWES, "Thucydides and the Persians", *Historia* 10 (Stuttgart 1961) 1-18.

66 Sidney G. SOWERS, "Did Xerxes Wage War on Jerusalem ?", *Hebrew Union College Annual* 67 (1996) 43-53, claims Julian MORGENSTERN, "Jerusalem -- 485 B.C.", *Hebrew Union College Annual* 27 (1956) 101-179; 28 (1957) 15-47; 31 (1960) 1-29 was overstated but would be valid if based on Ezra 4,8-23.

But when Athens supported the revolt of the Ionic cities, the threat to Judah came much closer[67]. Sidon was in open opposition to the Persians[68]. The coastal city of Dor south of Haifa was a taxpaying Athenian city from 460 to 450 (including under Pericles in 454 B.C.E. as shown by a fragment). When Ezra arrived in Judah in 458 with "well equipped and armed Jewish volunteers", this is seen as a promise to Artaxerxes of protection from his enemies[69].

Meanwhile after the death of Xerxes it was the king of Libya, Inarus, who around 460 induced the Egyptians to open revolt (Thucydides 1,104; Herodotus 7,7; Diodorus 11,71.77). Egypt had the support of Athens; but the Athenian fleet was defeated by the Persians[70]. Inarus was captured but

---

67 Jack M. BALCER, "The East Greeks under Persian Rule; a Reassessment" & Mario CORSARO, "Gli Ioni tra Greci e Persiani", in *Achaemenid History 6*, ed. Heleen SANCISI-WEERDENBURG (1991) 55 f & 11-53.

68 Josette ELAYI & Jean SAPIN,, "Numismatics and Economic History", in their *Beyond the River* (*JSOT* supp. 250, Sheffield 1998) p.126, but they resist the "temptation" to link with this political situation the simultaneous diminution of [silver content in] Sidonian double shekels by two grams. -- Paul NASTER, "Les monnayages satrapaux, provinciaux et régionaux dans l'Empire perse face au numéraire officiel des Achéménides" in *State and Temple Economy* (1979 → ftn. 48) 2,597-605. Perhaps relevant also is the *yehud*-coinage treated on p. 131; see also John W. BETLYON, "The Provincial Government of Persian Period Judea and the Yehud Coins", *Journal of Biblical Literature* 105 (1986) 633-642. -- Numismatics may also gain in importance for the debate over whether only silver was acceptable for the Persian tax (? "governor's bread", Neh 5,14 in ftn. 10 above); and over "Liberation from Debt Slavery after the Exile in Second Isaiah and Nehemiah", treated by Klaus BALTZER in Fest. F. CROSS (1987 → ftn. 81 below; 477-484) p. 481 on Neh 5,1-13.

69 Fritz M. HEICHELHEIM, "Ezra's Palestine and Periclean Athens", *Zeitschrift für Religions-und Geistesgechichte* 3 (1951) 251-3, further claiming that at that time the book of Job was being composed under the influence of Attic tragedy. No support of these views is apparent in D. GILLIS, *Collaboration with the Persians*: Historia Einzelschrift 34; Wiesbaden 1979.

70 A. ARGENTATIS, "La spedizione in Egitto (459-454 ?) nel quadro della politica esterna ateniese", *Acme* 6 (1953) 379-404. -- Jon L. BERQUIST, *Judaism in Persia's Shadow: a Social and Historical Approach* (Minneapolis 1995, Fortress) p.107 f stresses Persia's aid from Sparta, secured by the satrap-diplomat Megabyzus, who brought the Persian army toward Egypt through Palestine and near Yehud, but later defected. -- Eric M. MYERS, "The Persian Period and the Judean Restoration: from Zerubbabel to Nehemiah", in Fest. F. CROSS, *Ancient Israelite Religion*, ed. P.D. MILLER, al. (Philadelphia 1987, Fortress; 509-521) p.511.

(according to Ctesias *Persica* 32-36) only after some years crucified[71]. Thus there was no place for any "volunteer army of Ezra" to enter the story. We may continue to maintain that his interests were scribal and priestly, leaving to Nehemiah any pro-Persian activism which may have been demanded[72].

e) Other socioeconomic data which have recently been exploited are even more remote from our own present Ezra-era concerns, though useful and likely to prove even more useful as the movement grows. This is clearly enough true for feminist studies[73]. The increasing importance of coinage has been noted in footnote 66 above. There had already been known some Judean triangle-impressions cognate to those of Babylonian Nippur where some Judeans were living[74].

An original and wide-ranging use of the returnee-Judahite and Persian Empire historical context has been made by Ska. He holds that the "kingdom of priests" promised in Ex 19,6 means *both* "a kingdom ruled by (Persian-authorized) priests" (Moran) *and* "a priestly kingdom". This is the formulation of a "societal project, more exactly 'the project of postexilic Israel' intentionally inserted at the outset of the Sinai pericope to give it the seal of both authenticity and antiquity". "The population develops what D.L. Smith calls a 'resistance culture' in order not to be absorbed and disappear. ... Its

---

71 Friedrich W. KÖNIG, *Die Persika des Ktesias von Knidos* (Archiv für Orientforschung Beiheft 18; Graz 1972; p. 1-27, Auszüge des Photios, Buch VII-XXIII, Greek and German) p.13, Ctesias XVI, §32-36.

72 Kenneth E. HOGLUND, *Achaemenid Imperial Administration in Syria-Palestine and the Mission of Ezra and Nehemiah* (SBL diss. 125, Atlanta 1992) p.208-226; p.92-96, "The Requirements for a New Synthesis of Historical, Archaeological, and Biblical Evidence"; H.H. ROWLEY, "Nehemiah's Mission and its Background", *Bulletin Rylands* 37 (1954) 528-561 [= his *Men of God; Studies in OT History and Prophecy* (1963) 211-245].

73 Tamara C. ESKENAZI, "Out from the Shadows; Biblical Women in the Postexilic Era", *Journal for the Study of the OT* 54 (1992) 25-43; of dismay to geographers will be her p.39 on Neh 3,12: it is "amusing" that "daughters" is taken as "daughter villages". -- R.J. COGGINS, "The Origins of Jewish Diaspora" in *The World of Ancient Israel*, ed. R. CLEMENTS (Cambridge 1989) 170: already A. CAUSSE, *Les dispersés d'Israël* 1929 & *Du groupe ethnique* 1937 identifies "an increasingly important role for women" in the postexilic period.

74 Hubertus C.M. VOGT, *Studie zur nachexilischen Gemeinde in Esra-Nehemia* (Werl 1966, Coelde) p.15-17, noted by Roland DE VAUX in *Revue Biblique* 73 (1966) 603. -- Perhaps relevant is Raz KLETTER, *Economic Keystones; the Weight-System of the Kingdom of Judah:* JSOT supp. 276, Sheffield 1998.

new frontiers are not so much geographical and political, but of the order of 'the sacred' and of a 'holiness' spread out to the whole people"[75].

As for a greater contribution of archeology to purely literary and historical studies of the Bible, its importance of course cannot be exaggerated[76]. But the impression is sometimes conveyed by the authors treated above that Palestine excavation has been ignored until they took things in hand.

Some even have even proposed that the time has come to write a history of "Israel" or rather 900-600 BCE Canaan from solely excavated discoveries and no biblical texts[77]. Less implausible is Philip Davies in the earlier chapters of his *Search* not unjustifiably deploring the *misuse* of archeology for "special pleading"; but even he when in spoof the name of W.F. Albright comes up, cannot ignore the immense diffusion of archeological data within biblical scholarship during the past century under his influence.

---

75 Jean-Louis SKA, "Exode 19,3b-6 et l'identité de l'Israël postexilique", in *Studies in the Book of Exodus*, ed. Marc VERVENNE (44th Louvain conference, August 1995; Louvain 1996, Univ./Peeters; 289-317); p.300; 291; 317: refurbishing (p.298-304) the contested view of W. L. MORAN, "A Kingdom of Priests" in the M. GRUENTHANER Memorial, *The Bible in Current Catholic Thought*, ed. J.L. McKENZIE (NY 1962, Herder) 7-20; and citing Daniel L. SMITH, "The Politics of Ezra: Sociological Indicators of Postexilic Judaean Society", in *Second Temple Studies I*, ed. P. DAVIES (JSOT supp. 117; Sheffield 1991; 73-97) p. 80. Vervenne's erudite surveys of the 30 papers of this conference (p.3-18) and of more general trends in Exodus-study (p.21-59) seem nowhere to indicate any question like "What was the *perspective* of the biblical author(s) in narrating the Exodus event(s) as having actually happened ?"

76 Ephraim STERN, *The Material Culture of the Land of the Bible in the Persian Period (538-332 B.C.E.)*, Warminster 1982; "The Archaeology of Persian Palestine" & "The Persian Empire and the Political and Social History of Palestine in the Persian Period", *Cambridge History of Judaism*, ed. W.D. DAVIES & Louis FINKELSTEIN (1984) 88-114 & 70-87. -- Note also the first essay of that volume, Dennis BALY, "The Geography of Palestine and the Levant", p.1-24; and also Edda BRESCIANI, "Egypt, Persian Satrapy", p.338-371.

77 J. Maxwell MILLER, "Is it Possible to Write a History of Israel without Relying on the Hebrew Bible ?", in *The Fabric of History*, ed. Diana EDELMAN (1991; → ftn. 36 above: 93-102): his answer seems to be No [as indeed already clarified in detail in his (with J. HAYES) 1986 *History of Ancient Israel and Judah*], or "a rather thin volume", alien to the current discussion (p.101), but he deals mostly with those who have *misused* the Bible/excavation relationship; excavated written documents tend to take precedence over artifacts in producing scenarios (p.93); despite the "Relying" of his title, his p. 100 (like the 1986 book) admits that the Bible is "of course not a reliable source" but not totally irrelevant either.

Our general conclusion must be that for the era and problem we are exploring, there is much to be hoped for from the stress on socioeconomic evidence. It may well seem to support, or perhaps rather to reflect, the approach of Davies among the several maintaining an "invented Biblical Hebrew". But we have not yet seen in it much that is new for determining the likeliest *time* when that translation-event could have taken place (leaving apart the simultaneous heavy burden of creating out of virtually nothing the whole of biblical history).

5. Sabbath-Development as Key to Torah in Ezra-Nehemiah

a) The relevance of a recent and very original volume of Nodet might not be guessed from its title[78]. Actually it deals mostly with the origins of a weekly Sabbath observance among the Samaritans and Maccabees. But at the very beginning and at the very end it has headings on Ezra, whose Torah could not have included such a sabbath; and Nehemiah, linked with a strong sabbath-enforcement.

Joshua is barely mentioned as "the one who locally established in writing a statute and a law at the Shechem assembly" (p.12). We will be warned on p. 388 that "it is certainly excessive" [? and thereby somehow hinted] to connect to Ebal and Gerizim the obscure origins of the Samaritan schism and their own Pentateuch which they edited "with some emendations .. at a time difficult to determine" before 100 B.C.E. (p.126; even 200, p.153). But "the ancient Samaritans always had a book of Joshua which was their own, before any Jewish or other influence" (p.197, abbreviated as "JosS").

b) Many biblical texts deal with the Sabbath. Most of them concern the week and the weekly rest of the solar year (with which must be associated the sabbatical year, since it is described in similar terms). Others more or less clearly link it to the moon's phases: either full moon (Passover, 14/15 Nisan, Lev 23,10; Sukkot, 15 Tishri, Lev 23.39); or (rather in the prophets) new moon (Isa 1,13; 66,23; Hos 2,11; Amos 8,5).

"The weekly sabbath, based on the seventh [solar] day, was well adapted to what has been called the city of Nehemiah, but fitted in poorly with accounts of wars in ancient times", says p. 94; and what follows insists

---

78 Étienne NODET, *A Search for the Origins of Judaism, from Joshua to the Mishnah* [*Essai sur les origines du Judaïsme*, Paris 1993, Cerf] tr. Ed CROWLEY: JSOT supp. 248. Sheffield 1997.

that the lunar references have been unduly bypassed. More discussion is merited by their relation to Babylonian *šapattum* (15th lunar day) and the entirely distinct "dangerous" days 7, 14, 19, 28, and 49 (21 of following lunar month); and p. 100 takes up the vexed "passage from lunar to weekly computation", and the Decalogue is the major but not insuperable difficulty.

"The prohibition of buying from foreigners on the Sabbath (Neh [13,20, unlike 13,15] was not biblical ... nor was the giving up of harvests and of debts every seven years [though] the exact content of the Pentateuch at that moment cannot be ascertained" (p. 364; p.116, Deut 15,2 requires only "the return of personal effects that had been kept for the payment of a debt"; the debt-cancellation required by Neh 5,11 is not based on *šemittâ* or any pre-existing law[79].

c) A capital point for Nodet is the petition (Josephus Ant 13,251-264) to Antiochus IV 166 B.C.E. by "Sidonians" (of Shechem p.148; called Canaanites in Joshua 13,4; in Ant 1,133-140 Sidonians and Samaritans are juxtaposed). The petition mentions a "drought" and a "custom of observing the day which the Jews call 'sabbath' ". Nodet suggests on p.145 that the word could mean simultaneously the (weekly or originally lunar) repose and the seventh year fallow. At that time (as late as 166, p.378:) "the Samaritans, who were not yet really enemies of the Jews, admitted having received the Sabbath from them".

Another key point is that the citation of 2 Chr 36,22 in Ezra 1,1 is immediately preceded by 2 Chr 36,21 summing up the exile, "to fulfill the word of YHWH by the mouth of Jeremiah, 'so that the land might enjoy its sabbaths'; all the days that it lay deserted it kept the sabbath to a full seventy years". Nodet p. 349 remarks that Jer 29,10 speaks only of 70 years filled out for Babylon; the allusion to "the land enjoying its sabbaths" from Lev 26,34 is in this context a creation of the Chronicler.

d) The real meat of Nodet's thesis is that no Jewish war-leader before Mattathias (1 Mcb 2,41) in 167 B.C.E. had any scruple about fighting on the Sabbath. "How is it that such an elementary security problem only came up at such a late date ?" (p. 11). The answer is that what he calls "the Nehe-

---

79 So already N. P. LEMCHE, "The Manumission of Slaves -- the Fallow Year -- the Sabbatical Year -- the Yobel Year", *Vetus Testamentum* 26 (1976) 38-59 -- among the many intervening publications with which my *Sociology of the Biblical Jubilee* (Analecta Biblica 4: Rome 1954) will have to be updated. But a mass of factual data remains valid, especially in my "Maccabean Sabbath Years", *Biblica* 34 (1953) 501-505.

miah model" severely imposing ritual repose *every* sabbath, and *not* contained
in the Torah of Ezra, had been made obligatory only shortly before.

This legislation was made on the basis of non-biblical oral traditions,
in loose connection with Simon the Just and the *Pirqê Abot* "Men of the
Great Assembly" ('an imprecisely defined entity', p. 278 & 383) -- itself
surprisingly connected with the Library founded by Nehemiah[80], but not
with any of his several Assemblies (p.282), though it is a "configuration ..
like the 'city of Nehemiah', a restored quarter of Jerusalem".

It was this Simon [II not I, around 200] the Just who obtained the
"Jerusalem charter" from Antiochus III and "effected the synthesis between
the Judaism of Nehemiah [with its weekly sabbath], the law of Moses [under
a form earlier than the one we know] and the Temple ... Just before him
[c.250 B.C.E.] exchanges between Samaritans and Jews led to a Pentateuch
close to the present one, integrating in particular the weekly Sabbath (p.383)
... The proclamation of the law of Moses by Ezra created something new *in
Jerusalem* (p.384). ... What Cyrus had prescribed [Ezra 1,2; 6,3] was the
Temple, not the Law of Moses" (p.386); the Law which Ezra proclaimed
[Neh 8,3] was a transformation of the Pentateuch "reinterpreted through
Babylonian customs" under Antiochus III (p.386): here "Artaxerxes was
certainly a loan name" [as was Ezra also therefore ??].

e) So when did *our* Pentateuch with its obligatory weekly sabbath
come into being ? The question should rather be re-phrased: When did the
whole Judaean people, with its sects and sub-sects[81], Zadokites, Hasideans,

---

80 Known only from 2 Mcb 2,13: [Besides Jeremiah's fire -- and Solomon's] "Nehemiah's
memoir reports that he founded a library and gathered the books about the kings and prophets;
also the writings of David, and letters of kings about vow-gifts".

81 Joseph BLENKINSOPP, "A Jewish Sect of the Persian Period", *Catholic Biblical Quarterly*
52 (1995) 5-20, though dealing mostly with the *hᵃrēdîm* of Ezra 9 f & Isa 66 (with a good
survey of various dichotomies especially in note 6), cites with approval S.TALMON, "The
Emergence of Jewish Sectarianism in the Early Second Temple Period", in *King, Cult and
Calendar in Ancient Israel* [Jerusalem 1986, Magnes; 165-201 [cf. in Fest. F. CROSS his
Ancient Israelite Religion 1987; 587-616]: the *gôlâ*-returnees community called itself a *yahad*
in his reading of Ezra 4,3: therefore an earliest "sect". Talmon's 1995 *Israels Gedankenwelt*
p.236 finds a further dichotomy between the "monocephalic" (David alone) Chronicles and the
"bicephalic" Ezra (5, Zerubbabel paired with priest Jeshua); similarly R.L. BRAUN,
"Chronicles, Ezra, and Nehemiah: Theology and Literary History", in *Studies in the Historical
Books of the OT*, ed. J.A. EMERTON (VT supp. 30, 1979; 58-64) p.63. -- Hugo MANTEL, "The
Dichotomy of Judaism during the Second Temple", *HUCA* 44 (1973; 55-87) p.56 warns that

Essenes, Hasmoneans, Pharisees and the rest, come to recognize the Samaritan (Shechem, p.152) as the *true* Pentateuch -- while adding to it the *weekly sabbath* ?

"The material in the Hexateuch should generally be attributed to [the Samaritans of] Gerizim, with the conspicuous exception of the weekly Sabbath" (p.12). "The transformation [though apparently not such as to constitute *the* Pentateuch or to include the weekly sabbath] based on the Law of Moses came from the priest Ezra ... to Ezra was precisely connected the written Law (all or part of the Pentateuch), with views about all Israel and a dominant high priesthood governing the Law and the cult; whereas under the name of Nehemiah and his library were gathered the traditions of the Elders, various writings and a Jewish nostalgia for a monarchy having control over the cult" (p.386 f; the "perspectives" which follow add "the preceding sketch should not be considered a collection of established facts but a sort of 'model' grouping together in a single plan some scattered and very diverse pieces of information .. to be verified and extended").

Our provisional conclusion would be that for the proponents of a (whole) Bible in an "invented" language, the Ezra era would gain less support from Nodet's thesis than a date even much later than 200 B.C.E.

6. Ezra and Torah-Plus in Jewish Tradition

a) Under a cognate rubric, Blenkinsopp's commentary includes the data of Josephus and Sirach which we treat under other headings, but may summarize as a suitable lead-in here. The roles of Ezra and Nehemiah are somewhat like those of unsuccesful priest Aaron and successful leader Moses, though they have been combined in the canonical book in order to give the priest his full due[82]. (Third Ezra ignores Nehemiah except for subjecting him to a fictitious Attharates (*ha-tiršātā'* 3 Ezra 5,40.)

S. ZEITLIN, "The Origin of the Sadducees, Pharisees, and Essenes" in his *History of the Second Jewish Commonwealth* (Philadelphia 1933) 41-56, ignores the fact that neither Pharisees nor Sadducees are mentioned in Ezra-Neh and wrongly calls the Pharisees "those that separated themselves from the Torah".

82   B. GOSSE, "L'alliance avec Lévi et l'opposition entre les lignes royale et sacerdotale à l'époque perse", *Transeuphratène* 18 (1995) 29-33, on Neh 10,1; 13,29. -- "Beginnings of a new institution, the Targum" are found by David BOSSMAN, "Ezra's Marriage Reform: Israel Redefined", *Biblical Theology Bulletin* 9 (1979) 32(-38): "Ezra(-Neh 9) transformed Israel's understanding of what it meant to be a Jew ... technique of reinterpreting Israel's traditions which notably transcended the Deuteronomic reforms".

Sirach's silence about Ezra was deliberate and polemical, not due to ignorance about Ezra (Pohlmann; Noth amounts to the same, his having as source only the Nehemiah-memoir) or to Ezra's non-existence (Torrey), nor in order to pair Nehemiah rather with Simon the wall-builder high-priest[83]. Rather Sirach's favor for Oniad Simon II reflects Nehemiah's feud with the Tobiads and political realism anticipating the Hasmoneans[84].

b) "With the ascendancy of Pharisaic rabbinism, after the suppression of the revolts against Rome, it was inevitable that Ezra the scribe rather than Nehemiah the political activist should become the model of leadership for the Jewish people"[85]. One wonders whether the recurrent "Woe to you scribes and Pharisees" of the New Testament conceals any hint of scribal involvement in some perhaps tendentious editing of the Hebrew Bible.

The Fourth Ezra Apocalypse is generally dated near 90 C.E.[86]. In it (14,24.39.44), Ezra after drinking a divinely-given fiery liquid dictated from memory (or divine inspiration) to five scribes in forty days (beside 70

---

83 Sirach 49,13; 50,2; Kurt GALLING, *Studien zur Geschichte Israels im persischen Zeitalter* (Tübingen 1964) 129 n.3. -- See now also A. SCHENKER, "La relation d'Esdras A' au texte massorétique d'Esdras-Néhémie", in D. BARTHÉLEMY Fest., *Tradition of the Text* (Fribourg Univ./Göttingen 1991) 218-248.

84 Peter HÖFFKEN, "Warum schwieg Jesus Sirach über Esra ?", *ZAW* 87 (1975; 184-201) p. 195, their ideologies differed, not on Torah but on mixed-marriages.

85 Joseph BLENKINSOPP, *Ezra-Nehemiah, a Commentary* (London 1989, SCM; 54-59 on Jewish tradition) p. 57.

86 Michael E. STONE, "Esdras, Second Book of", in *Anchor Bible Dictionary* 2 {1992; 611-614) 612: date before 96 C.E. following SCHÜRER; literary unity defended. [This article is distinct from his p.728 on "Ezra, Greek Apocalypse of"]. -- The English edition of GARBINI's *Storia e ideologia* (→ ftn. 94 below) p.152 says "Toward the beginning of the second century BC [should be AD/CE, also p.156 & 157 (Garbini letter of June 2, 1999, enclosing his list of other corrigenda) since he mentions a Christian addition which 'belongs to the second half of the century'], the redaction of the Apocalypse of Ezra took place, a reworking of an earlier Apocalypse of Salathiel with the addition of material relating to a Legend of Ezra [citing R. KABISCH 1899; G. BOX in R. CHARLES *Pseudepigrapha* 1913; W. OESTERLEY 1933, E. BRANDENBURGER, Zurich 1981; against unity of Fourth Esdras claimed by J. SCHREINER, Gütersloh 1981]; the Christian addition which forms the first two chapters of IV Ezra and which speaks of 'Ezra the prophet' belongs to the second half of the century".

esoterica) the entire 24 books of official Scripture[87]. Unless this was the Law he brought to Jerusalem, there is no other link with canonical Ezra.

c) *The Legends of the Jews* "call for careful form-critical analysis" though Ginzberg is outdated[88]. The whole medieval Jewish exegetical tradition now after the Enlightenment clamors for rediscovery. Ezra was seen as a pupil of Baruch, Jeremiah's scribe (Jer 26,4), and he esteemed Torah-study higher than Temple worship (bMeg 16b; in 2 Mcb 2,2 it is Jeremiah who gives the Torah to the departing exiles). Ezra is just like Moses (Parah 3,5; as at the end of Fourth Ezra). Around 300 C.E. was discussed a dictum of Rabbi Eleazar (bKidd 69a) concerned with "racial purity" rather than Torah.

"Ezra's principal achievement was to restore the Torah (bSukk 20a), so that if Moses had not preceded him, he would have received Torah directly from God himself (bSanh 21b)". In citing this oft-quoted phrase, Blenkinsopp seems to leave open the inference that not only Ezra but even his rabbinical glorifiers were not much concerned about the Prophets and the Writings, putting them on a level distinctly less worthy of Ezra than was the Torah. Chronicles entire at least was for them wholly of Ezra's own authorship; and so was the book of Ezra(-Nehemiah -- putatively, to cover over the possibility that it was due to arrogant Nehemiah: Baba Bathra 15a). Alleged Ezran authorship of Targum and Mishna is less relevant here.

At Cordova even an Arab, Ibn Chazm c.1050, held that our Pentateuch (with its discrepancies) is a copy dictated by heart by Ezra when the only existing copy was destroyed. We noticed above (ftn. 87) that the number of books edited by Ezra was equal to one of the existing counts of the books in what would later be called the canon. The Qur'ān itself (Sura 9,30) has the statement "The Jews said ' 'Uzair is the Son of God' " (this Uzair as name for Ezra is elsewhere attested as a place-name in Babylon[89]).

---

87 Christian MACHOLZ. "Die Entstehung des hebräischen Bibelkanons nach 4. Esra 14", in *Fest. R. Rendtorff* (Neukirchen 1990; 379-391), p. 387: 4 Ezra 14,44 says 94 books were written (minus 70 arcane; =) 24. This figure is given as the Syriac reading for 4 Ezra 14,44 in Jacob M. MYERS, *I and II Esdras* (Anchor Bible 42, 1974) p.321, but in some counts the figure is 22. Myers says "Vulgate omits", but the Sixtine edition gives in verse 44 "204 books" and in verse 46 "70 (esoterica)", leaving 134 canonical.

88 L. GINZBERG, *The Legends of the Jews*. Philadelphia 1909-1938. Presumably Jacob NEUSNER, not mentioned in BLENKINSOPP p. 58 or 28, is to be our most abundant resource here and in the next-mentioned "rediscovery".

89 H.L. ELLISON, "The Importance of Ezra", *Evangelical Quarterly* 53 (1981) 48-63; p.49.

Spinoza's *Tractatus* in 1670 held that Ezra collected various histories all the way down through our 2 Kings, but left them in a fragmentary state. Apparently some more specific declaration of the Jewish sages will be needed to justify any of the varying claims of the whole Bible rewritten in an "invented" language.

d) As for the Christian observers outdoing the Sages in glorifying Ezra: We mentioned Jerome and Bellarmine in this regard (p. 104 above). We find Justinian a century after Jerome saying that the whole of Jewish literature was restored by Ezra, though it is surprising that this is one of the concerns of *De cultu feminarum* (1,3). Abelard about 1100 credited Ezra with editing also other OT books. Photius too (MG 101,816) does not limit Ezra's needed services to the Torah. Tostado, bishop of Avila until 1455, attributes editing operations and insertions to Ezra.

From Renaissance times Houtman gives us more help than is generally available[90]. Catholic Masius in 1573 adds at least Joshua to Ezra's work. "In 1679 an able student, Thomas Aikenhead, was hanged in Edinburgh at the age of 18 for uttering wild statements among which was that Ezra was the author of the Pentateuch". Favor for Ezra by the exegetes Richard Simon, Jean le Clerc, Isaac de la Peyrère, and Samuel Reimarus is pretty much limited to the Pentateuch; so also Voltaire. But Thomas Hobbes' *Leviathan* §33 in 1651 credited him with the whole of Scripture as in Fourth Ezra.

Amid re-emerging favor for Moses as true author of Genesis (Astruc) and the whole Pentateuch (Eichhorn), one last exegete (E. Bertheau 1885) is credited by Houtman with attributing to Ezra Judges and Ruth down through 2 Kings. Then Wellhausen took over, but the allotting of some Pentateuch scribal activity to Ezra by him and C. Steuernagel was disallowed by Kuenen and Holzinger. More recently Eissfeldt and Cazelles are among the few who return to the view that "Ezra's Torah" was substantially the Pentateuch.

e) We must conclude by reiterating that Christians, especially those who expand Ezra's activity to the whole Bible or anyway beyond the Pentateuch, are under the influence of a long medieval Jewish glorification of Ezra, generally admitted although we were able to document it only sparsely

---

90 C. HOUTMAN, "Ezra and the Law: Observations on the Supposed Relation between Ezra and the Pentateuch", *Oudtestamentische Studiën* 21 (1980 meeting. Leiden 1981; 91-115) p, 86; *Inleiding in de Pentateuch* (Kampen 1980) §14 on MASIUS.

here above. Thus we have not gained much in our search for a possible Sitz im Leben for an alleged rewriting of our Bible in a language created for that purpose.

7. What is Really Meant by the Claim "Ezra Never Existed"

a) We may refer here to our *AnchorBD* article on "Ezra (Person)"[91]. It was of course not commissioned to treat a theme so negative as the above subtitle indicates. First we have a listing of the relevant passages, only twenty in Ezra 7-10 and Neh 8-12 and usually a single verse. Six of these exhibit really "personal" traits (Ezra 9,3.6; 7,27; 8,22; 10,6; Neh 9,6-37). Six others give titles (Ezra 7,12.21; 8,5; 10,10; Neh 8,1-9), "our firmest clue to the real Ezra"[92]. In Ezra 7,14-26, Artaxerxes decrees munificently various functions Ezra is commissioned to perform; but quite different are the only two verses which show Ezra actually functioning, Ezra 7,28; Neh 8,13[93].

There follows almost immediately among the alternatives to be "evaluated" the counter-claim that Ezra never existed, but was a post-Sirach rabbinic invention to serve as base for their claim of a Mosaic Law from which they could draw their authority. This problem was discussed almost wholly in dialogue with the original Italian edition of an essay in a book by Garbini. This book has meanwhile become available in English, so we seize this chance to update our documentation.

b) Ezra 7,1 declares that he was son of Seraiah, and his genealogy is then traced back to Aaron *ha-kohēn hā-ro'š* in 7,5. However, in 1 Chr 5,40H (our 6,14) Ezra is not mentioned, and Seraiah is the father of Jozedek. But in Ezra 3,2 Jozadak is father of the priest Jeshua, who along with Zerubbabel restores the altar and offers sacrifice, then in Ezra 5,2 "rebuilds

---

91 R. NORTH, "Ezra (Person), *Anchor Bible Dictionary*, ed. David N. FREEDMAN, 2 (1992) 726-8; also relevant is "Postexilic Judean Officials" 5,86-90.

92 Magne SÆBØ [the typographically-difficult ø of this surname was understandably suppressed as an *o* crossed out, not only in *AnchorBD* 2,726.728 but curiously also in the VOLTERRA-Festschrift above), "Esra: §3, Werk und Wirkung", *Theologische Realenzyklopädie* 10 (1982) 380f. In TRE vol. 24 (1994) 242-6, Arvid TÅNGBERG, "Nehemia", observes with understatement that unlike Ezra's [though not so noticeably in *TRE* 10], the date of his activity is virtually uncontested.

93 Henri CAZELLES, *Histoire critique d'Israël des origines à Alexandre le Grand* (Paris 1982) p.224.

the Temple", all with no mention of Ezra himself (though Neh 12,26 mentions Ezra as contemporary to Nehemiah and to *the son of* Jeshua).

This praise of Jeshua is repeated in Sirach 49,12. And again with no mention of Ezra, Sirach 49,13 quite forcibly acclaims, "Also Nehemiah's memory is enduring; he rebuilt our fallen walls with their renewed gates and bars, and made livable houses out of our ruins". For the silence of Sirach about Ezra, other hypotheses are considered, but it is generally concluded that neither his environs nor the source he was following knew anything about any Ezra in 180 or (the date of our translated text) 130 B.C.E. More relevantly to our present research, "the author is ignorant of the law promulgated by Ezra"[94].

Even on into the first pre-Christian century in Jason's history [c.120 B.C.E.] later epitomized in 2 Mcb 1,18.20.23.31.36, it is Nehemiah with no mention of Ezra who restores the cultus with recovery of the sacred fire. And in 2 Mcb 2,13 the attribution of this fire to Jeremiah, and comparison of the miracles attending its discovery to similar experiences of Moses and Solomon are said to be recorded in the Memoirs and in the Library of Nehemiah (p.164, ftn. 80 above).

We briefly noted above the contents of the Fourth Esdras Apocalypse and Garbini's view of its date and composite character. He continues, "It is from this work that the fortunes of the figure of Ezra grew in the Christian church ... half a millennium elapses [between his canonical] 'Memoirs' and the time when he began to be known in a fairly wide circle" (p.133). We will note below why he does not here consider as of more proximate importance the fortunes of Ezra within Judaism, on which he had begun his essay with three resounding quotations; and to which normally Ezra's fortunes within Christianity would have been due to some extent, strictly delimitable as in the case of Josephus and Philo.

Instead, only now Garbini turns to the *contents* of canonical Ezra and its undeniable disorderliness. "The inevitable conclusion is that the author of Ezra had remarkably confused ideas about the historical period in which his narrative is set, and therefore falls into innumerable contradictions and errors, an inexhaustible source of hypotheses and inferences (as useless as they are

---

94 Giovanni GARBINI, *History and Ideology in Ancient Israel* [*Storia e ideologia* 1986], tr. John BOWDEN (London 1988, SCM; ch. 13, "Ezra" p.151-169) p.152; then p. 153 takes issue with Morton SMITH's "irritable" remark about the Ezra-book, "Any proposal to contradict an apparently historical document must carry the burden of proof", in *Palestinian Politics and Parties that Shaped the OT* (London 1987 = NY 1971) p.91; Morton's p. 125 admits "Ezra's 'Book of the Law' disappeared with him".

unjustified) by biblical scholars who want at all costs to find a historical foundation in a text which is only 'apparently' historical" (p.154).

At this point he inserts that for a century already it has been recognized that Ezra was a "purely literary creation" based on the more defensibly historical model of Nehemiah: so Vernès in France in 1889[95]. Then in 1893 Ernest Renan's chapter on "Légende d'Esdras" argued that the reform itself was the work of Nehemiah, "and that later religious circles, who could not bear the fact that this was the work of a 'lay official', wanted 'a scribe, belonging to the priestly family, to have made at least an equal contribution to this great work of restoration"[96].

This position was taken up "by a young American student, C.C. Torrey, in 1896 in Germany ... denying the biblical book and the figure of Ezra all historical value ... a pure invention based on the figure of Zerubbabel"[97]. The Renan position was approved by Hölscher[98] (though Garbini p.155 finds Torrey preferable) and by the octogenarians Nöldeke and Loisy[99]. Torrey was rejected in "probably the worst volume of the prestigious ... International Critical Commentary"[100], and is now ... forgotten (well, not entirely, as some quite recent developments show)[101].

---

95 M. VERNÈS, *Précis d'histoire juive* (1989) p.582; and similarly a work of the same year by C. BULLANGÉ: to neither of which was Garbini able to have access. But the full contention of these scholars is said on p. 154 to be that Ezra was "a purely literary creation *by the Chronicler*" [Garbini p. 157 does not admit Chronicler authorship of Ezra-Nehemiah].

96 E. RENAN, *Histoire du peuple d'Israël* (Paris 1893, 96-106) p.97.

97 C.C. TORREY, *The Composition and Historical Value of Ezra-Nehemiah*: ZAW Beiheft 2, Giessen 1986. -- Further his *Ezra Studies*. Chicago 1910; reprinted by W.F. STINESPRING, NY 1970. [Garbini's note 22 (p.205) in translation says that for Pfeiffer "the Chronicler *was* Ezra" rather than as Garbini had written "the Chronicler *was the author of* Ezra".]

98 G. HÖLSCHER, *Geschichte der israelitischen und jüdischen Religion* (Giessen 1922) p. 140f; "Die Bücher Esra und Nehemia", in *Die Heilige Schrift des ATs*[4], ed. E. KAUTZSCH & A. BERTHOLET (Tübingen 1923, Mohr); WILLIAMSON comm. p.xxix.

99 T. NÖLDEKE, "Zur Frage der Geschichtlichkeit der Urkunden im Esra-Buche", *Deutsche Literaturzeitung* 45 (1924) p.1849-1856; A. LOISY, *La religion d'Israël*[3] (Paris 1993, Nourry) p. 27 f & 288 [English by Arthur GALTON (London 1910, Unwin). The first French edition of this work was by Picard in 1901; and see now Émile POULAT ed., Albert HOUTIN & Félix SARTIAUX, *Alfred Loisy* [1857-1940], *sa vie, son œuvre* (Paris 1960, CNRS).

100 L.W. BATTEN, *The Books of Ezra and Nehemiah*: ICC. Edinburgh 1913.

101 L.C.H. LEBRAM, "Die Traditionsgeschichte der Esragestalt und die Frage nach dem historischen Esra", in *Achaemenid History* 1, ed. H. SANCISI-WEERDENBURG (1983 Groningen

Meanwhile Torrey's position "was partly taken up again by R.H. Pfeiffer in 1941 = ²1952", says Garbini's p.155, but his long footnote is considerably more nuanced: Pfeiffer "does not deny the historicity of Ezra but stresses the improbabilities of the account which narrates his achievements; the Chronicler 'exaggerated the role of Ezra in such a fantastic way that it is difficult to recover the real historical framework of his contribution through the dense mist of imagination' (Pfeiffer p.256, cf.828)."

This formulation seems to me to correspond very well to the general view of all the exegetes of the past half-century who, without denying the existence of Ezra as a genuine historical figure, agree that it is so embroiled first by the disorderliness of the canonical book itself and secondly by the lavish embroideries of rabbinic tradition, that we can scarcely retrieve what belongs to the name as genuine history. In fact this is more or less just what I proposed in *AnchorBD* 2,727 as an alternative conclusion (I did not really consider it a "refutation") for the arguments marshaled by Garbini in support of his claim that "no Ezra ever existed"[102].

"Ezra is not a substitute for Moses but simply stands beside him ... not to symbolize the oral law of the Pharisees alongside the written law of Moses ... transmitted to 'the Men of the Great Synagogue' (Abot 1,1-5), i.e. according to rabbinic tradition, to those who returned from exile with

---

Seminar; Leiden 1987) 103-138, marshals the defects of the canonical and rabbinic Ezra-portrait just as severely as Garbini; but his mention on p. 135 of *two* independent Ezra-traditions seems to indicate that like Pfeiffer and my *AnchorBD* he admits that *some* Ezra really existed but was later enriched with invented attributes.

102 Upon receiving my photocopy of my *AnchorBD* article, Garbini wrote me under date of Jan.30, 1994, courteously giving the "honest reaction" I had requested: chiefly that to the *pars destruens* of his argumentation is somewhat sacrificed the more hypothetical *pars construens*. [Another part of his letter is cited above (p.94, n.93) in the chapter on "invented Hebrew".] -- Garbini has now sent me an offprint of his "La figura di Esdra nella letteratura e nella storia", from the 34th Settimana Biblica Nazionale, *Il confronto tra le diverse culture nella Bibbia da Esdra a Paolo*, ed. Rinaldo FABRIS: *Ricerche storico bibliche* 10,1 (1998) 59-66, noting that on his p.64 he is "trying to be *più buono*" by a paragraph admitting a "fairly painless .. irenical .. purely theoretical .. possible hypothesis" that Ezra could have been in fact a real person living in the Persian era; "but whether real or fictitious, in any case the figure of Ezra became 'historical' only at the moment when some began believing in the existence of this personage created by a literary work", presumably First Esdras before 100 BC (he still dates canonical Ezra first century AD p.59). His "new" formulation follows after citing on p. 64 some cautions of J.A. SOGGIN, "Esra. Zu einem Irrweg der Forschung", in Fest. M. SÆBØ, *Text and Theology*, ed. A. TÅNGBERG (Oslo 1994) 294-7.

[unacclaimed] Ezra[103]; ... Ezra stands outside this transmission of the oral law", as also in the Mishnah *Zugôt*, "Pairs" (Peah 2,6) c. 150 B.C., contemporaneous in origin to the Great Synagogue but more essential.

An Ezra thus "invented" to represent neither the written Mosaic Torah nor the Oral Law, must have represented the Canon[104], as suggested in Fourth Esdras 14,24.40.44 (p.167 above). "From the legendary Council of Jamnia [c. 90 C.E.] the fame of Ezra arose within Judaism: quite a different fame [from what we have identified as] the success of the figure of Ezra in the Christian era. The fact remains that at a certain moment, when problems of the canon did not exist [even for the Septuagint ??], a book called Ezra was written whose protagonist was connected with the Law; why ?"

Third Ezra, from which canonical Ezra is drawn, cites no source before 300 B.C.E., and is used not only thoroughly by Josephus but also by Philo *De confusione linguarum* 149 for 3 Ezra 8,29 around 30 C.E., possibly indeed as early as 150 B.C.E. by Eupolemos, who however draws rather from a source used by Third Ezra. By a preliminary analysis which he is carrying through in a university course, from the enormously signifcant liturgical reform program, "not a 'laicization' of the cult but a 'sacralization' of the people, all of whom are elevated to priestly rank" (p.162), Garbini concludes that Third Ezra represents the ideological projection of the destruction of the Temple wall separating male lay Israelites from priests begun by high priest Alcimus (earning the hostility of 1 Mcb 9,34). In Third Ezra 19,42 the high priest Ezra himself comes out from the Temple to be among the "sacralized people" women and all!

This Third Ezra ideology was at first popular; but hostility of the "sons of Zadok" priests led them to abandon the Temple and later found the Essene settlement at Qumran[105]. Opponents of Alcimus and Third Ezra would tell their story, much later [early A.D.!], in canonical Ezra, scraping

---

103 Garbini p. 156 citing I. LOEB. "La chaîne de la tradition dans le premier chapître du Pirké Abot", *Bibliothèque de l'École des Hautes Études. Sciences religieuses I* (Paris 1889) 307-322.

104 Garbini p. 157 "cannot but agree" with J. WELLHAUSEN, *Prolegomena to the History of Israel* (1883; Cleveland 1957 Meridian ed.) p, 409.

105 E. ULRICH. "Ezra and Qoheleth Manuscripts from Qumran" (4QEzra, 4QQoh^{a,b})", in Fest. J. BLENKINSOPP, *Priests, Prophets, and Scribes*, ed. Ulrich (Sheffield 1992) 138-157, is cited by Garbini, *Ricerche storico bibliche* 10 (1998: ftn. 102 above) p.62 as requiring a date earlier than his own "first centuries AD" for canonical Ezra -- unless these fragments are a modern falsification, as certain "elements" lead him to suspect.

around for a name which had never existed in Hebrew "but is virtually identical to *'azarah*, 'inner court of the Temple'" (p.166). "It is normal for a religious reform to be implemented with a reference to a tradition which is claimed   already to exist and to be associated with an important person" (p.165). "But why a non-existent person like Ezra ? Of course we shall never be able to provide an adequate answer to this question" (also p.165, earlier).

But p. 169, on the authority of Houtman and Wacholder (no page cited) against Yadin maintains that the Qumran Temple Scroll is, and itself calls itself "The Law", and adds "The problem of the Law of Ezra has thus been finally resolved". On the same page the article ends: "All [that which] revolves around the year 159 BC has a name [not Alcimus! but] -- Ezra. With this name, which no one ever bore, there really came into being ... Judaism".

Having thus tried to do full justice to the *pars construens* of Garbini's essay on how the name "Ezra" for a non-existent person came into use, I must end by saying that I find more convincing his summary of Pfeiffer above, and as in my *AnchorBD* article (fn. 102 above). There may well have been a real Ezra, even one acting as in his book (insofar as that can be detected behind the various confusions), who fell into neglect for some centuries of dominance by a hostile party, but with Pharisee ascendancy was honored and accorded new and extravagant titles as founder of Jerusalem and compiler of the Bible.

A rather recent essay of Garbini on Persian period biblical literature consistently does not even mention the name of Ezra (and Nehemiah only as a "simulation"), but constructively compares "Achaemenid Babylonian Hebraism" to the Spanish-Arabic period for original and modern interest in human existential problems: giving "new life to the distant and dramatic figures of the past, by breathing into them a humanity lacking in the annalistic tradition .. (Michal is perhaps the only woman in love in any ancient Near Eastern literature.) .. Under the domination of the Achaemenids, Hebraism knew its magical moment and Hebrew literature its golden age"[106].

Our final summation must be: Any possible occasion for the transfer of our Bible into a new language "invented" for that purpose would have to

---

106 Giovanni GARBINI, "Hebrew Literature in the Persian Period", in T. ESKENAZI & K. RICHARDS, ed., *Second Temple Studies 2* (*JSOT* supp. 175; Sheffield 1994) (180-) 188.

take into account the period when such materials were "ready at hand" to be worked on. From this point of view a date as late as the second or first pre-Christian century (as in fact opted by Naville) would be the most "manageable".

On the other hand, we have from that period no evidences of exuberant scribal activity such as during the period of Ezra. This period would be suitable for the books up to and including our Pentateuch ("his Torah" *pace* Nodet and some few others). And along with it there would be no historical or chronological objection to including the Psalms, possibly also the prophets and Writings (? leaving Daniel and Qohelet to be tucked in later). In the quite different ("heuristic") approach of Davies and many less-extreme recent scholars, the Ezra-era Persian administration of neighboring areas as well as Yehud is claimed to furnish hitherto-unnoticed clues to many things, including intense scribal activity.

Another conclusion must be, how surprising it is that among the extremely varying proponents of such transit of the Bible to an "invented" language, almost none take up the question of When and Why, or recognize how essentially intrinsic it is to any such "scholarly hypothesis".

Index of Authors Cited

(more than once on pages numbered in **bold-face**)

Scripture Citations

51,8: 25
51,28: 132

Lamentations
1,13: 12
2,11: 18
5,17: 12

Ezekiel
18,2: 16
21,21: 18
23,6: 132
27,25: 88n19
34,4: 26
37,6.8: 14
47,12: 26

Daniel
-: 86 144 147

Amos
8,5: 162

Hosea
2,11: 162
6,1: 26

Micah
7,6: 131

Haggai
-: 122
1,8f: 117
2,7: 117

Zechariah
9-14: 154n56
9,5: 131

Matthew
1,12: 122
5-7: 76
8,1-16: 65
8,24: 33
9,12: 33
10,36: 131
13,2: 73n3 77
13,42: 16
27,50: 77

Mark
1,43: 20
3,9: 74
3,21: 98
3,34: 98
4,1 **73-80**
4,1.10.36: 75
4,1-34: 74n4
    75n10,11
4,1-8,26:
    75n10
4,1-9: 74n9
4,3: 73n2
4,36: 74
5,21: 74n6
6,26: 9
6,33: 78
6,43: 77
6,44: 78n16
8,3: 19
8,9: 77
8,20 f: 77
8,22-26: 45
8,24: 15
10: 98
11,15: 77

Luke
3,27: 122
5,3: 73n3
4,18: 26
4,23: 9 33 57
5,31: 33
8,43: 33

John
6,10: 77
9,3: 24
21,11: 78n16

Acts
8,27: 128
12,24: 143n20
28,11: 23

Colossians
4,14: 33

James
5,13-20: 56

Index of Subjects, Semitic Terms, and Toponyms

(*Sites* in italics; also, in alphabetical order of transliteration, *Hebrew terms* DISCUSSED)

Finito di stampare
nel mese di febbraio 2000

presso la tipografia
"Giovanni Olivieri" di E. Montefoschi
00187 Roma - Via dell'Archetto, 10,11,12